The Economy of Deuteronomy's Core

Worlds of the Ancient Near East and Mediterranean

Series editor: Diana V. Edelman, University of Oslo

Worlds of the Ancient Near East and Ancient Mediterranean brings alive the texts, archaeology and history of the cultures of the regions around the Mediterranean Sea and eastward to ancient Iran and Iraq, from the Neolithic through the Roman periods (ca 10,000 BCE–393 CE). Studies of one or more aspects of a single culture or of a subject across cultures in the regions outlined will form the foundation of this series, in which interdisciplinary approaches are encouraged. Studies can be based on texts, on material remains, or a combination of the two, where appropriate. In the case of a project that focuses on either the memory or the reception history of a place, person, myth, practice, or idea that arose or existed within the prescribed time, chapters that trace ongoing relevance to the present are welcome. The volumes are meant to be accessible to a wide audience interested in how the inhabitants of these parts of the world lived or how they understood their own pasts, presents, and futures, as well as how current scholars are understanding and recreating their pasts or their future aspirations.

Published titles

A History of Biblical Israel: The Fate of the Tribes and Kingdoms from Merenptah to Bar Kochba
Axel Knauf and Philippe Guillaume

About Edom and Idumea in the Persian Period: Recent Research and Approaches from Archaeology, Hebrew Bible Studies and Ancient Near Eastern Studies
Edited by Benedikt Hensel, Ehud Ben Zvi, and Diana V. Edelman

Ancient Cookware from the Levant: An Ethnoarchaeological Perspective
Gloria London

Josiah: From Improbable Stories to Inventive Historiography
Lowell K. Handy

Leadership, Social Memory and Judean Discourse in the 5th–2nd Centuries BCE
Edited by Diana V. Edelman and Ehud Ben Zvi

New Light on Canaanite-Phoenician Pottery
Dalit Regev

Painting the Mediterranean Phoenician: On Canaanite-Phoenician Tradenets
Dalit Regev

Forthcoming titles

Burial Practices in Ancient Israel and the Neighboring Cultures (c. 1500–330 BCE)
Jürg Hutzli and Stefan Münger

Recovering Women's Rituals in the Ancient Near East
Julye Bidmead

The Economy of Deuteronomy's Core

Philippe Guillaume

SHEFFIELD UK   BRISTOL CT

Published by Equinox Publishing Ltd.

UK: Office 415, The Workstation, 15 Paternoster Row, Sheffield, South Yorkshire S1 2BX

USA: ISD, 70 Enterprise Drive, Bristol, CT 06010

www.equinoxpub.com

First published 2022

© Philippe Guillaume 2022

All rights reserved. No part of this publication may be reproduced or transmitted in any form or by any means, electronic or mechanical, including photocopying, recording or any information storage or retrieval system, without prior permission in writing from the publishers.

British Library Cataloguing-in-Publication Data

A catalogue record for this book is available from the British Library.

ISBN-13 978 1 80050 199 7   (hardback)
         978 1 80050 200 0   (paperback)
         978 1 80050 201 7   (ePDF)
         978 1 80050 252 9   (ePub)

Library of Congress Cataloging-in-Publication Data

Names: Guillaume, Philippe, author.
Title: The economy of Deuteronomy's core / Philippe Guillaume.
Description: Sheffield, South Yorkshire ; Bristol, CT : Equinox Publishing Ltd, 2022. | Series: Worlds of the ancient near east and mediterranean | Includes bibliographical references and index. | Summary: "Grounded in the text itself, The Economy of Deuteronomy's Core reads Deuteronomy 12-26 in light of what we know about Ancient Near Eastern economies. The results open new horizons regarding the origins of the Deuteronomic laws"-- Provided by publisher.
Identifiers: LCCN 2022018046 (print) | LCCN 2022018047 (ebook) | ISBN 9781800501997 (hardback) | ISBN 9781800502000 (paperback) | ISBN 9781800502017 (epdf) | ISBN 9781800502529 (epub)
Subjects: LCSH: Bible. Deuteronomy, XII-XXVI--Criticism, interpretation, etc. | Economics in the Bible.
Classification: LCC BS1275.6.E35 G85 2022 (print) | LCC BS1275.6.E35 (ebook) | DDC 222/.1506--dc23/eng/20220630
LC record available at https://lccn.loc.gov/2022018046
LC ebook record available at https://lccn.loc.gov/2022018047

Typeset by Sparks – www.sparkspublishing.com

Table of Contents

Abbreviations	vii
Foreword and Acknowledgements	ix
Introduction	1
Part I: Reading Deuteronomy 12–26 Economically	**13**
1. Expenses and Incomes	15
2. Deuteronomy's Economic Actors: Beyond a Single People of Brothers	54
3. Three Institutions and their Interplay: Beyond the Temple of Jerusalem	110
Part II: Focusing on Tithes	**155**
4. Yearly Tithes for Whom and How Much?	157
5. Claiming a Greater Share of Deuteronomic Tithes	166
6. Outlines of an Older Deuteronomic Core	174
Part III: Probing the History of the Deuteronomic Core	**197**
7. *Urdeuteronomium* After de Wette	199
Conclusion	215
Bibliography	221
Index of Authors	242
Index of Biblical References	245
Index of Subjects	248

ABBREVIATIONS

BHS	*Biblia Hebraica Stuttgartensia* (Stuttgart: Deutsche Bibelgesellschaft, 1990)
BHQ	*Biblia Hebraica Quinta* (Edited by C. McCarthy; Stuttgart: Deutsche Bibelgesellschaft, 2007)
HALOT	*The Hebrew & Aramaic Lexicon of the Old Testament* (Leiden: Brill, 1994–2000)
LSJ	*Liddell-Scott-Jones Greek-English Lexicon* (Oxford: Oxford University Press, 1996).
LXX	Septuaginta
MT	Masoretic Text
NETS	*A New English Translation of the Septuagint* (Edited by A. Pietersma and B. G. Wright; Oxford: Oxford University Press, 2007)
NRSV	*New Revised Standard Version* (New York: Oxford University Press, 1989).

Foreword and Acknowledgements

This work springs from correspondence with Diana Edelman in which she wondered if the tithing prescriptions in Deuteronomy 14 might serve as a thick cloud of smoke to hide the bare fact that the place YHWH shall choose is to be a tax collecting centre for the Empire. Picking up the challenge led on to consider Deuteronomy 14 in the context of the other economic passages concentrated in the Deuteronomic core.

I warmly thank the colleagues from whom this study profited greatly, through stimulating discussions in informal settings, in the Bernese *Oberseminar*, in conferences of the European Association of Biblical Studies, as well as through the generous sharing of published and unpublished ideas by Peter Altmann, Ehud Ben Zvi, Edmon Gallagher, Susanne Haury von Siebenthal, Georges Mills, and the members of Oslo Research Group headed by Diana Edelman, Benedetta Rossi, Anne Fitzpatrick-McKinley, Kåre Berge and Philip Davies, whose death in June 2018 was a most cruel loss.

Introduction

Jerusalem 649 BCE. Josiah ben Amon becomes king of Judah at the tender age of eight. The pious party behind the assassination of his father acts as regent and ensures that the young king will do what is right in the eyes of the Lord and walk in all the ways of his father David, turning neither to the right nor to the left. In the eighteenth year of his rule, Josiah dedicates the funds collected over the years by the keepers of the threshold to renovate the temple of his god. As carpenters and masons proceed in earnest, lo and behold, the book of the Torah is discovered in the house of the Lord. It is read aloud before the king who immediately tears his clothes and orders his high ranking officers to inquire of the Lord how to quench the divine wrath Josiah's fathers kindled against the people and the kingdom. Instead of unreliable court prophets, Huldah, an obscure prophetess is consulted. She reports that the Lord is inconsolable and that the fate of the kingdom is sealed. Josiah is granted a temporary respite on account of his piety. He will be gathered to his ancestors in peace and not witness the oncoming disaster.

The tall story of 2 Kings 22 offered an invaluable compass for biblical scholarship to navigate the mass of Old Testament material. It provided a badly needed reference point to anchor the formation of the Torah in the history of the Kingdom of Judah. The *sefer ha-torah* stowed away in the treasury of the Temple of Jerusalem and forgotten until it was discovered in the days of King Josiah became *Urdeuteronomium*, an early version of the Book of Deuteronomy. Thanks to Wellhausen's *Prolegomena zur Geschichte Israels,* Josiah's *Urdeuteronomium* entered in every Old Testament textbook because Josiah's reform became the watershed for the history of the Hebrew Scriptures.[1] Before Josiah, the Covenant Code in Exodus. After Josiah, the Holiness code of Leviticus. In between, the Deuteronomic Code.

A Josianic context for *Urdeuteronomium* raises problems of its own. The curious portrayal of a politically idle king in Deuteronomy 17:14–20 hardly fits with the very busy Josiah of 2 Kings 22–23. The ongoing failure to

---

1   Rogerson, *De Wette*, 267. See De Wette, *Dissertatio critico-exegetica*.

retrieve the sightliest extra-biblical evidence for King Josiah is another issue, considering that other Judahite monarchs of that period are attested to outside the Bible. The lack of any mention of Jerusalem in Deuteronomy, as also in the entire Torah, is equally problematic.[2] The story of 2 Kings 22 could simply have drawn on Deuteronomy to portray Josiah as a pious follower of Moses, even if Deuteronomy had originated in northern Israel, as long-suspected.[3] Nevertheless, the reign of Josiah continues to be viewed as the great turning-point in the formation of biblical literature because it is hard to give up such a convenient historical anchor.[4] It has been easier to question the historicity of the story of the book-finding than to work out a comprehensive alternative to Josiah's reform for the origins of *Urdeuteronomium*.[5]

After De Wette?

The idea that an early form of the book of Deuteronomy originated in the days of Josiah was already being challenged at the end of the nineteenth century, when a number of scholars argued that *Urdeuteronomium* was composed over a century later than Josiah.[6] They pointed to laws ascribed to *Urdeuteronomium* that Josiah could not have decreed. For instance, it was inconceivable for the entire pre-exilic Judean population—120,000, slaves included—to have gathered in the courts of the temple while no one was left at home to care for the herds and flocks.[7] The slaughter of an entire city to eradicate idolatry (Deut 13) could only be conceived once national existence had been cancelled or suspended so that theories could be produced without worrying about their practical application.[8] Under such conditions, Deuteronomy 13:12–18 could be written without noting the implications of such a set of laws. As 2 Kings 23 and Zephaniah 1 state that astral worship was practiced in Jerusalem in the days

---

2   Knoppers, "Rethinking," 399–404.
3   Knoppers, "Northern Context," 162–83.
4   Among many others, see Tigay, "To Place His Name," 17–26.
5   On the dubious historicity of the book-finding episode, the recent studies are Na'aman, "Discovered Book," 47–62; Davies, "Authority of Deuteronomy," 39–41.
6   D'Eichthal, *Mélanges*; Vernes, *Nouvelle hypothèse*; Vernes, *Précis d'histoire*, 467–70, 603–606; Horst, "Etudes;" Fries, *Gesetzesschrift*; Cullen, *Book*; Hölscher, "Komposition," 161.
7   Hölscher, 186–87.
8   Horst, "Etudes," 141.

of Josiah, Deuteronomy would have required torching Jerusalem and its entire population—including Josiah and the priests who had produced the law.[9]

Two arguments based on economic considerations made a more lasting impact. First, that the consumption of a tenth of the yearly yield at the *maqom* (Deut 14:22-26) was excessive for wealthy families and outright unwise for the less affluent ones.[10] Second, that debt release (Deut 15:1-6) is an idealistic measure to exonerate poor people from reimbursing debts they could not honor but would effectively dry out credit if applied to the entire society.[11]

These arguments made no dent in the popularity of de Wette's hypothesis but they aired key notions that remain popular in Deuteronomic research: 1) that tithe payers only consume a fraction of their tithes at the *maqom,* 2) that the debt release is unpractical, 3) and that it is a humanitarian measure.

Laws that seek to alleviate poverty may be motivated by noble idealism, but if they have no practical impact, they might be little more than wishful thinking, however high-minded their intention. Though the poor present a central figure in the study of Deuteronomy 12-26, if the application of the laws is impossible or their effect on the actual condition of the poor is negligible, then their humanitarian thrust is questionable, unless humanitarian means a morally noble stand possibly laced with condescension.

The same issues pertain to the laws of the Code of Hammurabi, of Lipit-Ishtar and other Ancient Near Eastern legal collections discovered in the early twentieth century CE. Were they binding laws, and to what effect? Do they merely reflect royal ideology and thus legitimate the ruler's prerogatives? If they are not binding, can they be designated as laws?

The humanitarian thrust of the Deuteronomic Code is easier to defend on the basis of comparisons with parallels in Exodus and Leviticus. As an "instruction of the people in humanism", the Deuteronomic Code supposedly upholds human life and the dignity of those at the margin of society, as well as animal life such as mother birds and treading oxen.[12] Including the latter stretches the scope of humanism to such an extend that humanism becomes a watered-down notion.

Then, the concept of utopia entered the discussion to account for the transmission of the Deuteronomic Code presented as Moses' testament

---

9 Hölscher, "Komposition," 193.
10 Reuss, *Histoire sainte*, 307; Hölscher, 184.
11 Reuss, 308; Hölscher, 195-96.
12 Weinfeld, *Deuteronomy 1-11*, 241-42; Weinfeld, *Deuteronomy and Deuteronomic School*, 282-97.

immediately before the conquest of Canaan. Deuteronomy is utopian because "its location in history is not unequivocally clear" and because the "biblical setting is fictitious".[13] The public reading in Deuteronomy 31 supports the understanding of the aim of the laws as the formation of a common memory rather than the publication of edicts regulating the life of the entire Israelite society. As a *"dream for a better life"*, the kind of utopia Deuteronomy displays would have practical applications for "the small circle of literati themselves".[14] Its laws would be useful (humanitarian?) for the elite even though they might be impractical or devoid of practical effects on the condition of others. As debt release is not expected to eradicate poverty (Deut 15:11), did the writers expound a utopia for the consumption of the general public and for the preservation of their own social hegemony?

Utopia as indicator of actual conditions

Most biblical texts were not intended to give a complete representation of the worlds in which they were written. What was well known to the writers and readers was taken for granted.[15] Not so Deuteronomy. Its central chapters offer more than a mere vocalization of the libretto of the opera imagined by the writers. Numerous references to economic practices offer glimpses of daily life in rural Palestine.

Or is the wealth of economic detail in Deuteronomy the clue that what is deployed before the reader is no insight into ordinary economic reality but a utopia that needed to be elaborated in some detail precisely because it differed from what everyone knew?[16] To appreciate the utopian nature of the Deuteronomic economy would require the ability to gauge the differences between the reality its primary audience experienced on a daily basis and what Deuteronomy envisaged. The main challenge today is that our present understanding of ordinary economic reality in ancient Israel is limited. Yet, the study of the utopian solutions proposed in Deuteronomy can supplement our limited access to that ancient reality. The utopia can profitably contribute to our understanding of ordinary economic practices because the gap between what was factually the case and the proposed new reality cannot be too wide. The solutions it proposes to the predicaments faced by its addressees must be perceived as workable to have the least appeal and credibility. One can dream of living in Eden,

---

13 Levin, "Rereading," 49.
14 Berge, "Literacy," 7–8.
15 Yamauchi and Wilson, *Dictionary of Daily Life*, 1.
16 Berge, "Literacy," 1–19.

but few would accept bearing the risks of change for mere pie-in-the-sky promises. Therefore, the utopian nature of Deuteronomy's laws are more a help than a hindrance to access the general nature of the economic reality in which the writers lived: to be acceptable, utopia cannot be entirely otherworldly but must bear a reasonable semblance of familiarity.

Unheeded: Norbert Lohfink and Georg Braulik

Besides the clues of economic practices that can be drawn from utopian laws, some valuable points were published decades ago, but they were either dismissed or they have not yet been fully absorbed due to the influence of Josianic hypothesis. Two points are particularly relevant to the present study.

First, the expression *"personae miserae"* (miserable persons) is often encountered in studies of Deuteronomy. It is a convenient shorthand for the tetrad that is often encountered in Deuteronomy 12–26: the Levite, the alien, the widow and the orphan. To designate them as miserable implies dire economic circumstances. In the early 1990s, Norbert Lohfink demonstrated the inadequacy of this expression because Deuteronomy never equates Levites, aliens, widows, and orphans with the destitute (§2.1.9). This point has major implications for the significance of triennial tithes.

Second, Georg Braulik published in the 1980s several versions of a study of the function of joy in Deuteronomy's cultic theory (§§4.1; 5.1–2). Joy is what makes the meals partaken at the chosen Place unique. Joy is highly relevant to the allocation of yearly tithes, which Deuteronomy 14 distinguishes from triennial tithes, a distinction that calls for a greater attention to economics than has been the case so far in Deuteronomic scholarship.

Defining economy

To be sure, economics is a modern concept for which the ancient Egyptians and the Hebrews had no term. Yet, the Bible is replete with references to food and drink, hunger and thirst, feasting and fasting, peace and war, rain and drought—all of which are elements of the challenges faced when securing the basic necessities of life. Hence, mentions of economic practices are numerous: credit, debt-cancellation, slavery, self-indenture, marriage, land tenure, transport, sowing, harvesting, winnowing and coping with storms, crickets, pests, and famines. Biblical texts do provide figures, ranging from calendars (the matrix of credit) and amounts of silver and gold paid as tribute or taken as loot, to administrative districts, city sizes, numbers of inhabitants or tax payers and even how many boys were mauled by two she-bears near Bethel. Yet, these numbers are insufficient to serve as quantitative data of statistical significance and it is legitimate that in theological exegesis such numbers be dismissed as irrelevant quantities. Figures given for tribes, families, armies, and prices are notoriously inflated, while the date of the texts transmitting those numbers are exceedingly difficult to ascertain due to later editing and the projection of conditions at the time of writing onto earlier contexts.

Yet, biblical texts refer to practices that bear striking similarities with laws and economic records from Mesopotamia and Egypt that are numerous enough to determine performance and identify trends. As no such records are available for the Levant, biblical exegesis can provide no measure of economic performance such as levels of production, growth, consumption and well-being—the backbone of economics. Therefore, looking for economic elements in a theological work such as Deuteronomy may seem hopeless. Among other things, economics deals with debt while theology deals with sin, though ironically—or maybe not—both use the terms remission and forgiveness.[17] Theology, as much as economics, has a deep interest in moral concerns, which shows that they are no strangers to one another. Studies of the Medieval perspective on economics have referred to the poetry of Dante's *Divine Comedy* and its Jewish counterpart, Immanuelo Romano's *Ha-Tofet ve-ha-Eden*.[18] Contrary to Dante, Romano's Jewish perspective features neither Purgatory nor a Lady Fortune to turn the wheel on the rich and redistribute wealth.[19] It is the Lord who strips the rich because they have ignored Deuteronomy's injunction to open their hand to the poor. Romano is immune to, or reacts against, the Franciscan commendation of poverty that deeply influenced Dante. As a Jew, Romano remains closer to the Hebrew Bible, in particular to the passages of Deuteronomy that discuss poverty.[20]

If it is possible to study Dante and Romano to get a sense of the Medieval perspective on economics, it should be possible to study Deuteronomy to understand the perspective of southern Levantine scribes on economics in the first millennium BCE.

That neither the Hebrew Bible nor Medieval literature used the word economics "does not mean that the worlds of work, human choices and

---

17 See Anderson, *Sin*, 27 on the influence of Aramaic using the same word for sin and debt.
18 Epstein, "Economics," 437–46. Romano, *Tophet and Eden*.
19 Epstein, 446.
20 Havely, "Poverty," 229–43.

exchanges, and the ethical problems surrounding money did not exist."[21] Today, economics readily evokes stock markets and unbridled greed such as the figure of Gordon Gecko in Oliver Stone's 1987 *Wall Street*. In this study, economics is understood as the study of human choices, of how people maximize their welfare under constraint.

"Welfare" avoids the narrow locution of "profit" and broadens the domain of economics to a wide range of human behavior, including non-market behavior, in line with the economic approach of Gary Becker (1930–2014; Nobel laureate 1992). Becker's approach is based on three assumptions:

1. Whether they are selfish, altruistic, loyal, spiteful or masochistic, individuals maximize welfare *as they conceive it*.
2. Their preferences are stable because they are defined by fundamental aspects of life such as health, prestige, pleasure and others that do *not* bear a stable relation to market goods and services.
3. These preferences are fairly *similar* over time and across social backgrounds and cultures.[22]

Becker's approach to welfare maximization is valid for first millennium BCE Mesopotamia:

> The economic choices that were made by any of the agents in the Babylonian economy were rational, one can assume, in that they were aimed at maximizing the utility that could be derived from them, but the range of choices, and the very definition of utility, were socially conditioned.[23]

The notion of maximizing behavior involving choices on the basis of available opportunities and constraints is equally valid for Deuteronomy. The presence of choice is obvious in the framing chapters of the book that present themselves as Moses' last exhortation to Israel to choose life and obedience to YHWH's command. The Deuteronomic core relies less on threats than the prescriptions found elsewhere in the Pentateuch to incentivize compliance.[24] In this sense, the Deuteronomic legal collection can be read as a series of guidelines on how to make the best choices to maximize welfare in an agrarian society.

Economics is used here in a broad sense as the analysis of "the outcomes of social interactions between agents in a system of incentives."[25]

---

21 Epstein, "Economics," 437.
22 Becker, *Economic Approach*, 5–6; Becker, "Economic Way".
23 Jursa, *Aspects*, 54.
24 Schmid, *Literaturgeschichte*, 106.
25 Wagner-Tsukamoto, "Economic Reading," 116.

In ancient Israel, as much as anywhere else today, farmers, artisans, and merchants both produce and consume goods and services. As economic agents, they are all expected to contribute capital in one form or another while expecting "to receive capital distributions in return."[26] In other words, economic systems are social games—very serious games to be sure—played out in more or less cooperative ways by self-interested agents who have conflicting interests and face dilemma that can be resolved by contributions of capital by each agent. Failure to resolve the conflict resulting from the dilemma can be expected to lead to mutual loss.

That the players each have conflicting interests is fundamental. Co-operation is not the result of free choice. It is forced upon the players when they estimate that greater losses will be incurred if they fail to cooperate. The fear of mutual loss does not always lead opposing parties to strike a compromise between their conflicting interests. Compromises by definition satisfy neither side. The seller always obtains a price for his goods and services lower than what he considers a fair price. Purchasers always pay more than what they consider the fair price. While some transactions fall through, even at the cost of mutual loss, many transactions are completed at a price that fully satisfies neither party but reflects seasonal and other causes for variations in offer and demand.

Seasonal fluctuations and variations from one decade to another in the prices of barley, sheep, slaves, dates, wool and land are now well attested to in first millennium BCE Babylonia.[27] Factors such as droughts, wars, epidemics and technological innovations influenced offer and demand. Hence prices of any given staple do reflect actual conditions and some degree of pragmatism in reaching an equilibrium between the conflicting interests of different agents. Beyond this, gains in adducing any of the supermodels of Ancient Near Eastern economic history are minimal. Each model foregrounds certain factors of economic causation, but none of these models "can nowadays claim to be fully convincing on its own".[28]

In addition to supermodels, ragbag notions of the poor (i.e. helpless farmers in general) versus the rich (i.e. all powerful parasitic city-dwellers) are best avoided.[29]

---

26 Wagner-Tsukamoto, 116.
27 Jursa, *Aspects*, 734–53.
28 Jursa, 16.
29 Ro, *Poverty*, 217 weds *homo economicus* with *homo religiosus*, but the main achievement of *homo religiosus* does not get beyond the obvious "production and development of theological thoughts and concepts".

Method: Purpose first

The designation of Exodus 21–23, Leviticus 17–27 and Deuteronomy 12–26 as law codes has long been recognized as misleading.[30] Codified laws establish regimes of civil law. The extent to which the biblical legal collections reflect legal practice is virtually impossible to evaluate due to the lack of judicial records recovered from the territories of ancient Israel and Judah.[31] The biblical collections of laws may have reflected customary law, unless the scribes who produced these collections sought to present an ideal society rather than rules to be enforced in a particular society at a particular period.

Another issue is the renewed interest in the parallels between Deuteronomy and Neo-Assyrian treaties. The recent discovery of a copy of the loyalty oaths of Asarhaddon's vassality treaty at Tel Taynat in Syria seems to offer a long-awaited external substantiation of de Wette's dating of *Urdeuteronomium* in the days of Josiah.[32] The parallels are deemed too close to be coincidental and they are used to claim that they "point to a seventh century date for the core of the book."[33] The parallels, however, apply to Deuteronomy 6:4–9; 13 and 28 only—passages that are very different in nature from the legal core of the book. Hence, the bearings of these chapters on the date of the legal collection is minimal. A Neo-Assyrian date is possible, but the Josianic connection remains as hypothetical as ever.

Therefore, the present study focuses on the Deuteronomic laws—whether they are precepts, recommendations or utopian—to recover a feeling for the kind of society imagined and desired by the producers of these texts. It has been more common to compare individual laws in the different collections and to reconstruct stages in the formation of these collections. A major hurdle with these approaches is that the question of Deuteronomy's dating has taken priority over the question of its purpose.[34]

For instance, Eckart Otto's monumental commentary on Deuteronomy splits the text into the usual main phases: a late pre-exilic Deuteronomy based on the revision and extension of the Covenant Code, an exilic Deuteronomy, and a post-exilic Deuteronomy integrated into the Torah.[35]

---

30   Wells, *Law of Testimony*, 11–15.
31   Fitzpatrick-McKinley, *Transformation*, 99–100.
32   Lauinger, "Esarhaddon's Succession Treaty," 87–123; Steymans, "Deuteronomy and Tayinat," 1–13. But see Radner, "Assyrische uppi adê," 251–78.
33   Römer, "How to Date," 369.
34   Davies, "Authority," 27.
35   Otto, *Deuteronomium 1–11*, 231–56.

This traditional scheme functions as a grand narrative that reduces the complexity of the material and allows the formulation of hypotheses on the processes that generated Deuteronomy.

Though it focuses on economics, Peter Altmann's monograph makes assumptions about dates when establishing a corpus of pre-exilic biblical texts as well as those from the Persian period.[36]

Any critical study of Deuteronomy's laws requires certain presuppositions about the origins of *Urdeuteronomium* and the formation of the biblical legal corpora.[37] Therefore, much attention has been given to parallels with Exodus 21–23 and Leviticus 17–27.[38] The problem is that we have no access to the collection of laws the first Deuteronomic writers would have used. Comparing the treatment of similar issues in different books of the Torah entails plotting the changes on an evolutionary framework for which the exilic period functions as a hinge.[39] The integration of the different legal collections into a single Torah is likely to have led to the insertion of additions and harmonizations in every legal collection, additions that prevent the recovery of the earlier legal collection that may have inspired *Urdeuteronomium*. The ongoing process of legal elaboration spurred a complex process of harmonization that is often too hypothetical to be useful.[40]

We are on firmer ground within Deuteronomy where it is fairly clear that the legal collection makes sense without the theological framework of chapters 1–11 and 27–34, while "the framework does not make sense without the law."[41] Therefore, the present study assumes the existence of a legal collection, traditionally identified as Deuteronomy 12–26, around which the theological framework developed, though this does not imply that everything within Deuteronomy 12–26 is older than the theological framework.

To be in a position to determine when Deuteronomy was produced, and under what circumstances, requires asking what it was seeking to achieve. What are its implied objectives and its vision of Israelite society? Knowing its purpose can eventually lead to pinpointing its initial audience.[42]

---

36 Altmann, *Economics*, 65–78; 188–20.
37 See Wells, "Interpretation," 234–66.
38 Otto, *Deuteronomium im Pentateuch*, Kratz, *Composition*, 130; Otto, *Deuteronomium 1–11*, 231–37.
39 Rütersworden, "Concerning Deut 14," 95–103.
40 See for instance Bartos and Levinson, "Manner of Remission," 351–71.
41 Kratz, *Composition*, 116.
42 Davies, "Authority," 27.

To this aim, chapter 1 approaches Deuteronomy 12–26 from the point of view of a token Israelite farmer to consider the implications of these chapters for his budget. Some laws imply profits and savings, others expenses. Actual expenses and revenues are not always assessable, but the mass of data transmitted in Deuteronomy 12–26 can easily be split into gains and losses, as would the profit and loss account of the token Israelite. Chapters 2 and 3 then focus on the different economic actors involved and on the different institutions that are mentioned. At this point of the analysis, the objectives of the laws and the contours of the Israelite society they imply become clearer, except that, instead of pinpointing the primary purpose of the laws, the study ends up with the identification of two opposing purposes within Deuteronomy 12–26 itself. Hence, prior to attempting a reconstruction of the history of the Deuteronomic legal collection in chapter 7, chapters 4, 5, and 6 below sort out material that reflects the interests of two economic actors with opposing interests.

Nomenclature

A set of technical terms is used throughout the present study. The term "core" designates Deuteronomy 12–26 as a whole, in opposition to the term "frames" to designate Deuteronomy 1–11 and 27–34.

The terms "Torah" and "Pentateuch" are commonly used as synonyms to designate the body of text between Genesis 1 and Deuteronomy 34. Here, however, each of these terms conveys a specific nuance. "Torah" designates the process accomplished by the Deuteronomic frames and specific passages within Deuteronomy 12–26, in particular (Deut 12; 16; 18:1–8; 26, see Part II). "Pentateuch" is used when the first five scrolls of the Hebrew Bible are referred to in general.

PART I

READING DEUTERONOMY 12–26 ECONOMICALLY

Chapter 1
Expenses and Incomes

Though a literary work, the Deuteronomic core evinces a large enough amount of economic material to draw up a fairly comprehensive list of the costs and gains a token farmer could expect when complying with Deuteronomic laws as he went about his everyday work. More so than Exodus and Leviticus, Deuteronomy discusses tithes, firstlings, first fruits, meat cuts, gleanings, loans, interest, pledges, debt, slaves, wages, alms, weights, transport costs and silver. Despite this wealth of material and the precision of Deuteronomic prescriptions dealing with financial matters, exegetes tend to read Deuteronomy in light of modern practices and ethics. Or they claim that no biblical text is specific enough to reconstruct a functional tax system in Israel or *Yehud* at any given time.[1] This claim is correct in so far as quantitative data is absent. There are no indications of yields, number of animals, prices or actual quantities to be earmarked for tithes and meat cuts for the simple reason that the ability of each farmer to produce enough food to cover his own needs is presupposed.

The lack of actual quantities is therefore no hurdle for the reconstruction of a theoretical profit and loss account based on the percentages extracted from and allocated to different social actors as well as on non-assessable expenses, revenues and savings that would occur when the various laws are taken into account.

1.1 Levies and Expenses

In the wake of Mary Douglas' work, the dietary prohibitions in Deuteronomy 14 and their parallel in Leviticus 11 received much scholarly attention.[2] Less ink has been spilt on the second part of the chapter devoted

---

1 Stackert, *Rewriting*, 175.
2 See Nestor, "We Are Family," 38–53.

to tithes.³ Yet, compared with the treatment of tithes in Leviticus 27 and Numbers 18:20–32, Deuteronomy 14:22–29 presents some significant differences in the way they are collected and as to who benefits from them. Tithing prescriptions in Deuteronomy and in the Priestly Legislation are more dissimilar than other parallel laws. Deuteronomy divides the tithes between multiple recipients (the Israelite farmer, the poor, the Levite) and prescribes different procedures for tithe distribution and consumption in different years. The Holiness author, by contrast, does not allow the Israelite farmer or the underclasses to partake of the tithe at all but rather assigns it all to the Levites and to the priests.⁴

Deuteronomy 14 only assigns to the Levite a share of the tithe of the third year while Numbers 18:21 grants the tithes of every year to the Levites and only to them.⁵ The difference is not negligible and speaks volumes about the identity of the expected beneficiaries of the texts. It is highly unlikely that Deuteronomy 14:22–29 was drafted by or for people drawing much of their revenues from an established sanctuary. Chapter 6 below identifies economic actors for whom a temple, in Jerusalem or elsewhere, would represent a burden rather than a source of revenues.

1.1.1 Tithes and firstlings (Deuteronomy 14:22–29)

Deuteronomy 14:22–29 delineates two different tithing methods for agricultural produce: a yearly and a triennial tithe. Verse 22 specifies that the yearly tithe applies to the "seeds coming out of the field" (זרע היצא השדה). Verse 23 has a longer list of produce to be brought to the *maqom*: wheat (דגן), fermented drink (תירש), oil (יצהר) plus the firstlings of the herd and flock.⁶ The discrepancy is routinely taken as the clue that the all-encompassing list of foodstuffs in v. 23 is secondary.⁷ This is possible and the difference between verses 22 and 23 would be crucial if the yearly tithes brought to the *maqom* were taxes. They are often considered as such, but this is doubtful.⁸ If these tithes are consumed by the families who produced them, the identification of actual products need not be as precise as would be the case if they were collected to feed others. The difference between grain only (verse 22) and wheat, fermented drink, oil and

---

3   Pagolu, *Religion of the Patriarchs*, 172–78; Salonen, "Über den Zehnten," 1–62. Recent bibliography in Stackert, *Rewriting*, 169 n. 8.
4   Stackert, 167.
5   Stackert, 182.
6   The word מקום is left untranslated because the common designation "central sanctuary" is misleading.
7   Schaper, "Geld," 47; Morrow, *Scribing the Center*, 88.
8   See Herman, "Tithes as Gift," 51–73.

firstlings (verse 23) would be highly significant if these verses identified taxable products. Tax-collectors as much as farmers would need to know if the tithe strikes every kind of grain or only wheat, and if animal products, wine and oil are tax-free or not. On the contrary, the difference between grain only and wheat, wine, oil and meat is only a matter of the victuals self-consumed during the feast. The difference is not negligible but it is a matter of prestige rather than tax. Farmers would deliver as little as possible to save taxes, but the same farmers readily bring more than enough of their best products when the aim is to throw a big party (see §1.2.1).

Contrary to verses 22–23, verses 28–29 apply the tithe of the third year to all produce (כל מעשר תבואה). The triennial tithes are a levy. They are collected by the local Levite who redistributes them to the local alien (henceforth *ger*), the orphan, and the widow who "shall eat and be satiated so that YHWH may continue to bless everything the Israelites do".[9] As the proceeds of the triennial tithes are deposited (הנח) at the gate of each settlement, the triennial tithes apply to field and garden produce. Animal products are not explicitly included, which makes sense as they are not storable at the gate. As the matter here is taxation, one would expect wool and meat to be listed explicitly. At best, their non-mention suggests that farmers are free to provide animals and meat as gifts but not as taxes.

Whether or not the third-year tithes delivered at the gate of the settlement supplant the tithes of the other years is debatable. Many exegetes distribute the tithes on a seven-year cycle, arguing that the yearly tithes applies only to years 1, 2, 4, and 5 while the triennial tithes apply to years 3 and 6. For year 7, the sabbatical year of Leviticus 25 is evoked to argue that no tithes are raised, as in that year there is no planting or harvesting.[10] Such a scheme is a far cry from what the Deuteronomic text specifies and reflects attempts at harmonizing the Deuteronomic tithes with those in Leviticus.

As the aim here is to retrieve Deuteronomy's own economic system, the temptation to harmonize the different tithing systems is resisted. Therefore, evoking the sabbatical year of Leviticus 25 to understand how Deuteronomy's two tithes are articulated is methodologically unsound.

A seven-year cycle is indeed found in Deuteronomy, but for credit operations between brothers (Deut 15:1–12; 31:10). Nothing in Deuteronomy

---

9   The word גר is also left untranslated to avoid clarifying Deuteronomy's view of this term by importing notions from other biblical books. See Ebach, *Fremde*; Awabdy, *Immigrants*.
10 Soss, "Old Testament Law," 331; Lundbom, *Deuteronomy*, 482–83; Otto, *Deuteronomium 12,1–23,15*, 1317.

supports the idea that there is no sowing and harvesting during the seventh year. Deuteronomy expects yearly tithes to be collected on a yearly basis with no exception or interruption. In this case, the tithes collected by the Levites are charged over and above the yearly tithes. Tobit 1:7, the LXX on Deuteronomy 26:12 and Josephus, *Antiquities* IV 8.22 take it as such. Some commentators consider that a double tithe on the third year is unlikely.[11] For instance, Jack Lundbom considers that "Two tithes meant an annual tax of 20 percent on one's yield, which was too high, making implementation of tithe laws nigh unto impossible".[12] In fact, a double tithe raised on a yearly basis does not amount to an annual tax of 20 percent because a triennial tithe collected yearly corresponds to 3.33%, not 10%. Hence, a double tithes means a moderate 13.33 % yearly levy on field produce (grain, wine, and oil): 10% yearly plus another 10% every third year, thus a yearly average of 13.33%, i.e. ([10% × 3] + 10%) / 3. A yearly rate of 13.33% is not unthinkable: Mesopotamian tithes, for example, were not always collected strictly at the rate of 10%.[13]

While the basic principle is the collection of a tenth of the produce of the third year (בשנת ההוא), in practice it is best for everyone concerned to collect the triennial tithes yearly at a constant rate of 3.33% rather than every third year at the full rate of 10%. The tax burden is the same, but the amounts collected are not. When the harvest of the third year happens to be poor, there is no way of smoothing the hardship by using reserves stored from the previous years and the beneficiaries of the triennial tithes would have to rely on charity when everyone else was experiencing shortages.[14] As discussed below (§1.1.6), charitable gifts are indeed mentioned, but not for the beneficiaries of the triennial tithes.

With a smoothed collection of the triennial tithes at the annual rate of 3.33%, by the end of the third year (מקצה שלש שנים) every farmer shall have indeed delivered 10% of his yield at the gate to feed the Levite, *ger*, widow, and orphan living in his village.

Another benefit of the collection of the triennial tithes on a yearly basis at a constant rate of 3.33 % is that the discussion whether or not farmers travel to the *maqom* on the third year becomes a purely academic debate. As the produce of the yearly tithes reverts to their producers, farmers need not abstain from the *maqom* festivities on the third year in order to avoid relinquishing 20% of that year's yield.

All in all, the tithes of Deuteronomy 14 correspond to a very low yearly levy of 3.33%. Farmers are expected to relinquish 3.33% of their yearly

---

11   For instance, Jagersma, "Tithes," 116–28; Mayes, *Deuteronomy*, 246.
12   Lundbom, *Deuteronomy*, 482–83.
13   Stackert, *Rewriting*, 170.
14   See Na'aman, "Sojourners," 237–79.

field and garden produce to the landless, while 6.66% or even 10% of their yearly yield and firstlings are dedicated to their own consumption at the *maqom*. This point is one of the most striking aspects of the Deuteronomic economy. It sets Deuteronomy apart from the rest of the Hebrew Bible where tithes are collected to support priesthood and royalty.[15]

A different reading of the initial words of the passage on tithes may be attempted to resist the strange notion of the bulk of tithes benefitting the tithe payers. Instead of reading "tithing you shall surely tithe" (עשׂר תעשׂר) in Deuteronomy 14:22 as a standard emphatic form involving a prepositive infinitive verbal form in front of the *iqtol* of same root that simply underlines the importance of the act of tithing, עשׂר תעשׂר may be read as "you shall set apart the tithe of the tithe", i.e., 10% of 10%. In this case, instead of consuming all the products they bring to the *maqom*, the farmers and their families would eat and drink 10% of what they bring to the *maqom*, leaving 90% of the yearly tithe behind for the priesthood serving there.

The presence of priestly personnel at the *maqom* is indeed mentioned in Deuteronomy 18:6–8 where it is stated that a Levite is free to travel to the *maqom* where he is to receive the same amount as his colleagues there. Verses 3 and 4 even specify the exact amount: a shoulder, the two jowls and the stomach of every ox or sheep, plus first fruits and first fleeces. These are designated as the priests' dues (משפט הכהנים) rather than tithes, and rightly so. Except for the wool, they concern the same agricultural produce brought or bought at the *maqom* by the farmers, but their purpose is entirely different. Whereas Deuteronomy 14 grants the Levite no revenues at the *maqom*, the priests' dues are a tax collected from the tithes at the *maqom* for the Levitical priests defined as the entire tribe of Levi (Deut 18:1). Whereas Deuteronomy 14 grants the Levite a share of the proceeds of triennial tithes stored in every settlement, chapter 18 introduces a tax collected at the *maqom* for Levitical priests. Chapter 18 presupposes the tithes of chapter 14 but increases the revenues of a prebendary group, priests that it avoids identifying simply with the Levite of chapter 14. Chapter 18 thus implies that the food set apart by the farmers for the Levite is insufficient to satiate him—contrary to the claim in Deuteronomy 14:29—and that by traveling to the *maqom* the Levite can supplement his (meager) revenues with those granted to Levitical priests, revenues chapter 14 fails to mention.

The tension between chapters 14 and 18—Levite and Levitical priests, yearly tithes for self-consumption and priestly dues—tends to be passed over because reading עשׂר תעשׂר in Deuteronomy 14:22 as a tithe of the

---

15 Altmann, *Festive Meals*, 231.

tithe solves several issues. It avoids admitting that Deuteronomy 14 keeps the Levites within your gates and away from the *maqom*, it saves considering whether Israelite producers can learn to fear YHWH by eating and drinking as much as their hearts' desire without the supervision of priestly personnel (see §4.3), and it explains away the difficulty of how families can eat and drink the whole of their yearly tithe within the days of the pilgrimage. Instead of putting the Levites on a diet while the rest of the population is gorging itself at the *maqom* with the whole of their yearly tithes, 90% of the yearly tithes are set aside to a *maqom* priesthood.

There is, however, a major hurdle. To express the notion that the audience must tithe the tithe, i.e. to set aside for their own consumption only 10% of the tithes they deliver at the *maqom*, a formulation such as תעשר את מעשר would be expected, with the noun tithe rendered with the participial form of the root עשר, i.e. מעשר, as is the case every time a tithe rather than the act of tithing is mentioned.[16] As far as I know, tithe is always מעשר, never עשר. To argue that עשר תעשר means a tithe you shall tithe requires postulating an unattested form of the noun tithe placed before the verb as can be the case in poetic texts, rather than after the verb as is regular in narration.

Two passages do mention a tithe of the tithe. Numbers 18:26 requires the Levites to set apart a tithe of the tithe they receive for themselves and offer it to YHWH. In this case, the tithe of the tithe is rendered as מעשר מן מעשר, literally "the tithe from the tithe". The notion of a tithe of the tithe is picked up in Nehemiah 10:39[Eng 38] where it is stated as מעשר המעשר. Again, tithe is designated with the initial letter *mem* and the genitive is rendered with the construct state, indicated by the regular absence of the article in front of the first member of the genitival group. In both cases, a verb expresses the action of setting aside the tithe of the tithe, לקח in Numbers 18:26 and עלה in Nehemiah 10:39. No such verb is found in Deuteronomy 14:22 if the two words עשר תעשר are already used up to express the notion of a tithe of the tithe.[17]

The tithe of the tithe in Numbers 18:21 may in fact react against the revenues Deuteronomy 14 grants to the Levite. Instead of Deuteronomy's 3.33% of all field produce to be shared out with *gerim*, widows, and orphans, Numbers 18:21 insists that YHWH has granted the Levites *every* tithe in Israel (את כל מעשר בישראל). The priests' dues (Deut 18:1) introduce

---

16   Gen 14:20; Lev 27:30–32; Num 18:21–28; Deut 12:5.11.17; 14:23.28; 26:12; Ezek 45:11.14; Amos 4:4; Mal 3:8.10; Neh 10:38–39, 12:44; 13:5.12; 2 Chron 31:5–6.12.
17   In a private conversation, Diana Edelman pointed out that in Deut 26:12 לעשר את כל מעשר could refer to the sacred portion removed from the house (verse 13), which would constitute a tenth of the tenth. If so, the secondary nature of chapter 26 is even more obvious.

within Deuteronomy itself the matter of the allocation of resources to the priesthood. Once the Torah is read canonically, the allocation of *all* tithes in Israel to the Levites (Num 18:21) turn the tithing system of Deuteronomy 14 into the introduction of a tax system that is more generous with the priesthood (see below §§4–5).

Read on its own account, the section on tithing in Deuteronomy 14:22–29 can hardly start with a mention of the tithe of the tithes before the tithe itself has been delineated. The yearly yield must be tithed before a tithe of the tithes can be extracted from it. According to Numbers 18:21 and Nehemiah 10:39, it is the duty of the Levites to set apart the tithe of the tithe as an offering for YHWH because they are the ones who receive the tithe from the producers. In Deuteronomy 14, however, the Levite is not involved in the collection of yearly tithes and he is not entitled to any of them. On the contrary, he shares the triennial tithes with the *ger*, the widow and the orphan in your gates. Hence the call not to abandon (לא תעזבנו) the Levite who remains in your gates in verse 27 (echoed in 12:19). Yet, the warning not to abandon the Levite has been read in the opposite way (see further below §4.3). As Deuteronomy 12:12, 18; 16:11, 14; 18:6; 26:11 mention the Levite besides the households at the *maqom* celebrations, the call not to abandon the Levite becomes a warning not to leave him behind. In the framework of de Wette's identification of the *maqom* as the temple of Jerusalem, the disenfranchised Levites are given menial tasks in Jerusalem to compensate for the loss of revenues at the peripheral sanctuaries they served before Josiah closed them. Therefore, the two verses in Deuteronomy 14 that keep the Levite away from the *maqom* can be dismissed, all the more so since the idea that Deuteronomy 14 grants the farmers the whole of the tithes they bring to the *maqom* leaves nothing for the priests and the Levites at the temple of Jerusalem. Elsewhere, sacrificial tariffs ensure that a large amount of foodstuffs go to the support of the temple priests (e.g. Lev 7). This is exactly what is found in chapter 18.

1.1.2 Priestly dues: meat cuts, first-fruits, and first fleeces (Deuteronomy 18:3–4)

As discussed in the previous paragraph, Deuteronomy 18 grants the Levitical priests a shoulder, the jowls, and the stomach of every sacrificed animal plus the first-fruits of the grain, wine, oil, and wool, plus the first fleece from every sheep (Deut 18:3–4).[18] These priestly prebends are pre-

---

18   A sheep produces about 2 kg of wool yearly: Dalman, *Arbeit und Sitte*, VI.180.

sented as compensation for the lack of shares of communal land (Deut 14:27.29; 18:1).

Contrary to the proceeds of the triennial tithes, these products belong exclusively to the Levitical priests. The Levite is entitled to them when he travels to the *maqom,* but orphans, widows, and *gerim* have no share in them. Even though Deuteronomy 18:3 makes no mention of the *maqom,* it seems that the meat cuts are collected from the carcasses of male firstlings sacrificed at the *maqom.* It can only be inferred that the firstling lambs were shorn there before the sacrifice. As for the first fruits, it is only in Deuteronomy 26:2 that they are mentioned again (§1.1.3).

In terms of quality, the Levites collect choice cuts though not necessarily the best ones.[19]

Besides the meat cuts, first fleeces belong to the Levitical priests. The cost of the allocation of first fleeces can be figured approximately by reckoning an average of ten live lambs born to every adult ewe. In this case, it amounts to a tithe on wool and goat hair, though the overall burden is higher since male firstlings are to be sacrificed before their first shearing (Deut 15:19).

Contrary to the meat and wool taxes, the first fruits mentioned in Deuteronomy 18:4–5 represent hardly any financial burden to the farmer. First fruits are mentioned again in Deuteronomy 26 where the ceremony during which they are collected involves a mere basketful of produce.

At this point, some remarks on the relation between tithes and priestly dues are possible. First, the meat cuts (Deut 18:3) answer the apparent lack of meat in the proceeds of the triennial tithes, since Deuteronomy 14:28 only mentions the produce of the field (כל מעשר תבואתך בשדה). Second, the list of non-meat produce (Deut 18:4) clearly specifies these products as first fruits, not as tithes. Third, the approximate 10% collected as tax on wool seems to be patterned on the yearly tithes (Deut 14:27–29). Therefore, the generous allocation of food to the Levitical priests (Deut 18:1–8) begs the question of the relation of this passage to the triennial tithes in Deuteronomy 14:27–29 (see §2.2).

1.1.3 First-fruits for a *maqom*-priest (Deuteronomy 26:2–4)

First fruits have already been encountered in Deuteronomy 18:4. Deuteronomy 26 clarifies what remains ambiguous in chapter 18. First fruits are to be presented at the *maqom* to the priest on duty on these days

---

19   At Borsippa, the shoulder was a choice piece, but not as favored as the thigh: Waerzeggers, *Ezida,* 262–63. The jowls probably included the tongue: Lundbom, *Deuteronomy,* 545.

(יהיה בימים ההם). This is one of the few occasions when the word "priest" is used alone without the qualifier "Levitical" and one of the few occurrences of an altar in Deuteronomy. The altar for YHWH (Deut 27:5–6) belongs to the framing chapters, though it agrees with the presentation of that altar in Deuteronomy 12:27; 16:21; 26:4.[20] The Levitical priest (Deut 18:1) is identified here as a priest, suggesting that Levites can serve as priests, a pivotal point in the scenario of the Levites as disenfranchised clergy from the local sanctuaries closed by Josiah,[21] though the term "high places" (במות) never appears in Deuteronomy.[22]

The notion of a single priest officiating at the time is coherent with the omission of Ithamar (Num 3:4) in Deuteronomy 10:6 where Eleazar alone succeeds his father. The priests (plural) who stood beside Moses when he was still alive (Deut 27:9; 31:9) leave the stage at the same time as Moses. Hence, there is considerable disagreement between the different textual traditions over the identity of the personnel of the high court of justice (Deut 17:9): "Levitical priests and a judge" (MT), no one in the Greek of Codex Vaticanus, and "the priest or the Levite or the judge" (Syriac). In verse 12, the Masoretic Text has only one priest "or the judge"; some Samaritan texts and the Vulgate have "the priest *and* the judge". A similar problem appears in the "law concerning witnesses" (Deut 19:17) where a singular form of the verb היה is attested to in some Masoretic and Samaritan texts though the subjects are priests and judges. These textual variants reveal the presence of editorial activity spurred by the importance of the issue at hand, the nature of the *maqom* and the beneficiaries of the generous prebends (Deut 18:1–8).

Much ambiguity remains over the beneficiaries of first fruits. In verse 11, the Levite and the *ger* are to rejoice in the bounty expressed by the basket of first fruits. The next verse adds the quartet of beneficiaries of triennial tithes from Deuteronomy 14:29, as though to justify the attribution of the first fruits to the priest only. The Levite and the *ger* may indeed rejoice, but the orphan and the widow are to be satisfied with triennial tithes only. Though a basket of first fruit presented to the priest on duty at the *maqom* is a negligible financial burden for the token farmer, the sum of produce from the basket presented by each Israelite family

---

20 First fruits to be delivered at the *maqom* are not mentioned in the products of the tithes in Deut 14:22–29. The first fruits constitute a common theme besides the priest and the altar and a clue to the presence of secondary insertions within the core in chapters 12; 16 and 26 under the influence of the framing material, in particular chapter 27. The matter of insertions into the core is discussed in the final chapter.
21 See Cook, "Stubborn Levites," 155–70.
22 Knoppers, "Rule of Law," 139.

would amount to significant quantities of foodstuffs. For this reason, a clear identification of the recipients of the baskets would be crucial in real life. Instead, Deuteronomy 26 generates fuzziness over these recipients, as though the aim is to resist any attempt to establish a coherent economic model. This is in sharp contrast to the allocation of tithes in Deuteronomy 14, and the option it grants to far-away farmers.

At this point of the inquiry, it is clear that Deuteronomy 12–26 cannot be taken as a coherent whole. The tension discernible over the revenues of the Levites suggests the existence of a prior text based on the tithing system of chapter 14, which granted minimal revenues and space to the Levites. As Deuteronomy 18 and 26 significantly raise the revenues of the clergy and at the same time introduce priestly personnel at the *maqom*, it is plausible that the tithing system of chapter 14 granted no such role to its Levites at the *maqom*, and that these Levites who only benefited from a share of the triennial tithes in each settlement were meant to be the sole representatives of any clergy, in sharp contrast to the previous books of the Torah. Before being in a position to substantiate further this claim, it is necessary to pursue the inquiry from an economic angle in order to grasp the originality of the society envisaged in the earlier Deuteronomic core.

1.1.4 Price fluctuation between home and *maqom*

In distant settlements, the farmer's decision to convert his annual tithes into silver presupposes the existence of a local buyer at home and a market around the *maqom* that allows him to convert his silver back into food. That being the case, it follows that the smaller the proportion of nearby farmers to distant farmers, the greater the demand for food at the *maqom* and consequently the higher the price. In the same way, the greater the number of far-away farmers flooding their local market in preparation for the pilgrimage, the lower the price they obtain for their produce and livestock. Hence, the concession to exchange tithes and firstlings against silver to save on transport costs entails potential costs that would work mainly in favor of those selling the produce and livestock at the *maqom*.

Those benefiting the most on the *maqom* market would be, first, the producers in the vicinity of the site of the banquet in front of YHWH who could sell their surplus to their distant colleagues; second, the agent supplying the silver and effecting the exchange; and, third, anyone with the ability to transport goods from the distant markets to the *maqom* in time for the arrival of the pilgrims, unless trade barriers were raised to protect the market around the site.

Deuteronomy ignores trade barriers and nothing indicates that it is utopian to the point of ignoring seasonal and market price fluctuations to postulate ideal silver equivalents such as 1 shekel of silver = 1 *kurru* (300 liters) of barley mentioned in legal codes.[23] It is impossible to evaluate the financial burden the price difference between the local market and the *maqom* could represent in the budget of the distant farmer. It would fluctuate from year to year, depending on the amount of surplus and the distance of the settlement from alternative outlets. With or without trade barriers around the *maqom* a 20% price variation does not seem exaggerated.

In the real world, the use of different weight systems such as the 20-gerah holy shekel (Lev 27:25) and the ordinary 24-gerah shekel would cause a further loss of purchasing power at the *maqom*.[24] The writers are aware of this possibility and Deuteronomy 25:13–14 prohibits explicitly the possession of different weights, "stones large and small in your purse" (בכיס) and "ephah large and small in your house" (Deut 25:13–14).

This burden borne by the distant farmers is a gain for the suppliers of the *maqom* market. The farmers living close to the *maqom* stand to benefit the most. Finding themselves next door to a captive market on which they can sell their surpluses to their colleagues coming from afar, the benefits they draw from their location entails no expenses, contrary to merchants who would incur transport costs when shifting produce from local settlements towards the *maqom*. Therefore, two different categories of producers arise. Those living close to the *maqom,* who benefit from the centralization and the others who, living at a greater distance, bear an extra 20% burden, through the loss of value of their tithes and firstlings, a burden which can be added to their fiscal burden which now corresponds to 23.33%. Thus, to the distant farmer, the total cost of his tithing—including the annual 3.3% levy as triennial—might amount to around 30% of the value of his total production for that year, despite the fact that his annual tithes do not represent a tax burden *per se,* since he consumes them with his family at the *maqom*.

1.1.5 Non-assessable costs: remission of debts (Deuteronomy 15:3–6)

On top of the outright expenses the Deuteronomic farmer incurs in the form of triennial tithes and the possible losses entailed when distant farmers exchange their annual tithes into silver, Deuteronomy 15 and 24

---

23   Jursa, *Aspects,* 814.
24   Kletter, *Economic Keystones,* 143–48.

discuss transactions that would represent extra expenses any economic agent would bear in the real world. These costs cannot be assessed but they should be taken into account as they reveal the different economic actors and institutions at work in Deuteronomy's core.

Together with the distinction between annual and triennial tithes and their allocation to different groups, the remission of debts delineated in Deuteronomy 15 constitutes the heart of the Deuteronomic economy. For this reason, this chapter is a pillar of biblical ethics, though the comprehension of this chapter is impaired by a number of fallacies. A first hindrance is Gregory Chirichigno's claim that Deuteronomy does not envisage the pledging of persons and restricts pledges to non-essential items such as a garment (Deut 24:10–13). In fact, the mention of work for six years (Deut 15:12) indicates that Deuteronomy 15 considers loans reimbursed by supplying an equivalent value in labor to the creditor (antichresis).[25] In this context, it is crucial to understand that the slave to be released in the seventh year is no chattel slave. Male or female, that person provides the creditor with labor to reimburse an antichretic loan, but the creditor does not own the debtor's person.

In ancient Oriental practice, antichresis was common, despite qualms about the exact terminology.[26] Many loans were paid back by granting the usufruct of the pledge to the creditor, rather than to the debtor as is common today.[27] When a person is pledged against an antichretic loan, manumission (another ambiguous term) is the result of the extinction of the lien the loan created between debtor and creditor. Hence, Deuteronomy's discussion of loans is congruent with ancient Near Eastern practice. Since the early second millennium BCE, a major motivation for agricultural lending was to secure a source of labor from the borrower rather than drawing revenues through the charging of interest.[28] For this reason, creditors were not necessarily in a hurry to press for full reimbursement of loans and debtors were not necessarily in a hurry to reimburse loans because debts fostered complex networks of interdependence between debtors and creditors.

In practice, the loans contracted by ordinary farmers would be repayable within twelve months at most, but usually less because during the months following the harvest farmers have no immediate need to borrow. Ancient farmers did not finance long-term projects such as land development with irrigation or assets such as buildings and expensive machinery, which have to be amortized over years or even decades. The

---

25   Against Chirichigno, *Debt-Slavery*, 270.
26   Zaccagnini, "Nuzi," 223–29.
27   On antichresis see Prov 22:7 and Guillaume, *Land*, 195–96.
28   Steinkeller, "Money-Lending," 109–37.

farmer in antiquity would have borrowed grain to feed his household, pay taxes, rent, any overdue interest he has to capitalize, and any principal he has not been able to repay from previous years' borrowings. Therefore, the seven-year cycle of Deuteronomy 15 exceeds the duration of agricultural/subsistence loans, most of which had shorter terms measured in months before the next harvest.

The cancellation of outstanding debts at the end of seven years (מקץ שבע שנים) concerns commercial operations between brothers. It is crucial to recognize that Deuteronomy 15 does not deal with short-term subsistence loans granted to farmers, the shortest being secured by a garment (Deut 24:10–13).

The cancellation of outstanding debts at the end of the seventh year is essential for the maintenance of a healthy credit market. Before reading any humanitarian ideal into the *šemiṭṭah,* it must be clear that a healthy credit market requires excluding defaulting payers, and that the cancellation of debts has a cost to both parties. The lender obviously loses the unpaid sums while, for the beneficiary, the released sums are not a net gain because it entails a serious loss of reputation and thus of further credit.

A good reputation is hard to acquire and is easily lost. Being unable to honor one's debt is a major dent in one's reputation and a loss of social capital. The brother who benefited from the *šemiṭṭah* will not find other brothers ready to grant him further loans at the preferential conditions that prevail within the brotherhood. Throughout the next cycle of lending and borrowing, he will find it more difficult to obtain loans. To compensate the higher risk taken by potential creditors, the loans he may obtain can logically be expected to be shorter, smaller, subject to interest, and debarred from any entitlement to further release. Because credit is crucial to social interaction, in finance as much as in marriage, the humanitarian aspect of the release resides in the second chance given to the defaulter. If he succeeds to honor all the debts he contracted during the next seven-year cycle, he might regain his previous status and re enter the commercial loans market.

Therefore, the Deuteronomic *šemiṭṭah* is the opposite of the Babylonian *andurārum.* The *šemiṭṭah* cancels outstanding debts in the form of commercial loans rather than debts of which the date of refund had not expired on the date the edict came into effect.[29] Contrary to the *andurārum,* the *šemiṭṭah* is not decreed by a monarch in search of popular support but within an association operating in isolation from any court and from the populace. The members of that association are also

---

29 Olivier, "Restitution," 12–25.

one likely source of shorter term agricultural loans for ordinary farmers. Such loans create a lien that is beneficial to both parties. For the lender, subsistence loans ensure a privileged access to surpluses, when there are any. For the borrowers, those loans produce a dependence that they consider beneficial because when there are no surpluses, and seeds and foodstuffs must be found in order to survive until the next harvest, lenders have a vested interest in finding the necessary resources to keep their debtors alive. Reimbursement is not the primary aim of these loans. As antichretic loans, they are paid back in labor-days, which enables the lender to tap into the local pool of manpower and beast of burden power at preferential rates.

Seven-year commercial loans are of an entirely different nature. They cannot be left running indefinitely. The credit market is at risk if it is not purged at regular intervals because, although interest-free, the sums and the risks these loans involve are greater.

Risk is controlled by calibrating the size of loans in proportion to the time left until the date of the *šemiṭṭah*, hence the calls to give loans even when the seventh year is close (Deut 15:9). Yet, all loans involve risk. To persuade the audience to accept the risk and to bear the costs of the *šemiṭṭah* release, Deuteronomy 15:7 insists that only the outstanding debts of a rare brother in one rare settlement (אחד אחיך באחד שעריך) are likely to have to be remitted.

1.1.6 Non-assessable costs: gifts to released pledges (Deuteronomy 15:13–14)

After limiting the term of commercial loans to a maximum of seven years when outstanding debts must be erased, Deuteronomy 15:13–15 urges creditors to mark the release of pledges with shows of generosity. The labor of these pledges reimbursed antichretic loans, which have been calibrated so as to be fully paid back at the end of six years. At the maturity of the loan, the creditor is urged to "neck" (ענק) the pledges associated with the loan with gifts from the flock, the threshing floor, and the wine vat. No actual amount is prescribed. As gifts, their size is left at the discretion of the giver. The silence over the oil press and the herd (בקר), which is always mentioned next to the flock when firstlings are discussed, indicates that the value of the gifts is low. The actual cost of these gifts is offset in a number of ways. First, the hope of receiving gifts at the end of the labor contract motivates pledges to work as hard for the debtor as they would when working for themselves. Hence, the gifts are incentives and their actual cost is balanced by greater productivity. Second, gifts call for counter-gifts and oblige the recipients of the gifts. The reciprocity sustains social cohesion.[30] Finally, end-of-contract gifts maintain the reputation of the giver whose access to the local pool of dedicated laborers of good repute depends on his reputation as an employer. An employer known as fair and generous also saves on the costs of supervision.

1.1.7 Non-assessable costs: daily payment of wages (Deuteronomy 24:14–15)

A day laborer (שָׂכִיר) is to receive his wages at the end of the day (Deut 24:14–15). This prescription represents a burden for the hirer when it involves an advance of funds, as would be the case if daily wages were disbursed before the fruit of the labor is converted into revenues. If, however, the hirer pays the hired laborers in kind, for instance grain or grapes at harvest times, or wool at shearing time, he saves on the cost of storage and the daily payment does not represent an advance of funds. Moreover, verse 14 introduces a number of qualifications. Daily payment only concerns the weakest category of workers, designated as עני and אביון. The meaning of these terms is discussed below (§2.4).

All in all, the actual financial burden of this prescription is quite light. Moreover, the mention of guilt (חטא) at the end of verse 15, where it is presented as the result of the worker crying out to YHWH, is a warning to the hirer. Besides the threat of divine wrath, delaying the payment of wages is detrimental to the reputation of the hirer who would find it hard to find reliable manpower and would end up having to hire less productive workers. Again, these verses underline the crucial matter of manpower in the world of the writers. It is in the interest of the hirer as much as in that of the hired to abide by this admonition. As is the case with end-of-contract gifts, discussed above, the quality of the manpower available to any potential employer depends on his social capital. The value of a good name is far from negligible. A good name is an important element of one's wealth broadly defined to include a wide range of social behavior, including non-market behavior. Hence, the daily payment of wages is a humanitarian measure to protect the weak that entails positive returns for the hirer too.

1.1.8 Non-assessable costs: gleanings (Deuteronomy 24:19–22)

In addition to the triennial tithes, the Israelite brother is urged to abstain from going back to his field, olive trees and vines to collect what was overlooked or what ripened later. The gleanings are allocated to the *ger*,

---

30 See Steinkeller, "Practices," 109–37.

widow, and orphan, in addition to their share of triennial tithes. Gleaning rights involve pasturing rights. This is clear for wheat and barley cultivated on strips of communal land that return to their status of commons as soon as the harvest is completed.[31] Pasturing rights are also tied to gleaning rights when the vines mentioned in verse 21 are grown in association with trees and that these trees are planted on communal land too. In this case, access to communal land that was temporarily denied to protect the crops revert back to the owners of pasturing rights as soon as the reapers have vacated the land.[32]

The text sets clear limits to the exercise of gleaning rights. Contrary to Ruth who works right behind the reapers, drinks and eats with them and even gleans between the sheaves as they are still standing in the field (Ruth 2:8–15), Deuteronomy 24:19 mentions a forgotten sheaf (שׁכר עמר). As reapers are more likely to miss some broken stems than to forget an entire sheaf, the purpose of this forgotten sheaf is to signal that the gleaners have no access to the fields and orchards before the reapers have finished work and vacated the site. The meaning of the verb פאר, applied to the olive trees after they have been beaten, is unclear but the term אחריך "after you" that follows shows that the intention is the same as for the fields. It forbids the artificial prolongation, by the owners of the crops, of the ban on access to the land by those with gleaning rights. The crop owners cannot purposely leave a sheaf behind to signal that they have not finished, nor can they claim the grapes that mature later for themselves.

Though not assessable, the financial burden of the gleaning rights of the *ger,* widow, and orphan is light since the value of gleaned products exceed the cost of their labor, all the more so if the owner of the crops is using hired laborers.

Recapitulation of levies and costs
The taxes, levies and various costs shouldered by the token Deuteronomic farmer are presented in Table 1.1.

The most significant burden is shouldered by the distant farmer who converted his yearly tithes into silver before going to the *maqom*. This burden could reach 40 percent.

31 Guillaume, *Land*, 29.
32 It is conceivable that in theory the same system would have applied to land granted to officers in the imperial land-for-service system. In practice, however, granted land would not usually encroach on communal land (see Guillaume, *Land*, 92–93), except as gleaning rights granted to such imperial officers on fallow land and between harvest and sowing time. On some *gerim* as imperial officers, see §2.3.5 below.

Table 1.1 Summary of levies and incidental costs in Deuteronomy

Category	Produce	Rate	Recipients	Deut.
Triennial tithes	Crop and plant produces	3.33% of annual yield	Levite, *ger*, widow, orphan	14:27–29
Annual tithes	Wheat, oil, wine, male firstlings or silver equivalents	10% of annual yield	Tithing families at the *maqom*	14:22–23 15:19
Price fluctuations	Silver	Losses of up to 20% of value of tithes	Whoever sells victuals at the *maqom*	14:26
Different weights	Wheat, oil and wine	Losses of up to 16% of quantities	Whoever sells victuals at the *maqom*	25:13–14
Remitted debts	Loans	not assessable	Insolvent brother	15:3–6
Alms	Food	not assessable	Needy brother and others	15:7–11
Presents	Caprovids, grain, wine	negligible	Released pledges	15:12–15
Hired labour	In kind, silver, work-days	not assessible	Day laborers	24:14–15
Gleanings	Grain, olives, grapes	negligible	*Gerim*, orphans, widows	24:19–22
First fruits	Fruits and plants	one basket	Priest at the *maqom*	18:4; 26:2–10
Meat cuts	From bovines and caprovids	25% of every carcass	Levitical priests	18:3
First fleeces	Wool	> 10%	Levitical priests	18:4

For a distant farmer attending the *maqom*, it could be physically impossible or excessively costly to transport his tithed barley, dates, wine, and the firstlings from his livestock all the way from his home village. On arrival at the *maqom*, he would consequently need to purchase locally the produce and firstlings he could not bring with him. But the price of produce and firstlings at the *maqom* could be, say, 20 percent higher than back in the distant farmer's home village. Hence, the original tithe of 13.33 percent on harvested produce, such as barley, would cost the farmer an additional 20 percent, bringing the total cost of his tithe up to 16 percent (13.33% plus 2.67%) of his harvest.

In the case of firstlings, tithing cannot be expressed as a percentage of a farmer's livestock. But the surcharge for the farmer who is not able to bring his firstlings to the *maqom* remains the same, i.e. up to 20% of their original value back in his home village. This shows how crucial the setting of the *maqom* is as it has the potential to split Israel into those who benefit from the pilgrimage and those who lose out every year. Yet, Deuteronomy also envisages a number of situations that would significantly lighten the overall financial burden shouldered by farmers.

1.2 Savings

1.2.1 Yearly tithes consumed by the tithe-payers

The most significant saving to the token Deuteronomic farmer is the 10% of his yearly yield designated for self-consumption at the *maqom* (Deut 14:23). Unsurprisingly, "Neither the rabbis nor Christians, for example, adopted the annual tithe from Deuteronomy earmarked for a religious feast."[33] The notion of taxes reverting to the taxpayer is so different from the tariffs in the previous books of the Torah that it is tempting to include the Levites mentioned in Deuteronomy 14:27 along with the guests at the banquets.[34] Yet, Deuteronomy 14:26 does not list the Levites besides the addressee's household. At most, verse 27 could be read as a post scriptum, enjoining the farmers to hand out something to the Levites while recognizing that the yearly tithes do not belong to the Levites.

As the *setuma* between verses 26 and 27 indicates, verse 27 is in fact the introduction of the passage dealing with the triennial tithes. As one of the landless beneficiaries of the triennial tithes, the Levite has no right to the yearly tithes (verses 22–26) except as a guest in the festive meals at the *maqom*. It is left to the discretion of each producer to invite a Levite to the *maqom* banquets. This point is crucial for the understanding of *maqom*. According to Deuteronomy, the climax of the pilgrimage is not the slaughter of clean animals but the joy of a common meal in the presence of YHWH.

The killing of the animals is relatively insignificant in the light of the celebration of Israel's existence before the countenance of YHWH. The Israel that celebrates this festival is moreover a society where there are neither poor nor needy. This ideal society constitutes in Deuteronomy the true sacred.[35]

---

33 Eldevik, *Episcopal Power*, 41.
34 Tigay, *Deuteronomy*, 141. Awabdy, *Immigrants*, 61.
35 Lohfink, "Destruction," 104.

The self-consumption of yearly tithes in front of YHWH is part and parcel of the pedagogical function of the joyful meal. Learning the fear of YHWH (למד ליראה את יהוה) by eating one's yearly tithes in front of him is the Deuteronomic way to learn that YHWH is the "true owner of the land and giver of life, who takes the tithe and turns it back in yet another wave of generosity".[36] Halachic exegesis is less generous. It organizes the tithes in the Torah into a single system, reading Deuteronomy 14:22–27 and Leviticus 27:30–31 as a second tithe, taken from the 90% remaining after the first tithe of Numbers 18.[37]

Other scholars reduce the significance of the self-consumption of the annual tithes by presenting them as compensation to the farmers for the expense of transporting the tithes to the central sanctuary.[38] For Shigeyuki Nakanose, the distant peasants are only allowed to deduct their traveling expenses "from the amount of the tax due".[39] While distant farmers would indeed incur greater costs (§1.1.5), the yearly tithes are a tax from which travel expenses may be deducted. But are those yearly tithes a tax?

The Deuteronomic tithes are also unique in that their assessment seems to be left at the discretion of the producer himself, contrary to the livestock tithe in Leviticus 27:32, which mentions passing animals under a staff as part of a tallying procedure that would involve external tax assessors.[40] In sharp contrast to the complaint in Malachi 3:8–10 that some of the tithes did not reach the sanctuary's coffers, Deuteronomic taxpayers have no reason to evade taxes since they are the beneficiaries of the lion's share of the tithes. Bringing lesser amounts to the *maqom* would result in throwing a less impressive party at the *maqom*.[41] To "keep up with the Joneses", families would tend to bring more rather than less in order to avoid shame in front of relatives and neighbors.

The same principle would work at the local level. All the Levite is expected to do is wait at the gate of the settlement in which he resides to receive the proceeds of the triennial tithes and redistribute them to the defined beneficiaries: "Bring all your tithe... and they will eat and be

---

36 Brueggemann, *Deuteronomy*, 161; Hall, *Deuteronomy*, 246; McConville, *Deuteronomy*, 252.
37 Tigay, *Deuteronomy*, 41.
38 Claburn, "Fiscal Basis," 16.
39 Nakanose, *Josiah's Passover*, 75.
40 Milgrom, *Leviticus 23–27*, 2399.
41 On the basis of the Chronicler's description of Hezekiah's reform (2 Chron 31:5–6), Herman, "Tithes as Gifts," 71 found no competitive enthusiasm in the Pentateuch.

satiated so that YHWH your God will bless you in everything you have a hand in" (Deut 14:28–29).

The estimated financial burden on Israelite farmers is partially compensated for by the elimination of most of the usual beneficiaries of revenues, including YHWH who, even according to the Deuteronomic frames (Deut 10:12), insists that he requires nothing from his people other than reverent fear.

1.2.2 No expenses for the palace (Deuteronomy 17:15–19)

If the writers envisaged the presence of a king in their Israel, they expected that king to be self-supporting.[42] The spoils of war are granted to the warriors with no mention of any royal shares (Deut 20:14). There is no indication that the king is involved in the exercise of justice.[43] The expression "to do them" (לעשׂתם) in "He shall read it... to observe all the words of this Torah... in order *to do them*" (Deut 17:19) has been read as an indication of the involvement of the Deuteronomic king as judge, on the basis of episodes from the Deuteronomistic History.[44] In Deuteronomy itself, the king is one Israelite brother among others. Hence, there are no costs attributable to the support of a royal house to be listed in the profit and loss account.

1.2.3 No expenses for the elders, officers, judges, and prophet

Elders hold important functions at the local level. They send back a murderer on the run (Deut 19:12), deal with cases of unsolved murder (Deut 21:1–9) and arbitrate family conflicts (Deut 21:18–21; 22:13–29). Elders and judges are mentioned together when measuring the distance of two settlements from a murder scene (Deut 21:2). Hence, the officers (שׁטרים) who address the troop (Deut 20:5) and the judges (Deut 16:18; 17:12; 19:17–18; 25:1–2) are selected for a specific role in particular situations. They are "recognized leaders of a group of equals".[45] As is the case for the king, no revenues are attributed to the holders of official functions.[46]

---

42 Scheffler, "Criticism," 124–37 takes the portrayal of a dwarf king as the clue for an exilic date.
43 Lohfink, "Distribution," 340.
44 As does Weyde, "Narrative of King Solomon," 75–91.
45 Willis, *Elders of the City*, 307.
46 See also Tigay, "Role of the Elders," 89–96 who argues that the elders also served as notaries publicizing cases.

Nothing indicates that elders and judges must be brothers as the king must be, though they are not just any randomly picked Israelite. In societies with no professionalized offices, it is local worthies who are called to arbitrate disputes and perform other public functions on account of their wisdom and wealth. Wealth proves wisdom and vice versa, and these wealthy wise men accomplish their duties at no cost for the community.

1.2.4 No expenses for army, police, and judges (Deuteronomy 17:8–13; 22:1–4)

Besides taxes to build and maintain palaces and fortresses, the running costs of watchtowers and wardens can be dispensed with since farmers regulate matters of stray animals between themselves (Deut 22:1–4). The supreme court of justice is no court of appeal with the powers to reverse verdicts pronounced "within your gates". It arbitrates difficult cases at the *maqom* (Deut 17:8–13). No revenues are specifically allocated for the activities of the judge and possibly the priest or Levite who arbitrate the cases.[47]

1.2.5 No diviners and ritual specialists (Deuteronomy 16; 18:10–15; 22:5; 23:18–19)

Another source of savings for the Deuteronomic farmer is the elimination of a whole range of individuals who might otherwise draw revenues from farming populations: diviners, soothsayers, augurs, sorcerers, spell casters, ghosts and spirit consulters, necromancers (Deut 18:10–11) and some order of temple personnel referred to as sacred prostitutes, dogs (Deut 23:18–19) and transvestites (Deut 22:5).[48] Whatever the functions of these specialists, whether they are active in particular sanctuaries or ply their trade independently, they have no room in the world of Deuteronomy. They should not be heeded, contrary to a prophet like Moses (Deut 18:15). This leaves the Levite in your gates as the sole ritual specialist who gets a share of the proceeds of triennial tithes (Deut 14:27–29). The assault against traditional ritual specialists draws the attention on the status of the Levite in the festal calendar of chapter 16.

---

47   The critical apparatus of the BHS indicates the debate over the identity of the person besides the judge in Deut 17:9.
48   See Crouch, *Making*, 141–56; Bird, "Whores and Hounds," 352–64; Haworth, "Wolfish Lover," 7–23. On cross-dressing see Sacher Fox, "Prohibition," 49–71; Paganini, "Gesetz," 309–42. On *klbm*, *qrm* and *'lmt* on an inscription in fourth century BCE Kition, see Ribichini, "A servizio di Astarte," 59–60.

No Levite is mentioned in the description of the Passover sacrifice (Deut 16:1–8), as though each household takes care of the sacrifice, thus saving the fees of a ritual specialist, unless the meat cuts mentioned in 18:3 are also collected from the Passover lamb. The Levite is present at the *maqom* for the festivals of weeks and booths (Deut 16:11.14) but he is simply tagged along with the members of the celebrating households: you, your sons, your daughters, your male and female slaves, *and the Levite who is in your gates*. At most, the Levite joins the families for two festivals as a guest. This minimal involvement of the Levite fades further in the concluding verses of the festal calendar, which require all your males to appear at the *maqom* three times a year for the festivals of unleavened bread, weeks and booths. The presence of women becomes optional. The warning not to appear before YHWH empty-handed ignores the Levite. As a male, the Levite's presence would be required as carrier of his own gifts rather than as the beneficiary of the gifts brought to the *maqom* on these occasions. Hence, the festal calendar remains within the bounds set by the tithing system of Deuteronomy 14. The Levite's proper place remains within your gates where a share of the triennial tithes is set apart for him. During his occasional presence at the *maqom* where he plays no particular function, the Levite is entitled to the priests' dues that belong to the Levitical priests (§1.1.2).

1.2.6 Tax-free meats (Deuteronomy 12:15.22; 15:22)

Unlike beef, mutton, and goat meat, game is considered tax-free while Deuteronomy 14:5 underlines the importance of game with a list of permissible wild animals.[49] Meat from animals deemed unclean (Deut 14:3–20) can also be eaten at home, and thus are tax-free, if the *lectio difficilior* in Deuteronomy12:15.22; 15:22 is taken into account, as any *lectio difficilior* should be.

After the warning that all meat offerings must be sacrificed at the *maqom* and at the *maqom* only (Deut 12:13–14), verse 15 states that one can eat anything "in any of your gates". The second part of the verse specifies, according to the NRSV that "the unclean and the clean may eat of it, as they would of gazelle or deer": הטמא והטהור יאכלנו כצבי וכאיל (Deut 12:15b). The common understanding of this passage is that "the distinction between pure and impure refers to humans, not to the kinds of meats that are permitted." (*BHQ*: 87*). The MT is deemed ambiguous because it can be read as permitting the consumption of meats declared unclean in

---

49   Rütersworden, "Deut 14," 98.

the list of Deut 14:7–8, literally "the unclean and the clean (animal) he will eat some of it as (if) it was gazelle or deer".

To lift the ambiguity, in all three instances (Deut 12:15.22; 15:22) the LXX added ἐν σοί between the words clean and unclean:

ὁ ἀκάθαρτος <u>ἐν σοὶ</u> καὶ ὁ καθαρὸς ἐπὶ τὸ αὐτὸ φάγεται αὐτὸ ὡς δορκάδα ἢ ἔλαφον

The unclean *among you* and the clean together shall eat of it, like gazelle or deer. (NETS)

In Deuteronomy 12:22 and 15:22, a similar clarification is found in the Samaritan Pentateuch and 11QT^a 53:4 that insert בך/בכה between הטמא and והטהור. In every case, the words among you (ἐν σοί, בך) insist that the impure refers to the eaters not to the eaten.[50] This is a typical case of *lectio facilior* and the BHQ notes that all the expansions presuppose the Masoretic text. The *lectio facilior* is obviously motivated by the desire to align Deuteronomy with Leviticus 11.

The Vulgate, as much as the Samaritan and Greek texts, steers clear of the notion that impure animals can be eaten as long as the meal is partaken of at home rather than at the *maqom*. Yet, Jerome was aware that the impure in the Hebrew text refers to the meat rather than the person eating it. To avoid this reading, he aligned Deuteronomy 12:15 with the prohibition of sacrificing blemished animals (Deut 15:21). Hence, the Vulgate introduces several qualifications regarding meats from clean animals that are nevertheless unfit for sacrifices: *sive inmundum fuerit hoc est maculum et debile sive mundum hoc est integrum et sine macula quod offerri licet sicut capream et cervum comedes* "whether it be unclean, that is blemished and maimed, or clean, that is, whole and without blemish, which may be offered, such as the roebuck and the stag, you may eat." (BHQ: 87*) Specifying that unclean means blemished or maimed, Jerome steered clear of the suggestion that unclean animals could be consumed just like clean ones. Instead, what is allowed becomes the consumption of clean animals that are unsuitable for sacrifice due to imperfections (*maculatum et debile*).[51] In this way, impurity refers to blemished and handicapped animals and purity to intact and unblemished animals (*integrum et sine macula*).

The triple *lectio difficilior* of Deuteronomy 12:15.22; 15:22 ought to be a pivotal point in discussions of lists of clean and unclean animals, and even more so of the relation between the legal corpora of the Pentateuch. As far as I can see, the variant is not given the attention any *lectio difficilior*

---

50   NETS, 156; See Wevers, *Notes*, 219; Schiffman, "Septuagint," 280–81.
51   Weigert, *Hebraica veritas*, 170–71.

should receive from critical exegetes.[52] Dismissing it ignores a crucial aspect of the Deuteronomic world.

Granting the consumption of meats declared inedible in front of YHWH excludes the carcasses of unclean animals slaughtered or hunted on home ground from the meat cuts owed to the priest, that are specifically collected from bovines and caprovids (שור ושׂה Deut 18:3), the provision that, in their homes, Israelites may eat the flesh from any animal appears a concession to the extension of the meat cuts collected at the *maqom* to the same meat cuts collected at every Israelite settlement. In this case, Deuteronomy 12:15.22; 15:22 all belong to the same redactional stage as the priestly dues of Deuteronomy 18:1–8.

That Deuteronomy does not extend the *kashrut* to daily life in Israelite settlements is confirmed by the fact that there is no specification about the species of the eggs and fledglings that can be collected from the nest (Deut 22:6–7). At home, any bird, any egg, and any meat is permissible, which constitutes a significant source of tax-free meats since it is only from domestic bovines and caprovids that the Levites collect meat cuts.

Deuteronomy provides a number of ways in which Israelite brothers can obtain additional revenues besides ordinary farming activities. The actual amount cannot be estimated, but the sources of these additional revenues distinguish brothers from ordinary farmers.

1.2.7 Sale of carrion to foreigners (Deuteronomy 14:21)

Deuteronomy's core displays much interest in commercial interactions with non-Israelites. Deuteronomy 14:21 matches the prohibition of carrion consumption by Israelites with a provision that carrion (נבלה) may be given to the *ger* or sold to the foreigner (מכר לנכרי). The distinction between gift to the *ger* and sale to the foreigner is completed by a geographical distinction.[53] The *ger* is within your gates. The implication is that the foreigner resides elsewhere. The matter of distance is essential when dealing with corpses. Meat, fat, guts, and leather rot away beyond recovery within a few days, depending on the season. In practice, only the *ger* residing in the same settlement would be able to eat the meat,

---

52   See Rütersworden, "Deut 14," 95–103; Nihan, "Laws," 401–34; Chavel, "Deuteronomy 12," 85–108; Achenbach, "Systematik," 161–209; Nihan, *Priestly Torah*; Houston, *Purity and Monotheism*; Rütersworden, "Purity Conceptions," 413–28. Venter, "Dietary Regulations," 1240–62. Otto, *Deuteronomium 12,1–23,15*, 1138 and Lundbom, *Deuteronomy*, 435 mention the variants without drawing any implications for the meaning of the MT.

53   Rütersworden, "Purity," 419 misses the distinction and states that the "Israelites are allowed to sell נבלה to the foreigner (גר) who is living within their gates."

fat, and guts, as well as dry the abomasum of unweaned lambs, kids, and calves for rennet.⁵⁴ Hence, the gift of carrion to the *ger* is specifically designated for human consumption: (לגר תתננה ואכלה Deut 14:21), while this designation is omitted in the case of sales to the foreigner.

Other parts would be used, even from animals that had died before being slaughtered (Lev 7:24). Skins, wool, bones, and horns might be taken by the Israelite owner himself, who could use them because they are not edible.

While Deuteronomy 20:16–18 views the presence of the Canaanites as a threat to Israel's identity,⁵⁵ Deuteronomy 14 recognizes the economic benefits that can be drawn from such a presence. To modern readers, the sale of carrion feels like some ethnic joke to reinforce Israelite identity. To farmers, however, the premature death of animals is no laughing matter. The Israelite brother would hear the advice to recycle carcasses in every possible sense as a welcome concern for his needs. The frame displays an utopian view of a world entirely devoid of diseases (Deut 7:15) as long as Israel observes the divine decrees. The core, however, takes into account accidental losses of livestock and offers two ways to limit the loss. Sale to the foreigner offers some compensation. A gift to the *ger* excludes financial compensation but might still provide indirect compensation by ingratiating the giver in the eyes of the *ger*.

1.2.8 No interest on loans from brothers (Deuteronomy 23:20)

Loans between brothers are the only ones specifically designated as free from interest, contrary to loans granted to foreigners. The absence of interest thus represents significant savings, all the more so because these loans have terms up to seven years, whereas the vast majority of recorded loans run only over a number of months. This is true for commercial loans, and even more for the loans contracted by farmers who typically borrow between the sowing season and the harvest.⁵⁶

---

54 See Guillaume, "Curdle Milk with Rennet," 213–15; Guillaume, "Binding Suck," 335–37.
55 Crouch, "Threat," 546 n. 15.
56 Of the 27 usable commercial contracts for barley published in Pearce and Wunsch, *Documents*, a single one has a term of 12 months (No. 61) and another of 10 months (No. 94). Of the eight tablets published in Joannès and Lemaire, "Contrats", and Joannès and Lemaire, "Trois tablettes," two have terms of 11 months (J 1 and J 5). Of the 16 usable contracts involving silver, the longest term is 10 months (again No. 61). The others have terms between less than a month and 7 months. Though not relevant for Palestine, contracts dealing with date follow the same pattern.

Boer presents interest-free loans as a system of assistance based on trust that ensures "the mutual allocation and reallocation of all goods within the community".[57] Deuteronomy distinguishes three different regimes of credit. Besides foreigners who obtain interest-bearing loans and brothers who lend to one another interest-free, the neighbors to whom brothers grant secured loans at unspecified interest rates represent the village community (see below§2.3.4).

1.3 Non agricultural income

1.3.1 Interest from loans to foreigners (Deuteronomy 23:21 [English 20])

Besides the sale of carrion, Israelite brothers draw revenues from loans granted to foreigners.[58] The use of the term brother (אח) in the previous verse indicates that it is mostly Israelite brothers who are expected to have the means to engage in large-scale credit operations involving foreigners. Ordinary Israelite farmers are not directly concerned. The foreigners in question include any of Israel's neighbors except some Edomites who are declared brothers (Deut 23:8) and would thus not pay interest on loans. The other foreigners represent valuable sources of interest from loans that are shielded from the remission of debt.

1.3.2 Interest from loans to neighbors (Deuteronomy 24:10)

Besides foreigners, brothers are invited to grant interest-bearing loans to neighbors (רעה). Interest is not specified, thus reflecting the fact that interest was not the primary motivation of ancient lenders. Instead of interest, Deuteronomy 24:10 states that loans of any kind may be granted. The prohibition to enter the house of the borrower indicates that loans to neighbors are secured by a pledge because neighbors are not brothers, a crucial difference discussed at length below (§2.1). As relations between neighbors occur outside the inner circle of brothers, the higher risk is reduced by a collateral taken in hand the moment the loan is transferred to the borrower (possessory pledge), rather than in case of default (non-possessory pledge).

The difference between interest-bearing loans granted to foreigners and interest-free loans between brothers does not necessarily reflect an

---

57   Boer, *Sacred Economy*, 157–58.
58   Mutius, "Zinsgesetzgebung," 19–24 argues that the Greek text is an injunction: "you must exact interest from a stranger!"

anti-foreigner stance. It is, first of all, the logical consequence of saving on transaction costs. Potential lenders know best the financial situation and the credit-worthiness of people they are close to. For this reason, they need not devote extra efforts to assess the risk entailed by loans granted within their circle, although these loans, contrary to those granted to foreigners, are subject to the šemiṭṭah release. The šemiṭṭah and the absence of security are risk-increasing factors, but the risk is in fact lower than for loans to outsiders because default is less likely within the group than outside of it. Solidarity and transparency between brothers puts a high price tag on the cost of default. By contrast, one has less leverage over a defaulting neighbor and even less over a foreigner. For this reason, interest is the only way to reduce the inherent risk attached to granting credit.

It is important at this point to stress the importance of credit in agricultural economies ancient and modern. There is no escaping the symbiotic relationship between creditor and debtor. Therefore, the notion that the rich enrich themselves by pushing the poor into destitution is highly misleading. That the rich grant loans to the poor to make them even poorer makes no sense, unless poor implies in need of funds and creditworthy rather than destitute and unable to service a loan.

Another misrepresentation about the relationship between economic actors is that debt "functioned as a benevolent method to support the poor farmers rather than exploit them."[59] Debt, in fact, is a way to help farmers survive times of hardship so that they continue to reimburse their loans in the following years when yields are better. In other words, debt ensures that the creditor and the debtor *continue* to exploit one another. Contrary to the common usage, "to exploit" simply describes how the parties in any transaction use what they have in excess of their needs to obtain from each other what they lack, which may necessitate committing a minimal amount of loan capital to this aim.

Borrowing does not imply destitution.[60] On the contrary, destitution excludes one from the credit market in a more radical way than default. There is no point lending to someone who has no possibility whatsoever to pay back his debt. Destitution may be alleviated by alms, but the fact that someone was granted a loan proves that the borrower is not destitute, or that he has convinced the lender that there is a fair chance that he will honor his repayment obligations.

As Deuteronomy 15:11 states, there always will be needs in the land, and the credit market delineated in the Deuteronomic core is meant

---

59   Ro, *Poverty*, 216.
60   Against Levin, "Rereading," 67 who infers poverty from the fact that a loan has been contracted.

to answer to those needs in order to make destitution irrelevant. The šemiṭṭah preserves the commercial credit market by removing defaulting debtors from the preferential conditions that prevail among brothers. Instead of sucking borrowers into an irresistible spiral of debt, loans are calibrated to the financial capacity of each borrower: a maximum term of seven years between brothers, down to one day for the most modest borrowers who only have the mantle on their shoulders to pledge. Moreover, there is no evidence in Deuteronomy that shares of communal land are pledged, in contrast to Leviticus 25:23–28. Hence, even if barred from the preferential brotherly rates, the defaulting brother continues to grow the food his household needs in the gardens he owns and on his shares of communal land.

The Deuteronomic core refutes the simplistic view that loans are the hallmark of sharks while gifts are the hallmark of kindness. Wealth in the form of social recognition and prestige is obtained through creditworthiness, while charity benefits the giver more than the receiver of alms. Boer's elaborate distinction, between interest-bearing loans as the hallmark of extractive regimes and subsistence regimes characterized by interest-free loans that allocate and reallocate all goods within the community, is hardly more accurate.[61] Close interactions and blood ties within local communities can be very conflictual. Instead of a romanticized local community, the Deuteronomic core imagines a brotherhood that transcends local communities and the confines of Israel itself (§3.3).

Finally, the temptation to read the words עני and אביון in the Deuteronomic core in light of the Psalms in which the expression עני ואביון conveys a privileged access to divine favors should be resisted. The equation of righteousness with poverty in these Psalms ended up generating sayings such as "it is easier for a camel to go through the eye of a needle than for a rich man to enter the kingdom of God" (Matt 19:24). The spiritualization of poverty severs all moorings with economic realities. By contrast, Deuteronomy delineates a program that claims to be able to eliminate poverty, contrary to Psalm 140:12 that expects God alone to do justice to the poor and needy. Having seriously curtailed kingship, the Deuteronomic writers transferred the traditional role of the king as protector of the poor and needy to the brothers, who find themselves as the primary instance of patronage. The idea that for the Deuteronomic writers poverty was not a condition that ought to be overcome because "it is the mark of a religious group characterized by its special closeness to God"[62] can only be valid when the detailed economic guidelines of the Deuteronomic core are ignored.

61   Against Boer, *Sacred Economy*, 156.
62   Levin, "Rereading," 59.

1.3.3 Social capital from short-term loans to neighbors (Deuteronomy 24:12–13)

Deuteronomy 24:12–13 further reduce the risk incurred by the lender when the borrower is of low economic status (עָנִי). The common translation of this term as "poor" is the source of much confusion. The prohibition to sleep in the cloak that the poor borrower pledged has misled many in reading a humanitarian concern for the poor in these verses. Poverty is too vague a concept to account for the stipulations of Deuteronomy 24:12–13. In any credit market, what matters is creditworthiness.

At the risk of stating the obvious, a loan—any kind of loan—is not a gift. A loan must be paid back. Hence, the very fact that a loan has been granted indicates that the lender has considered, rightly or wrongly, that the borrower was creditworthy when the loaned capital was transferred from the lender to the borrower. Therefore, instead of being poor, the borrower in question here is better designated as of modest means. However poor he may be, he is considered creditworthy by the lender. His economic standing is modest. He might not own anything else than the cloak on his back and in which he sleeps at night. But he is evidently a valid person. For this reason, the lender takes the risk of granting a loan because the modest borrower has the ability to generate profit from the transaction and pay back the loan in time and in full.

Still, the lender mitigates the risk of default by reducing the duration of the loan. As with the prohibition to enter the house of the borrower (Deut 24:10), the prohibition to sleep in the borrower's pledged cloak has fooled many in reading humanitarian concerns in this straightforward principle of economic wisdom. The low value of the pledge is indicative that the loan is a small one. The return of the pledge by sunset (Deut 24:13) indicates an ultra-short term. This is a case of microcredit to be reimbursed by sunset and in full, at which point the pledge is returned.

Were the pledged cloak returned by sunset, though the due repayment date of the loan was longer than one day, the loan would no longer be secured, unless the debtor collected the pledged cloak morning after morning and returned it each evening until the loan was finally extinguished. Sunset, therefore, marks the duration of the loan.[63] Such very short-term loans may bear interest since the neighbor is not designated as a brother. The interest rates on these loans appear exorbitant when they are converted into annual rates.

Interest rates between 33% and 50% per annum can only be considered usurious in isolation of economic realities. Among socially integrated

---

63   Altmann, *Economics*, 258.

peasant societies, such rates are bearable.[64] They correspond to standard rates practiced today for microcredit transactions. High interest rates cover the proportionally high transaction costs incurred by the lender when small amounts are granted over short periods, in this case a single day. Hence the basic principle that interest rates are in inverse ratio to the size and duration of loans.[65]

The last part of Deuteronomy 24:13 presents the return of the pledged cloak at sunset in a very positive light for the lender: "so that your neighbor may sleep in the cloak and bless you; and it will be to your credit (צדקה) before the LORD your God." These words may be somewhat self-congratulatory, but it is important to note that they address loans, *not* charity.

Loans generate straight financial blessings for the lender in the form of interest. Blessing for the borrower comes in the form of credit based on his good reputation. By taking the risk and the trouble to lend to small economic actors, the creditor enables his debtors to generate extra revenues for themselves. The Nobel prize for economy was awarded to the founder of the Grameen Bank in 2006 for the precise reason that microfinance is seen by development agencies as an effective way of empowering small and micro-enterprises and traders.[66] Despite the high interest rates charged, these loan transactions are very effective, as their development shows, and they demonstrate the fallacy of placing limits on interest rates.

Cases of default are not even considered because the full reimbursement of micro-credit results in blessing as much for the borrower as for the creditor, with both standing to gain in material and social prestige. As with the big parties thrown at the *maqom*, the status derived from granting loans to borrowers of modest means is an important ingredient of individual welfare, a factor motivating human behavior.

With the loan, the creditor gains interest *and* social capital. Does this means that he should be viewed as a shark?[67] A lender is indeed a loan shark if his gains are a loss to the supposedly poor borrower. But this is hardly a common case because a loan gives the debtor a chance to make a profit from the loan. He can look his creditor in the eye when he pays back his debt on time and in full (including any interest) and requests the return of the collaterals. If indeed poor, the debtor is less destitute than before. Had he received alms rather than a loan, the alms-giver would have gained social capital all the same, but without taking any risk since

---

64 Renger, "Comments," 195; Vargyas, "Babylonian Interest Rates," 1102.
65 Duncan-Jones, *Economy of the Roman Empire*, 134.
66 Sider, "Evaluating," 120.
67 As does Boer, *Sacred Economy*, 156.

no returns would be expected beyond the social recognition gained from his generosity. As for the gains of the receiver of alms, they would be minimal. Poor in the sense of destitute, alms might have brought him an additional day of survival. Needy in the sense of looking for an advance of capital, the loan provided an opportunity to make a profit. Loans entail risks for both parties and consequently the possibility of benefits for both parties, in straight financial forms and in terms of reliability, creditworthiness and good reputation. Deuteronomy presents the ability to lend to many people as YHWH's blessing (Deut 15:6), blessing enumerated in straight economic terms.

1.3.4 War booty and captives (Deuteronomy 20:10–15; 21:10–14)

The license to marry a female war captive is a convenient means to obtain extra woman-power, a more significant asset than a man because of the ban on male castration (Deut 23:2) in a world where the first cause of adult female mortality is childbearing.

Keen as she is to demonstrate Deuteronomy's efforts to construct a distinctive Israeliteness, Crouch insists that the war captive's identity is "so unfamiliar as to pose almost no threat to be rendered an Israelite" and that "Isolation, both geographical and cultural, is the solution proffered".[68] In fact, nothing in the rules of warfare delineated in Deuteronomy 20 indicates that the culture and origins of the war captive are unfamiliar. Geographical distance (Deut 20:15) distinguishes between the towns that can be raided and those in Canaan that must be utterly destroyed with no booty taken. Once the genocide of the seven nations is accomplished (Deut 20:16–18), Israel is expected to find itself surrounded by foreign towns to be conquered to enlarge Israelite territory. The dynamic notion of a territory susceptible of being extended is congruent with the idea that, thanks to YHWH's blessing, Israelite farmers will find themselves at an ever great distance from the *maqom* (Deut 14:24).

More than giving time for shedding the foreignness of the woman, the month of mourning is the necessary time to find out whether or not she was pregnant when captured. Far more practical than Judges 21:11–12 that eliminates women who have lain with a man—hardly a foolproof criterion—Deuteronomy's only condition is that she be beautiful and desirable (Deut 21:12). Such a candidate to Israeliteness would be more likely to produce good-looking children, especially since her new husband is prevented from ever selling her as a slave and has thus no incentive to divorce her. This does not mean, however, that the writers condemn slave trafficking.

---

68 Crouch, *Making*, 202.

Is Deuteronomy's military law pacifistic?[69] Indeed, the rules governing war afford every potential fighter the chance to go back home before the battle because of fear, because he acquired a new house, planted a vineyard, became engaged (Deut 20:2–9), had a wet dream (Deut 23:9–11) or is newly wed (Deut 24:5). More than pacifism, these exemptions reflect economic concerns, ensuring that war does not disrupt procreation and agriculture. Deuteronomy's suggested pacifism actually means viewing war in economic terms, as a way to increase the community's assets. Cases of aggression by a foreign army are ignored because defensive wars present little opportunities for booty. The newly wed man and the one who recently built a new house would have to join the others to protect their wives and homes (Deut 20:11.14; 21:11).

The ban on the destruction of fruit trees (Deut 20:19–20) may be read as anti-Assyrian polemics.[70] It also reflects the concerns of an audience that has every interest in preserving the economic potential of regions about to be conquered in order to extend Israelite territory (Deut 14:24; 19:8).[71] Like the prohibition on taking the mother bird with its fledglings, the ban on felling trees is motivated by economic considerations: "that it may go well with you and you may live long" (Deut 22:7).[72]

Whether or not comparison with Hoplite warfare makes war in Deuteronomy "a democratic enterprise"[73] depends on the identity of the fearful trooper who may discourage his brothers (Deut 20:8). If brothers here are his companions in arms, nothing can be inferred as to the composition of the troop. If it refers to members of the inner circle in which credit is granted at preferential rates, Deuteronomic wars are as democratic as Spartan wars: they involve only the members of the upper class.[74] In any case, Deuteronomic wars are viewed as convenient ways to expand territory and increase resources.[75] Though fear is mentioned, defeat, retaliations, and casualties are not.

1.3.5 Slave trafficking (Deuteronomy 23:15-16; 24:7)

Another economic source of revenue is the slave trade. The existence of such a trade is implicit in the ban on the abduction (גנב) of any person (נפש) belonging to an Israelite brother (Deut 24:7). This is the only instance of the death penalty for stealing, though not because an Israelite may not

69   As claimed by Rütersworden, "Purity," 415.
70   Crouch, *Israel*, 175.
71   On trees and siege warfare, see Wright, "Warfare," 423–58.
72   As argued by Carmichael, *Laws of Deuteronomy*, 151–56.
73   Hagedorn, *Moses and Plato*, 199.
74   Hagedorn, 178 quoting Garlan, "War and Peace," 63.
75   On the link between war and economy see Trundle, "Coinage," 65–79.

be sold or bartered (Exod 21:16).[76] What deserves the death penalty here is the sale of a person *belonging* to an Israelite brother (מאחיו מבני ישׂראל).[77]

The issue is that the abductee belongs specifically to an Israelite *brother*. The centrality of the brotherhood is becoming obvious and it is discussed below (§2.1). Here, it is not the nationality of the abducted person that matters, but the identity of the owner.[78] The argument is precise. Enslavement (עמר) is followed by trading (מכר) but the two are not synonymous.[79] The sale is the logical outcome of the abduction because the kidnapper would soon be unmasked if he kept the abductee in his service. In itself, enslaving is no offense. It might even be voluntary (see §1.3.6).

That enslavement is no offense is confirmed by the provision that runaway slaves are not to be returned to their owners when they seek refuge among Israelites, or among Israelite brothers if the "you" is taken in a restrictive sense (Deut 23:15). The next verse grants slaves the choice of their place of residence, without specifying that they will be free. The injunction not to oppress them is not followed by the mention that they are to be considered as a brother or at least as a *ger*. The implication is that they are free to choose their new master, albeit retaining their servile condition. Hence, the idea that the beneficiaries of that law are "not the elite but those at the margin of society" requires qualification.[80] The condition of the fugitive slave may well be improved if the ability to choose his new master provides him with some bargaining power. Does this means that runaway slaves are expecting to arrive in Israelite villages and bargain with the locals before choosing the master offering the best work conditions? Perhaps. Whatever happens to the slave, his new master acquires a new slave for free.

In the real world, treaties of extradition were ratified to stipulate the return of runaway slaves seeking asylum elsewhere and thus defuse tensions resulting from the mobility of servile manpower. The prohibition to establish any treaties with other peoples in the frame (Deut 7:2–3) would make it possible to apply the stipulations relative to the runaway slave. In the absence of extradition treaties Israelites could not be accused of harboring runaway slaves.[81] Therefore, various forms of slave trafficking are envisaged as sources of revenues, as long as the slaves are not stolen from

---

76 Against McConville, *Deuteronomy*, 361.
77 Against Crouch, *Making*, 210. Levin, "Rereading," 66 dismisses the significance of the juxtaposition of the brother and the sons of Israel, claiming that they "are not connected, so that they give the impression of being variants."
78 Against Tigay, *Deuteronomy*, 224.
79 Against Levin, "Rereading," 66 who sees them as a doublet which he attributes to a brotherhood revision.
80 Baker, *Tight Fists*, 135.
81 So Craigie, *Book of Deuteronomy*, 301.

Israelite brothers. At this point, much depends on how the term brotherhood is conceived. If it does not necessarily include all fellow Israelites (see below), Deuteronomy does not explicitly condemn the abduction and the sale of Israelites who are not brothers. This facet of brotherly ethics is not congenial to humanitarian readings of Deuteronomy.

1.3.6 Self-indenture of pledges (Deuteronomy 15:16)

Less likely to generate tensions with neighboring countries than the welcoming of runaway slaves, self-indenture is another source of man and woman-power. Self-indenture is well attested to in ancient Oriental practice. Under certain circumstances, it conferred a level of security that could be considered preferable to freedom.[82] According to Deuteronomy 15:13–16, self-indenture is possible when the antichretic loan against which the borrower has pledged himself has reached its maximum term, on the day of the release. From that moment, the borrower is free to ask to remain with the creditor, if the pledge is the borrower himself. Otherwise the pledge returns to the service of whoever has pledged her/him. The motivation for self-indenture is presented paradoxically as love for the master (Deut 15:16). In practice, the acceptance of life-long indenture would rather be a charitable act on the part of the master. Deuteronomy turns the deal on its head and presents self-indenture as an act of love on the part of the slave since, in an ideal world free from want, love would be the only motivation left for such a practice.

In the ancient world, much of imperial taxation took the shape of labor requirement for military service, building projects, and institutional agriculture. This was the case in Babylonia during the Achaemenid rule. There is no reason to believe that it was significantly different from earlier practices.[83] In such contexts, the acceptance of self-indentured bodies within one's workforce would represent a significant capital for the master who could use them to provide the labor required by the overlords, without depleting his own ranks, while the self-indentured person's family may not be considered a taxable unit and thus be exempted from supplying labor. On the other hand, the support of self-indentured persons during their time spent in labor obligations would be partially or completely covered by the rations work-gangs received during their duties.[84] The situation was far more complex than the common designa-

---

82   Guillaume, *Land*, 194.
83   Silverman, "Judaeans," 18; Jursa, *Aspects*, 500–509.
84   Silverman, 20–22 discusses the rations for *kurtaš* in the Persepolis Fortification Archive.

tions of slavery suggests. Hence, the notion of self-indenture blurs the line between forced labor and voluntary employment.

Recapitulation of savings and non-agricultural income

The distance to the *maqom* remains decisive as Israelites residing closest to the site of the festivities stand to gain much from the sale of their surplus to fellow Israelites residing too far to transport their yearly tithes. The silence over taxes as tribute and workdays for the king or dues to officers, judges, and diviners would represent substantial savings if they were expected to be non-existent (Table 1.2).

Besides gains from the sale of foodstuffs at the *maqom*, access to cheap sources of labor from the corvée imposed on subdued cities, from runaway slaves and from self-indentured slaves would represent substantial revenues too. The non-agricultural sector would represent a third source of revenues for any brother with the ability to grant loans to foreigners and neighbors, while benefitting from interest-free loans from other

Table 1.2 *Summary of savings and revenues*

Savings	Amounts	Deut.
No tribute and corvée for any king	not assessable but not negligible	17:15-19
No prebends for diviners and other office holders	not assessable but not negligible	18:10–15; 23:18–19
No priestly cuts on game and unclean meats	not assessable but not negligible	12:15.22; 15:22
No interest on loans from brothers		23:20
Revenues		
Price fluctuation at the *maqom*	Up to 20% when closest to the *maqom*	14:26
Carrion sold to foreigners	not assessable	14:21
Interest from loans to foreigners	gains of 20% on silver and 50% on grain	23:21
Interest from loans to neighbors	gains of 20% on silver and 50% on grain	24:13
Plunder from conquered cities	not assessable	20:14; 21:10–14
Corvée from subdued cities	not assessable but not negligible	20:11
Slave sales	not assessable	23:15–16; 24:7
Self indentured slaves	not assessable but not negligible	15:16

brothers. Revenues from plundered cities and from the sale of slaves and carrion would be more aleatory.

1.4 Balancing expenses and revenues

The "You" to whom Deuteronomy's laws are addressed is no ordinary farmer. Besides producing grain, oil, wine, wool and meat, he also engages in commercial and financial transactions that far exceed the activities of ordinary peasants. He grants interest-bearing loans to foreigners, borrows from and lends to brothers at no interest. He mounts attacks on distant lands for booty, including wives. He conquers neighboring countries and sells slaves.

The most striking feature of the Deuteronomic economy is the refund of annual tithes that are consumed by the tithe payer and his dependents at the *maqom*. The only tax he pays are the triennial tithes he sets aside for the Levite, *ger*, orphan, and widow of his home settlement. If he lives too far from the *maqom* to bring his yearly tithes in kind there, the victuals he purchases at the *maqom* are much fewer than the produce he sold at home to obtain the silver needed to replace them. This loss of purchasing power is bearable if it is not recurrent (see 3.2.2). If, on the contrary, he happens to reside close enough to the site of the pilgrimage, he can sell his surplus to distant colleagues who brought silver with them. The *maqom* banquets thus play a fundamental role in the circulation of silver. The stated aim of these banquets is to learn to fear YHWH (Deut 14:23) by much eating, drinking, and rejoicing in front of YHWH (Deut 14:26).

The Deuteronomic Israelite wastes no resources on hiring divination and rituals specialists. Amulets and charms, supposedly creative responses of peasant cultures to the challenges of survival, are denounced (Deut 18:10–11).[85] As vows are also best avoided (Deut 23:22), one may wonder if Deuteronomy's economic networks really reflect a "sacred economy".[86] In the sections he devotes to Deuteronomy, Boer underlines the importance of communal land and the allocation of usufruct and labor rather than particular fields (Deut 19:14), a welcome corrective to the common focus on land ownership.[87] Village communes headed by their council of elders (Deut 19:12; 21:3) were a creative adaptation to ever-changing conditions and ensured the resilience of kinship-households.[88]

---

85 Boer, *Sacred Economy*, 56–57.
86 Boer, 8.
87 Boer, 72–73.
88 Boer, 103–104; Guillaume, *Land*, 56–66.

Boer's theoretical framework consists of institutional forms, regimes and modes of regulations. Of the three regimes (subsistence, palatine, and plunder regimes), Boer only considers the subsistence regime as allocative; the other two are deemed extractive.[89] To illustrate the difference between subsistence and extractive regimes, Boer argues that interest-bearing loans are not really loans because the aim is to keep the borrower in bondage while credit is supposedly a system of mutual assistance based on trust that ensures "the mutual allocation and reallocation of all goods within the community".[90] Boer also opposes credit and debt, debt being defined as interest-bearing loans and credit as interest-free loans as in Deut 15:7–9; 23:20–21. Credit supposedly reflects the (good) subsistence survival regime while debt belongs to (evil) extractive regimes.

True, the aim of landlords was to secure the labor of his debtors rather than to have the loan repaid promptly.[91] Less true is Boer's sharp opposition between subsistence regimes and extractive regimes, which leads him to romanticize the subsistence regime and to revert to the popular clichés of social-scientific exegesis to illustrate debt:

> The despised busybodies known as merchants (*tamkāru*) rolled into one bundle the tasks of acquiring preciosities for the rulers, management of estates as landlords, tax collecting, and loan-sharking. If one wanted a loan, the conniving merchant-cum-landlord-cum-shark was the first and often only person who could provide it. That is, both extractive forms, of (e)state and tribute exchange, cannot be understood without debt.[92]

Until the recent advent of banks, merchants were indeed the most likely source of loans thanks to their ready access to silver and foodstuffs.[93] Yet, the "merchant-cum-landlord-cum-shark" was himself as much a borrower as a lender. Borrowing implies neither poverty or wealth. For instance, the Neo-Assyrian Salmānu[...] was a powerful merchant (*tamkāru*) who received gifts of honor from Sargon II to whom he lent a huge sum for the building of the new royal capital. Yet, this apparently wealthy man wrote a letter to the king pressing him in frank language to pay back his dues because he was under pressure from the sons of his father's creditors.[94]

---

89   Boer, 217.
90   Boer, 157–58.
91   Boer, 159.
92   Boer, 156.
93   Jursa, "Silver," 69.
94   Radner, "Traders," 103.

This letter illustrates the complexity of credit networks into which the king, the merchant, and the heirs of the creditor of Salmānu's father found themselves. According to Boer's categories, Sargon represents the extractive palatine regime. But instead of outright plunder, Sargon's mode of extraction takes the form of loans. There is no way of knowing whether or not Salmānu charged interest on the sums he lent to Sargon, but the royal gifts Salmānu received motivated him to remain the king's creditor until the pressure of the heirs of his father's creditors became too great. What Sargon did and why Salmānu's creditors pressed for reimbursement is unknown, but it is clear that Salmānu's ability to lend to Sargon was partly based on funds borrowed by his father. Rather than hurrying to reimburse loans he had inherited from his father, Salmānu lent the borrowed funds to the king. Hence, Boer's understanding of debt as an unidirectional flow of wealth running from debtor to lender is too simplistic.[95] Sargon is neither at the receiving end of an extractive palatine regime, nor the innocent victim of Salmānu. If a "conniving merchant-cum-shark", Salmānu also qualifies as the victim of another "shark" who had granted a loan to his father. Rather than conspiratorial sharks, Salmānu's letter reveals wealth extraction in the form of a complex network of debt and credit. In sound economic practice, not all assets are hoarded. Salmānu still owed a debt contracted by his father because his father's creditors had not pressed for repayment.

Trade venture contracts frequently reveal that a creditor is also one of the debtors involved in the provision of venture funds.[96] In such ventures, interest rates hold secondary importance. In the particular case discussed by Karen Radner, half of the loans bear no interest while half of the interest-bearing loans carry interest lower than the usual 25%.[97] Boer's distinction between debt characterized by interest-bearing loans and credit characterized by interest-free loans is artificial.

Boer opposes the bondage that loans create to the system of mutual assistance created by credit, ignoring the element of security gained by the borrower. While loans keep the borrower in bondage, they also generate a degree of solidarity between borrowers and lenders. Any interest paid on a debt is similar to to the insurance premium paid today in order to buy the solidarity of other insurance contractors in case of an accident, disease, natural disaster, theft or loss. Salmānu started pressing Sargon when he was himself under pressure from the heirs of his father's creditor who were under pressure from their own creditors. The needs of these heirs sent signals across the chain of solidarity established by the

---

95 Boer, *Sacred Economy*, 161.
96 Radner, "Traders," 110–15.
97 Radner, 115.

debt. Thanks to the lien that ties up the debtor to his creditor, the debtor gains a level of insurance that the creditor will have to support him in case of hardships. Hence, extraction works both ways. Whatever interest was paid for the loan was an insurance premium. The lien that maintained the loan alive strengthened the mutual relation between lender and borrower. Claiming that the "major feature of debt is to ensure that the flow of wealth runs from debtor to lender" is an over-simplification.[98]

Boer is correct in describing the *mišarum* as ways to shift labor from one type of dependency and back to another,[99] but the opposition between subsistence and extractive regimes ignores the positive effects of dependence and perpetuates the portrayal of poor borrowers versus fat lenders described as "cockroaches, who also happen to be tax collectors, usurers, and landlords".[100] Though he recognizes the creative adaptation to ever-changing conditions that ensured the resilience of kinship-households, Boer only grants this capacity to adapt to ever-changing conditions to peasants who happen to live under subsistence regimes. The artificial opposition between allocative and extractive models turns the adaptable peasant into a passive victim of merchants, landlords, and monarchs. Refusing to consider regimes other than subsistence as beneficial to the community in general, Boer ignores the role credit and debt played in the construction and maintenance of a social bond essential to crisis management in regimes that are both allocative and extractive rather than either allocative or extractive.

The social-scientific propensity to oppose the mass of rural producers to urban elites, viewed as idle and parasitic, is a modern construct. The rural/urban divide is not marked by production on one hand and consumption on the other hand.[101] Deuteronomy has its audience engaged in activities typical of both urban and rural realms. The Deuteronomic brother cultivates fields and orchards, raises cattle and caprovids, shears his sheep, sells or gives carrion. He owns slaves, acquires some and sells others. He lends at interest to some people, at no interest to others, and borrows at no interests from his brothers. If he lives close enough, he trades off surplus to colleagues who arrive at the *maqom* with silver. He extracts revenues wherever he can, but he also disburses alms, gifts, and tithes. As with most functional economies, Deuteronomy's economy is both extractive and redistributive.

Before considering how the life of the Deuteronomic Israel is regulated, the different economic actors are considered.

---

98 Boer, *Sacred Economy*, 161.
99 Boer, 160.
100 Boer, 175.
101 Guillaume, *Land*, 100–106.

Chapter 2
Deuteronomy's Economic Actors:
Beyond a Single People of Brothers

A society is made up of individual players striving over limited resources. The competition results in economic exchanges that "cannot be viewed as secondary in importance to social, religious, or political agendas."[1] Deuteronomy identifies a dozen social categories involved in economic interaction. Given the dispersion of the relevant indications across the entire book and the number of inconsistencies that can be discerned, an overview is provided before each category is considered in detail. In decreasing order of space devoted to each economic agent, Deuteronomy identifies:

Brothers (אחים) are by far the most commonly mentioned economic actors. The forty-eight occurrences are listed in Table 2.1 below. In short, they are involved in disputes, inheritance, lost property, kidnapping, apostasy, and physical assaults. They take their yearly tithes to the *maqom* where they consume them. They deliver their triennial tithes to the gate of their settlement, wage wars, distribute land, obtain and grant loans, release other brothers from their debts, raise themselves to kingship and face famines.

Slaves (עבדים) must not be stolen from a neighbor or from a brother (Deut 5:21; 24:7), they partake in *maqom* banquets (Deut 12:12.18; 16:11–14, but not in chapter 14), they can be acquired by self-indenture (Deut 15:17), from runaways who are not sent back (Deut 23:15–16) and as war captives (Deut 20:11; 21:10). Unfaithful Israelites will offer themselves into slavery in Egypt (Deut 28:68).

Neighbors (רעים) must be protected from false witness, theft, and dishonor (Deut 5:20–21; 19:14; 27:17; 22:24.26), they are perhaps released from their outstanding debts (Deut 15:2), they might be involved in homicides (Deut 19:5.11; 27:24), handfuls may be collected from their standing crops (Deut 23:25–26). The loans they are granted are secured by a pledge (Deut 24:10).

---

[1] Miller, "Methods," 15.

Gerim receive a share of triennial tithes (Deut 14:29; 26:11–13). They receive or pay wages (Deut 24:14), have gleaning rights (Deut 24:19–21), could take control of unfaithful Israel (Deut 28:43) and swear faithfulness to the Torah (Deut 29:7; 31:12). They appear at the *maqom,* seemingly as guests to the festive meals instead of the Levite (Deut 12:18 LXX) or with the Levite, the widow and the orphan (Deut 16:11, 14).

Levite/s partake in *maqom* meals (Deut 12:12.18; 16:11.14; 26:11), receive and redistribute triennial tithes (Deut 14:27–29; 26:12), may move to the *maqom* (Deut 18:6), list curses (Deut 27:14) and carry the ark (Deut 10:8; 31:25). They have no gleaning rights but they have some unspecified paternal possessions (Deut 18:8).

Widows and orphans (אלמנה ויתום) are protected by YHWH (Deut 10:18; 27:19), receive triennial tithes (Deut 14:27–29; 26:12), partake in *maqom* meals (Deut 16:11.14; 26:12–13 but not in chapters 12 and 14), hand over pledges to receive loans (Deut 24:17) and have gleaning rights (Deut 24:19–21). The wife of the dead partner in Deuteronomy 25:7 is not granted the status of widow.

Levitical priests arbitrate difficult cases with the judge (Deut 17:9), supply a copy of the Torah to the king (Deut 17:18), collect meat cuts, first-fruits, and first fleeces (Deut 18:1–4), supervise hygiene (Deut 24:8) and stand beside Moses (Deut 27:9).

The **needy** (אביון) in the land receive charity (Deut 15:11), short-term secured loans (Deut 24:12) and daily wages (Deut 24:14–15).

A rare **needy brother** should be granted a loan (Deut 15:7).

The **foreigner** (נכרי) buys carrion (Deut 14:21), his debts are never remitted (Deut 15:3), he cannot become king in Israel (Deut 17:15), he pays interest (Deut 23:21) and might witness the devastation of unfaithful Israel (Deut 29:21).

The labor of **Hebrews**, males and females, can be traded between brothers (Deut 15:12–16).

2.1 Brothers: more than farmers

Deuteronomy calls Israel to regulate their lives according to a set of rules meant to ensure their welfare. While the Levites are always referred to in the third person, the "you" of the addressees are the producers of primary goods, animals, grain, wine, oil, wool, gleanings, and carrion. Hence, the addressee is clearly a farmer, but a farmer involved in credit operations that exceed the requirements and scope of ordinary agricultural activities. The Deuteronomic "you" systematically addresses a brother

(אח), but modern translators tend to render this term in different ways.[2] It is thus necessary to list the forty-eight occurrences of the term in Deuteronomy (Table 2.1).

2.1.1 Brothers as siblings

Three times at most, the word brother designates a true sibling. The brother who entices to worship other gods must be stoned to death, even if he is the son of your mother (אחיך בן עמך Deut 13:7). Following the Samaritan Pentateuch and the LXX, the NRSV renders this closest degree of brotherhood as "your brother, your father's son or your mother's son", thus ignoring the difference between uterine brothers (same mother) and agnate or consanguine brothers (same father).

Moses will die outside Canaan like his brother Aaron (Deut 32:50). They are siblings too, but not necessarily uterine brothers.

Less precise is the brother to whom food will be begrudged when Israel will follow other gods (28:54).

2.1.2 Brothers as fellow tribesmen

In three cases, the Deuteronomic brother is a member of the same tribe within the framework of the twelve-tribe system: Joseph is a prince among his brothers and Asher is the favorite among his brothers (Deut 33:16.24). The Levite from one of your gates may depart from anywhere he has migrated to in Israel and join his brothers the Levites at the *maqom* to minister there in the name of the Lord (Deut 18:6–7).[3]

2.1.3 Brothers as fellow Israelites

The Deuteronomic brother in references to episodes from the books of Exodus and Numbers (Deut 1:16.16.28; 3:18.20; 18:15.18) is clearly a fellow Israelite.[4] Levi is deprived of land among his Israelite brothers (Deut 10:9; 18:2) and he ignored his Israelite or tribal brothers (Deut 33:9).

2   A fact deplored by Morrow, *Introduction*, 247.
3   The text insists that the move from your gates to the *maqom* is the result of free choice (בכל אות נפשו), a clause reminiscent of Mesopotamian sales records that consider sale under duress nil. The notion of Levites disenfranchised as a result of Josiah's reform is foreign to Deuteronomy.
4   Judges appointed in the wilderness (Exod 18:13–26), Horeb (Exod 20:18), spies sent in Canaan (Numbers 13) and the Transjordan tribes serving as vanguard (Num 32:17–42).

Tab 2.1 Deuteronomic brothers and their renderings in the NRSV

Deut		Context	NRSV
1:16,16	אחיו ובין בין־איש משפט־צדק אחיכם בין ושמע	Arbitration	fair hearings for members of your community and judgments between one person and another, citizen or alien
1:28	את־לבבנו המסו אחינו	War	our kindred made our hearts melt
2:4,3	אחיכם/אחיכם בני־עשו	Edom	your kindred/our kin, sons of Esau
3:18,20	החלוצים לפני אחיכם בני־ישראל	War	the vanguard of your Israelite kin
10:9	היה ללוי חלק עם אחיו לא	Land	no allotment for Levi with his kindred
13:7	אחיך בן־אמך	Apostasy	your brother, your father's son
15:2,3	לא יגש את־רעהו ואת־אחיו / את אחיך	Debts	a member of the/your community
15:7a	מאחד אחיך / בארצך תמאחיך	Loans	a member of your community
15:7b,9	אחיך האביון / אחיך האביון	Loans	your needy neighbor
15:1b	אחיך האביון בארצך	Alms	poor and needy neighbor in your land
15:2	אחיך איש עברי	Antichresis	a member of your community, a Hebrew
17:15,15	איש נכרי אשר לא אחיך הוא	King	who is not of your community
17:20	מאחיו לבב רום	King	above other members of the community
18:7	הלוים אחיו	Prebends	other members of the community/fellow-Levites
18:15,18	מאחיך / מקרב אחיהם כמוך	Prophet	among your/their own people
19:18,19	עד שקר ענה באחיו	False witness	another
20:3	את־לבבכם אל־ירך	War	melting the hearts of his comrades
22:1-4(6x)	אחיך שור...	Strays	your neighbor's ox...
23:3	כי אחיך הוא	Edom	they are your kin
23:20,21	לא תשיך לאחיך נשך	Interest	to another Israelite
24:7	מאחיו מבני ישראל נפש גנב	Kidnap	other Israelite
24:14	שכיר עני ואביון מאחיך או מגרך	Wages	poor and needy laborers, whether other Israelites or aliens
25:3	אחיך לעיניך	Flogging	your neighbor will be degraded
25:5–9(4x)	ישבו אחים יחדו	Partnership	when brothers reside together...
25:11	אנשים יחדו איש ואחיו	Brawl	men in a fight with one another
28:54	אחיו ובאשת חיקו	Famine	begrudge food to his own brother
32:50	אחיך אהרן	Sibling	your brother Aaron
33:9	ואת אחיו לא הכיר	Tribe	Levi ignored his kin
33:16	נזיר אחיו	Tribe	Joseph prince among his brothers
33:24	רצוי אחיו	Tribe	Asher, favorite of his brothers

Four cases deserve special attention since the writer states explicitly that the brother in question is a fellow Israelite (Deut 17:15.15.20; 24:7).

The king to be chosen by YHWH among your brothers (מקרב אחיך) must not be a foreigner who is not your brother (איש נכרי אשר לא אחיך). The man who kidnaps someone for his brother from the sons of Israel (מאחיו מבני ישראל) must be stoned to death (Deut 24:7). If all it takes to be a brother is to be an Israelite, a brother "from the sons of Israel" is as superfluous as a foreigner who is not your brother. Otto explains the insistence on the Israeliteness of the king as a reaction against positive descriptions of non-Israelite rulers in Isaiah 44:28; 45:1 and Jeremiah 25:9; 27:6; 43:10.[5] Levin views the brother in front of the sons of Israel as a late insertion he attributes to a brotherhood revision.[6]

There is no need to look beyond Deuteronomy to understand why it is necessary to insist that the king must be an Israelite brother who is not a foreigner. There is no need to postulate a late insertion to understand why the kidnapping of someone from a brother from the sons of Israel is particularly grievous. The simple reason is that there are non-Israelite brothers in the world conceived by the Deuteronomic writers. Who are those non-Israelite brothers?

2.1.4 Edomite brothers

Three times brothers are designated as sons of Esau or Edomites (Deut 2:4.8; 23:8). Had the sole requirement for the king been that he be a brother, an Edomite assimilated into the brotherhood would qualify to rule Israel.

According to Levin, the brotherhood ethic of Deuteronomy reflects a humanitarian ideal that expresses "the special relationship obtaining among members of God's people."[7] As an Edomite brother does not fit a special relationship, Levin simply ignores the Edomite brother (Deut 23:8), though such a brother would have made a great contribution to the ethical aspect of the postulated revision.

Quoting Deuteronomy 15:7–11 and 22:1–4, John van Seters writes that "the law code sets forth the view that one should treat all fellow-Israelites, one's neighbors, as brothers (and sisters)." Van Seters adds that "… this brotherhood only includes those of the community of Israel. No such compassionate attitude holds for the foreigner who has another religion and way of life".[8] The problem is that the Edomite brother appears

---

5 Otto, *Deuteronomium 12,1–23,15*, 1482–84.
6 Levin, "Rereading," 66.
7 Levin, 67.
8 Van Seters, *Pentateuch*, 111.

immediately at the end of the section that excludes Ammonites and Moabites from the *qehal-YHWH*, while the next verse clearly states that third generation Egyptians may be admitted to the same *qehal-YHWH* (Deut 23:9 [8]). The *qehal-YHWH* is discussed below (§3.3), but it is already clear at this point that the Edomite brother and the Egyptian in the *qehal-YHWH* are not viewed in the same way as the Ammonites and Moabites are. At the very least they belong to a different category of foreigners. Are they considered as equals, as was the case in Bronze Age diplomacy when a foreign ruler of equal rank was designated a brother?[9]

Given Deuteronomy's minimal interest in kingship and the economic context in which the term brother appears, the Edomite brother is best considered in light of Egyptian letters from Elephantine where business partners address each other as brothers independently from any shared ethnicity. For instance, the letter TAD 1:A3.10 Berlin 23000 concerns non-Judeans who own a boat, or share a boat in partnership. Spendata son of Fravatipata addresses Ḥori son of Kamen and Peṭemachis as their brother, showing that, in Aramaic, the term brother was applied to anyone with whom one had established business dealings or ties, forming a personal economic network.[10] The difference between a brother, a companion (אחבר)[11] and a colleague (כנת)[12] in the Elephantine papyri is not clear, but it is fair to argue that it is economic ties that differentiate brothers from mere companions and colleagues.

Closer to Israel, brothers are attested by the Yavne-Yam ostracon that records the complaint of a harvester who states that his brothers (אחי, lines 10–11) are ready to testify to his innocence. These brothers are co-workers who are best qualified to testify, though of course some of these co-workers could also be the plaintiff's siblings.[13]

If ethnicity is less relevant than economic ties in the definition of brotherhood, the presence of Edomite brothers and third generation Egyptians is hardly surprising.[14] These non-Israelite brothers belong to

---

9 Tugendhaft, "To Become a Brother," 89–104; Ebach, "Walk Exactly," 168; Moran, "Note on the Treaty," 173–76.
10 Porten and Yardeni, *Textbook*, 48–49. Other letters were discussed by Diana Edelman in a paper presented at the joint 2017 EABS/ISBL Berlin conference.
11 Porten and Yardeni, *Textbook*, vol. 4: 7.56 line 2.
12 Porten and Yardeni, vol. 4: 1.32:14; 3.45:6.
13 Pardee, "Meṣad Ḥashavyahu," in lines 10–11.
14 The favorable attitude to Edom and Egypt in Deut 23 is remembered in Neh 13:1, which recalls the exclusion of Ammon and Moab. Though Jer 49:7 adds a series of judgments on Edom to those on Egypt, Ammon and Moab, the Edom it refers to is Arabia (Teman and Dedan). Moreover, besides the recall of Bozrah, Jer 49:11 has a strange note on orphans and widows that recalls the prescriptions relative to the third-year tithes, festive meals and gleanings in Deut 14 and 24.

a circle half-way between the narrowest sense of someone born of the same mother or father and the broadest sense of any fellow Israelite. This circle deals in economic rather than political matters, which were the prerogative of the local communities (in your gates) and of the *maqom* assembly.

Levinson notes that the singular form אח occurs 28 times in Deuteronomy and 18 times in the legal code.[15] What Levinson does not note is that almost all the occurrences of the word brother in the frames lend a clear ethnic sense to the word used to designate fellow Israelites.[16] Therefore, the frames could have been broadening the brotherhood to every fellow Israelite because the core restricted the circle of the brotherhood to members of the *qehal-YHWH* mentioned in Deuteronomy 23:8.[17] The admission of Edomites and Egyptians in the *qehal-YHWH* is a thorn in the flesh for those upholding the notion that the Deuteronomic brother is a fellow Israelite, especially since the frames themselves do not counter the notion of Edomite brotherhood. Though using the expression sons of Esau instead of Edomite, Deuteronomy 2:4.8 equally uses the term brother and integrates Edomite brotherhood within the context of the Exodus and Conquest. The framing process merely broadened the Deuteronomic understanding of brotherhood to every fellow Israelite and intervened within the core itself at two of the eighteen verses mentioning the word brother:

1. A neighbor (רעה) was added as beneficiary of the *šemiṭṭah* release in Deuteronomy 15:2.
2. A second mention of the word אח at the end of Deuteronomy 23:20 has been dropped in the Masoretic text, though it is attested to in the Septuagint. It downplays the exclusivity of interest-free loans for brothers only.

---

15   Levinson, "Manumission," 317.
16   See Deut 1:16.28; 2:4.8; 3:18.20; 10:9; 28:54; 32:50; 33:9.16.24. The exceptions are Deut 2:4.8, which refer to Esau as your brother // 23:8. Note that Deut 13:7, traditionally counted as part of the legal core, also has a clear ethnic sense, which supports my contention that this entire chapter, like chapter 12 and most of chapter 14, belong to the framing process.
17   On general Israelite brotherhood see Deut 1:16.28; 3:18–20; 10:9; 13;7; 28:54; 32:50; 33:9.16.24; including Edom as well (Deut 2:4.8). On narrow brotherhood see Deut 15:2.3.7.9.11; 17:15.20 (the king more likely chosen from within the guild than from the general Israelite populace); 22:1–4; 23:20.21; 24:7.14; 25:3.11. Other types of brotherhood besides *qehal-YHWH* membership are blood brothers (Deut 25:5–10), brothers-at-arms (Deut 20:8) and Levite brothers (Deut 18:1–18), which obviously excludes other Israelites.

The frames retain the unique status of Edom in the core while downplaying the unique status of the brotherhood within Israel. Just as a given quantity of salt is easier to dissolve in a greater rather than a smaller volume of water, so does the frame dilute the significance of the Edomite brother by absorbing him into a greater number of brothers. Including all Israelites in the brotherhood reduces the ratio and wards off the danger of saturation. The Edomite brother becomes a smaller quantity in a greater whole, which modern scholarship makes even greater by adding slaves and sisters,[18] or by turning the Edomite brother into a quasi-Israelite who has been living long enough among Israelites.[19]

From a guild of Israelite, Edomite, and Egyptian traders, the *qehal-YHWH* takes on a more ethnic meaning, albeit a shaky one, as the restrictive sense of the guild was never entirely erased. Israelite and Edomite ethnicities can hardly function as proper ethnic markers if at least some Israelites and some Edomites belong to a narrow brotherhood that excludes most Israelites and Edomites. These cousins remain brothers, unless brotherhood is taken in its widest possible sense. It is this unresolved tension over the delimitation of brotherhood between the Deuteronomic core and its frames that Leviticus 25:46 clarifies by adding בני-ישראל immediately after אחיכם to remove any doubts as to the identity of the brothers who are never to be enslaved permanently. No Edomites among the brothers in Leviticus, and no *qehal-YHWH* either.

The Edomite must not be abhorred because he is your brother (כי אחיך הוא) while the Egyptian is not to be abhorred because you were a *ger* in his land. This mention of Egypt may belong to the integration of the core into the Exodus and Moses narrative. By contrast, Edom's brotherhood implies no reference to the Exodus. It is the frame that makes the connection with the Exodus (Deut 2:4–8). Edomites are not to be abhorred because they are brothers and that brotherhood entitles them to admission to the *qehal-YHWH*.

The centrality of brotherhood in Deuteronomy has been obscured by arguing that there is no difference between brothers and neighbors—despite the different designations in Hebrew—and that the original sense of blood relative can be extended to include neighbors.[20] It is preferable to retain the common meaning of Hebrew and Aramaic terms and avoid viewing brothers and neighbors as synonyms. Neighbors are thus discussed among other non-brothers (§2.3.4).

18 Van Seters, *Pentateuch*, 111.
19 Crouch, *Making*, 198 n. 240.
20 As argued by Perlitt, "Volk von Brüdern," 56.

2.1.5 Brothers in court (Deuteronomy 19:18–19)

Like the first occurrence of the word אח in Deuteronomy—brothers to be given a fair hearing (Deut 1:16)—the witness who accuses his brother falsely (Deut 19:18–19) may refer to fellow Israelites since the entire passage describes daily life at home among neighbors and brothers (Deut 19:4–5.11).

2.1.6 Brothers in arms (Deuteronomy 20:8)

The release of the timorous fighter (Deut 20:8) is justified with the same expression as the result of the disheartening report of the spies: "to make our heart melt" (Deut 1:28). Though in chapter 1 the brothers are indeed fellow Israelites, in chapter 20, the brothers in arms can only refer to fellow Israelites if all Israelites are enrolled. General conscription does not necessarily apply here. Only a certain elite may be expected to join the militia.

2.1.7 A brother's strays and lost garment (Deuteronomy 22:1–4)

The rules regarding the return of lost property use the term brother instead of son of Israel to designate the rightful owner (Deut 22:1–4). The NRSV broadens the application of that law by rendering אח as neighbor. Yet, apart from the garment mentioned in verse 3, it is mostly the members of an inner circle of wealthy owners who are likely to suffer the loss of livestock and other kinds of property from the simple fact that they own more assets than ordinary farmers and are thus unable to supervise them as closely as the owners of smaller flocks would. Therefore, these mentions of brothers are not necessarily referring to fellow Israelites.

2.1.8 Brothers lending to one another (Deuteronomy 23:20–21)

Loans of silver, food or any other staple to your brother must not bear interest, contrary to loans to foreigners (נכרי). The mention of foreigners could support the idea that the brother is a fellow Israelite, but as Edomite brothers are present, the prohibition of interest-bearing loans applies to them, but not necessarily to all Israelites. In fact, three categories of loans can be distinguished. Loans to neighbors are secured with a pledge (Deut 24:10) and are not subject to the *šemiṭṭah* release, contrary to loans between brothers, which are interest-free but are subject to the release. Loans granted to foreigners bear interest (Deut 23:20) and they are to be recovered by any means (Deut 15:3). This leaves open the matter of interest on loans granted to neighbors, left to the discretion of the lender. It is not clear whether all neighbors are fellow Israelites, but it is possible that some Israelites are not brothers.

2.1.9 Brothers hiring day laborers (Deuteronomy 24:14)

Deuteronomy 24:14–15 stipulates the daily payment of the wages of hired laborers from your brother or from your *ger* in your land, in your gates. The particle *mem* in front of your brother and in front of your *ger* (מא־חיך או מגרך) is usually taken as a reference to the laborer himself. The *ger* being commonly designated as one of the *personae miserae*, the particle *mem* is read as the indication of the status of the laborer. Once the *ger* is deemed miserable, the brother of Deuteronomy 24:14 must also be poor and needy, which in turn proves that the Hebrew slave of Deuteronomy 15:12 is indeed one of your brothers.

In fact, Norbert Lohfink long noted that the four beneficiaries of the triennial tithes (the Levite, *ger*, orphan, and widow) are never identified with the so-called poor and needy (עני ואביון), the only category that experiences financial difficulties. On the contrary, the needs of the Levite, the *ger*, the orphan, and the widow are covered by the regular delivery of the proceeds of the triennial tithes.[21] Unless one follows Harold Bennett's opinion that these tithes cannot possibly cover the basic needs of Levites, *gerim*, orphans, and widows, the *ger* here is not a poor laborer among poor brothers but the employer of day laborers as is the brother.[22] These laborers must be paid at the end of each day, whether they are employed by a brother or by a *ger*. Awabdy accepts Lohfink's view that the Deuteronomic *ger*, orphan, and widow are neither poor nor needy, but he does not apply this view to the *ger* in Deuteronomy 24:14.[23] Reading this verse as a reference to an impoverished brother and an impoverished *ger*, Awabdy argues that although the *ger*, orphan, and widow do not represent a separate class of the poor, "they have the potential, just as the native does, to become impoverished (see 24:14)."[24]

The notion of the potential impoverishment of the natives fails to recognize the difference between brothers and natives. Deuteronomy has no place for any potential impoverishment of brothers. Why abide by a set of precepts that retains the possibility of impoverishment? The idea that the *gerim* remain under the threat of potential impoverishment is

---

21 Lohfink, "Poverty," 34–50.
22 See Bennett, "Triennial Tithes," 7–18.
23 Awabdy, *Immigrants*, 109 and 214.
24 Awabdy, 89.

countered by the claim that the triennial tithes ensure that their beneficiaries eat their fill (Deut 14:29). The idea that brothers remain under the threat of potential impoverishment ignores the statement that the Levite and the *ger* celebrate the bounty the Lord has given to the brothers who have set those tithes aside to ensure they can eat their fill (Deut 26:11).

Certainly, Deuteronomy 15:11 recognizes the ongoing presence of need in the land (אביון מקרב הארץ), but not among brothers (Deut 15:4) nor among the beneficiaries of the triennial tithes such as *gerim*. There is no contradiction between the needy laborer of Deuteronomy 24:14 and the eradication of need among brothers (Deut 15:4) when the two *mems* are taken as indications of the origin rather than the identity of the laborer (see also Deut 24:7). The letters *mem* in מאחיך או מגרך indicate that the laborers who need to be paid daily come not from the addressee's workforce but are tied to the workforce of another brother or of his *ger*. These laborers are thus providing occasional work on the farm of a colleague of the man for whom they usually work, either as slaves or, as is the case with the Hebrews (Deut 15:12), as reimbursement of antichretic loans (see below §2.3.3). In either case, your brother and your *ger* are the occasional employers of the laborers in question. It is all the more crucial to pay the wages of these hirelings daily. Any unpaid workdays they provide is otherwise reckoned against what the laborers owe to the master who sent them, as well as against what that master himself owes to the person for whom the labor in question was given. Such intricate networks of mutual debt are well attested to in the archaeological record and in the biblical story of Jacob's labor for Laban.[25] Antichretic loans could be reimbursed partially or fully with the supply of a dependent, resulting in levels of interdependence that could become too complex to be accounted for properly. This is the kind of complexity in credit networks the *šemiṭṭah* seeks to prevent by enacting a clearing of all accounts every seventh year.

Understanding the brother and his *ger* as employers of day laborers rather than day laborers themselves is thus coherent with Lohfink's notion of the absence of *personae miserae* in Deuteronomy. The *ger* who hires laborers, even if only on an occasional basis, must have more means than someone who survives by eating what he earned that very day. The social standing of this *ger* is discussed below (§2.3.5).

---

25 Rossi and Guillaume, "Hebrew Slave," 9–20.

2.1.10 Preserving the honor of a guilty brother (Deuteronomy 25:3)

The number of lashes to punish a brother found guilty is limited to a maximum of forty (Deut 25:3). This seemingly humanitarian concern may apply to any fellow Israelite, though it can also display the same concern as the maiming of a wife discussed in the next paragraph (Deut 25:11). If only forty lashes could display a humanitarian concern for one's brother, cutting the hand of the woman who tried to save her husband does not. What connects these two measures are the criteria enumerated for admission to the *qehal-YHWH* (Deut 23:2–9). These criteria concern ritual purity expressed by the verb תעב (Deut 23:8). They recall criteria attested to for Babylonian temple personnel. Initiation required a thorough check of the undressed body of the candidate before washing and shaving.[26] Moral integrity being a prerequisite, signs of corporal punishment such as traces left by lashes on the body of the candidate revealed a criminal record that barred one from admission to temple duties as surely as defective testicles.[27] Grabbing testicles and lashing have the potential of rendering their victims unfit as much as leprosy would (see Deut 24:8–9). Though forty lashes might be enough to leave scars on the culprit's body for life, the limitation to forty lashes may nevertheless belong to the criteria barring one from the *qehal-YHWH:* being an Ammonite or a Moabite, a first or second generation Egyptian, and physical defects caused by leprosy, emasculation, and accidental injuries. In this case, the main concern of the limit set at forty lashes is the physical integrity of the members of the brotherhood.

2.1.11 Brothers in partnership (Deuteronomy 25:5–11)

The next verses present two cases of brothers who could be siblings, though not necessarily so. The brothers who live together (ישבו אחים יחדו Deut 25:4–9) refer to partners who work an undivided estate. Tablets recovered from Emar use a similar expression to express the action of *sitting down* together in order to have a will drawn up rather than living together in the sense of working an undivided estate. Nevertheless, Sarah Milstein admits that Deuteronomy 25:5 "may well imply joint ownership", while pointing out that such laws reflect the proceedings of small-scale legal councils dealing with the transfer of property using standard legal

---

26 Lambert, "Qualifications", 144.
27 Defective testicles are listed along other disqualifying physical defects such as squinting eyes, chipped teeth, cut off fingers and leprosy: Waerzeggers and Jursa, "Initiation," 13.

language.[28] This situation would be common for siblings who inherited their father's estate and decided to cultivate it in partnership instead of splitting it, but it also applies to partners in trade ventures who address one another as brothers though they have no blood ties.[29] The consequence of the death of a partner who did not beget a son is the same whether the associates are siblings or not. The issue is who is going to inherit the assets of the deceased partner. Raising the name (יקום על שם) involves the fate of the partnership that depends on who inherits the assets of the dead partner. This issue is discussed below (§2.1.14).

At this stage, only the two brothers of Deuteronomy 19:18–19 can be securely added to the initial fifteen fellow Israelites identified above. These seventeen fellow Israelites with five blood brothers and fellow tribesmen leave a remaining twenty-three out of the total of forty-eight cases to be examined: 17 fellow Israelites + 5 blood brothers and fellow tribesmen + 3 Edomites + 23 = 48.

2.1.12 Arrears of a neighbor besides those of a brother? (Deuteronomy 15:2–3)

The seven occurrences of the word אח in Deuteronomy 15:2–12 can now be considered. The double mention of his neighbor in the introductory verse (רעהו Deut 15:2) is the cornerstone of the notion of Deuteronomic humanitarianism and brotherly ethics. Verses 1–2 set out the prescriptions relative to the debt release (*šemiṭṭah*, שמטה) at the end of the seventh year. Verse 1 is termed in a general manner: "At the end of the seventh year, *you* will call a release" (מקץ שבע שנים תעשה שמטה). Verse 2a continues with third person singular forms:

וזה דבר השמטה שמוט כל בעל משה ידו אשר ישה ברעהו

This is the manner of the release: every creditor is to drop any loan held against *his neighbor.*

The release is designated as outstanding debts held against a *neighbor*. Verse 2b further explains the release procedure by indicating what should *not* be done:

לא יגש את רעהו ואת אחיו כי קרא שמטה ליהוה

no one shall press his neighbor and *his brother* when a release for YHWH has been declared.

---

28 Milstein, "Will," 56.
29 For instance *ḫarrānu* business ventures in CUSAS 28 #40, 55, 61, 97.

A brother appears besides the previously mentioned neighbor, as though the terms אח and רע were synonymous. The next verses delineate the practical application of the *šemiṭṭah* and of labor contracts, using over sixty second person singular prefixes and suffixes, which all refer to your brother since "his neighbor" (רעהו) never occurs again in Deuteronomy 15 after verse 2.

The Septuagint ignores the words "his neighbor and" in Deuteronomy 15:2 and limits the practical application of the release to his brother only:

ἀφήσεις πᾶν χρέος ἴδιον ὃ ὀφείλει σοι ὁ πλησίον καὶ τὸν ἀδελφόν σου οὐκ ἀπαιτήσεις

you shall remit every personal debt which your neighbour owes you, and you shall not ask it back of your brother (NETS)

The other textual differences besides the Septuagint reveal a debate over the crucial issue of who exactly should benefit from the *šemiṭṭah*. Two opposite strategies can be seen at work, either inflating or deleting.

In light of the Septuagint, it is possible to argue that the Masoretic text reflects the inflationary tendency: the words "his neighbor and" were added to an older form of the Hebrew transmitted by the LXX. In this case, the older Hebrew text of verse 2a sets out a general rule (remission of a neighbor's debt) followed by the practical application of that rule to brothers in verse 2b. In light of Otto's approach to the possibility of changing yearly tithes into silver when the distance is too great, the neighbor in verse 2a would belong to the *lex generalis,* while the brother in verse 2b reflects the *lex specialis*.[30] Otto, however, does not apply the *lex generalis* and *lex specialis* distinction in Deuteronomy 15:2. He argues instead that the Greek translators deleted the second occurrence of the word neighbor, which they supposedly considered superfluous as it is already mentioned in the first part of the verse.[31]

Otto is correct if, without the second neighbor, the Greek text appears as the *lectio facilior*. The juxtaposition of his neighbor and his brother in verse 2b is awkward and it is clear that the Greek translator managed to separate them by introducing the first clause with ἀφήσεις and make the neighbor the beneficiary of the release: "you shall remit every personal debt which your neighbor owes you" (ἀφήσεις πᾶν χρέος ἴδιον ὃ ὀφείλει σοι ὁ πλησίον) and then adding "and you shall not ask it back of your brother" (καὶ τὸν ἀδελφόν σου οὐκ ἀπαιτήσεις).

---

30 Otto, *Deuteronomium 12,1–23,15*, 1312 argues that Deut 14:24–26 reflects the *lex specialis* based on the *lex generalis* of Deut 12:21–24 which deals with profane slaughter also attributed to the distance from the *maqom*.

31 Otto, 1329, Schenker, "Literalistische Übersetzungen," 154–55, though Schenker's article deals with 3 Kingdoms.

The argument, however, can be reversed. If the Greek translator improved the version transmitted in the Masoretic text, a clearer reading for the whole of verse 2 would have been obtained by deleting the brother rather than the second neighbor in verse 2b. This is exactly what is attested to by a single Hebrew witness mentioned in the critical apparatus of the BHS, which suggests deleting ואת אחיו to obtain a smoother reading involving neighbors only. This suggestion contradicts the basic rule of textual criticism since it is attested to by merely a single manuscript. With no brother at all, Deuteronomy 15:2 would have requested the remission of all debts held against any neighbor, as humanitarian readings do, thus avoiding the issue of the difference between a neighbor and a brother.[32]

The Samaritan Pentateuch provides another take on the issue. In the Samaritan text, the second occurrence of the word רעהו in Deuteronomy 15:2b is sometimes attested to without the conjunction between his neighbor *and* his brother.[33] The missing copula can be interpreted as a *lapsus calami*, a scribe having simply missed the copula. Or the missing copula represents an intermediary phase between an older Hebrew version attested to in the LXX with no neighbor in verse 2 and the reading attested to in the Masoretic text with both his neighbor and his brother but without the copula (see Table 2.2).

With no copula, the intermediary text sets the brother in apposition to the neighbor: "no one shall press his neighbor, i.e. his brother" (את רעהו את אחיו), to specify that the actual beneficiary of the release is really a brother. With the mere addition of the copula between his neighbor and his brother, the final text extends the release to the debts of neighbors.

The Septuagint reflects the apposition of the brother to the neighbor by presenting the *lex generalis* in verse 2a (πλησίον) and then the *lex specialis* (ἀδελφός) in verse 2b: "no one shall press his neighbor, i.e. his brother". The absence of any neighbor in the rest of the chapter shows that the release concerns first and foremost, if not exclusively, the debts held against brothers.

Finally, a single Dead Sea scroll fragment preserves a section of Deuteronomy 15:2. Dated paleographically between 150 and 100 BCE, 4Q30 (4QDeut) fragment 26 line 4(3) has neither neighbor nor brother in verse 2b: שמ]טה ל[א יגש כי קרא.[34] Despite its fragmentary state, this line

---

32 Combining humanitarian kindness with the notion of the impracticality of the release that goes back to Hölscher, "Komposition," 161–255, saves readers from delving into practical ways to care for the poor in general.
33 Von Gall (ed.), *Pentateuch der Samaritaner*, 396.
34 Crawford, "4QDeut[c]," 24 pl. V. Ulrich, ed., *Biblical Qumran Scrolls*, 211, and http://dssenglishbible.com/scroll4Q45.htm and http://www.deadseascrolls.org.il/explore-the-archive/image/B-368456 Plate 1087, Frag 7.

Table 2.2   Postulated growth of the Hebrew text of Deuteronomy 15:2

LXX's Vorlage*	אחיו כי קרא שמטה ליהוה	לא יגש את
Intermediary text (one Hebrew ms + SP)	את רעהו את אחיו כי קרא שמטה ליהוה	לא יגש
Final text (MT)	את רעהו ואת אחיו כי קרא שמטה ליהוה	לא יגש

states "d[o not collect when a release has been called]", clearly omitting את רעהו ואת אחיו.

Is the omission of his brother and his neighbor a *lectio facilior* or a *lectio difficilior*? A firm answer would require the full text of verse 2 to know if a neighbor or a brother or both were mentioned in the first part of the verse. Unfortunately, the last two words of verse 2a are not preserved. It begins with וזה ד[בר at line 2. As line 3 begins with verse 2b, it is clear that more than half of the column is preserved and that only a dozen letters are missing. There is space for one or two words where the Masoretic text has eight words (שמוט כל בעל משה ידו אשר ישה ברעהו). There is no way to decide whether there was any brother or neighbor in the void, but it is clear that 4QDeut^c transmitted a shorter version of Deuteronomy 15:12, for both parts of the verse:

- With a neighbor in the void, 4QDeut^c had the *lex generalis* in verse 2 and the *lex specialis* in the next verses mentioning your brother.
- With neither neighbor nor brother in the void, 4QDeut^c also had the *lex generalis* in verse 2 and the *lex specialis* in the next verses mentioning your brother.
- With a brother in the void, 4QDeut^c had no *lex generalis* in verse 2. The brother was mentioned throughout.

In the case of Deuteronomy 15:2, the identification of textual improvements, either through deletions or additions is not secure and the recovery of the earliest form of the verse by comparing the available textual witnesses remains speculative.[35] Nevertheless, with or without neighbor, brother and a copula between them, the practical application of the release concerns the debts held against a brother. This brother may be a fellow Israelite, a sibling, a friend, an associate, a fellow tribesman or even an Edomite.

2.1.13 No shortage among brothers (Deuteronomy 15:4)

Recognizing the difference between brothers and fellow Israelites somewhat resolves the tension between Deuteronomy 15:4, which promises

---

35   See McCarthy, *Biblia hebraica quinta 5*, 98*.

an absence of shortage among brothers and verse 11a, which recognizes ongoing shortage outside the brotherhood, i.e. in the land:

(Deut 15:4a) אפס כי לא יהיה בך אביון כי יברכך יהוה

(Deut 15:11a) כי לא יחדל אביון מקרב הארץ

"Among you" in verse 4 refers to the brothers mentioned in verse 3. The promise of verse 4 is conditioned by the application of the release of a brother's debt, not of the debts of neighbors. Neighbors stand outside the inner circle of brothers, in the land where, according to verse 11, need and shortage prevail.

The difference between a narrow circle of brothers and the situation in the land in general justifies two different attitudes regarding the practice of credit:

In the brotherhood	šemiṭṭah	no shortage	lend to many goyim (Deut 15:2–6)
In the land	no šemiṭṭah	shortage	open the hand to brother and needy ones (Deut 15:11)

It may seem counter-intuitive to derive the absence of shortage from the practice of the šemiṭṭah. Yet, from an economic point of view, it is crucial to purge the credit market regularly, identify borrowers in dire straights, clean their slate even when no interest is accruing, and protect the actors on the credit market by excluding defaulting debtors. The opposition between the brotherhood and the land presupposes a narrower definition of the brotherhood than fellow Israelites.

From a rhetorical point of view, the promises of prosperity conditioned by the application of these measures (Deut 15:4–6) lose all credibility if the šemiṭṭah is unable to protect brothers from serious impoverishment. For this reason, it is crucial to identify the beneficiary of alms in verse 11.

2.1.14 Brothers of indistinct ethnicity

Of the forty-eight occurrences of the word brother in Deuteronomy, three are blood brothers, three are fellow tribesmen, sixteen are fellow Israelites, and three are Edomites.[36] The remaining twenty-three brothers can

---

36 Siblings (Deut 13:7; 28:54; 32:50), tribal brothers (Deut 18:7; 33:16.24), fellow Israelites (Deut 1:16.16.28; 3:18.20; 10:9; 17:15.15.20; 18:2.7.15.18; 19:18.19; 24:7), Edomites (Deut 2:4.8; 23:8).

be either Israelites or Edomites.[37] Ethnicity is not the defining factor, as as been shown here.

These twenty-three brothers occur in economic contexts, though at first sight, the case of the brawling brothers (Deut 25:11) seems to be an exception. In light of the brothers who live together (ישבו אחים יחדו) a few verses earlier (Deut 25:4-9), the offense of the grabbing wife takes on a more economic turn. Living together implies a community of interests that has direct implications on inheritance rights.

The case in Deut 25:4-9 is that one of the associates dies prematurely with no heir. Hence, the conventional solution is for the deceased's wife to marry his brother, which would result in the post-mortem birth of a heir—presumably a son, though the LXX has a child (παιδίον).[38] But what if the deceased had had a son? As heir, the son would obviously have inherited his father's estate. What would happen to his mother? Would her son also inherit his father's duty to provide for his mother? This is not necessarily the case. In Mesopotamia, some husbands had tablets drawn up to adopt their wife as "father-and-mother" of their estate to protect her from his legitimate heirs.[39] In exchange, the widow lost the liberty to marry outside the clan. It is this possibility that Deuteronomy 25:4-9 seeks to avoid.

There is indirect evidence that biblical writers did not consider wives as legitimate heirs of their husbands' estate.[40] Therefore, the general principle is that in the absence of testamentary dispositions to the

---

37 Deut 15:2-12 (7×); 20:8; 22:1-4 (6×); 23:20.21; 24:14; 25:3-11 (7×).
38 The child in the LXX is a likely harmonization of Deut 25 with the prescription relative to the inheritance of daughters in Num 27:1-11 (Tigay, *Deuteronomy*, 231).
39 See Démare-Lafont, "Eléments," 55-56. Hammurabi §150 insists that any asset a husband may bequeath to his wife must be duly recorded or the sons will claim it. §172 merely grants the usufruct of the deceased husband's home to his widow.
40 Laban's daughters imply that they expect no share of their father's estate (Gen 31:14). Naomi (Ruth 4:3) and the Shunamite (2 Kgs 8:16) are no proof of the contrary. They are only entitled to the usufruct of the husband's estate, which is why they lost it while away. The Shunamite has to appeal to the king to recover her usufruct. Naomi can trade her late husband's usufruct—not the land itself—because she is back to claim it. For Westbrook, *Property*, 83, the Torah does not grant widows their husbands' estates. The case of Zelophehad who only fathered daughters is far from normative. First he died for his own sin (Num 27:3), suggesting a criminal case. Then, a long discussion is necessary for his daughters to be granted land from their father's tribe (Num 27:1-8; 36:1-12), which shows that it was against tradition for daughters to inherit their father's usufruct of communal land. Hence, the case of Zelophehad is not relevant to the inheritance of a husband's usufruct by his widow.

contrary, the wife of a man who died *ab intestat* found herself at the mercy of the heirs even if she had borne sons to that man.[41] If, as is the case here, the marriage had produced no son, the situation of the wife was even more precarious. With no husband to ensure her daily upkeep, no son to establish her as guardian and no testament to establish her as dowager, all she can hold on to is her dowry. i.e., what she received from her father when she married.

The case in Deuteronomy 25:4–9 is even more complicated because the two brothers ran their affairs in partnership, which raises three separate but entangled issues: the identity of the heir, the upkeep of the bereaved wife and the fate of the partnership, indeed a borderline case.[42] Beginning with the last issue, the death of one of the partners dissolves the partnership, unless a *post-mortem* heir secures the dead partner's assets and prevents the immediate dissolution of the partnership. The beauty of the arrangement is that the birth of the *post-mortem* heir solves all issues in one stroke.

As mother of the *post-mortem* heir, "the wife of the dead brother" functions as his tutor. As there is no reason to assume that a woman could not take over her late husband's role in the partnership, she administers her late husband's assets in the partnership until her son reaches adulthood. What would happen then to his mother is unclear, but this issue need no immediate resolution and by then she might have gone to her own fate.

Why is it important that the *post-mortem* heir is sired by the surviving brother rather than by the stranger mentioned in verse 5? The stated aim is to ensure that the wife of the dead is "not outside for a stranger" (לא תהיה אשת המת החוצה לאיש זר Deut 25:5)? This stranger is distinct from a foreigner (נכרי) or a resident (גר), which leaves open the possibility that "outside" does not mean outside the community but outside the partnership. In this case, the law looks beyond the immediate interest of the surviving brother to consider the risk the dissolution of any partnership entails for individual partners.

The dissolution of the partnership and the move of the wife of the dead brother outside the partnership can be detrimental to the surviving brother. If, as would often be the case, the deceased brother had invested all or part of his wife's dowry in the partnership, the surviving brother would have to find the resources needed to return the dowry of the wife of the dead brother. The untimely death of one partner may occur at an unfavorable time to free up sufficient funds to reimburse the dead brother's wife and release her. In such a situation, the surviving brother might, for instance, have to approach a merchant for a bridging loan until such

---

41 See the comprehensive discussion in Otto, *Deuteronomium 12-34*, 1850–53.
42 Otto, 1850.

time the funds tied up in the partnership's investments reach maturity and his share in them becomes available to reimburse his creditor.

If the birth of a *post-mortem* heir can solve so many issues, why does the text put so much emphasis on convincing the surviving brother to comply? At no point is his right to decline the offer pressed on him by the "wife of the dead brother" challenged. By law or by custom, the surviving brother-partner has every right to refuse to comply. He cannot be forced to take the wife of the dead and sire the *post-mortem* heir. In fact, in most cases he has every interest in refusing to comply.

Though it is not necessarily the case, brothers "who resided together" could be and often would indeed be siblings. Therefore, the surviving brother is by law or by custom the heir of his brother's estate.[43] Therefore, the wife of the dead is advised to apply all the social pressure she can muster on the unwilling surviving partner who has no economic interest whatsoever in complying if by refusing to do so, the entire estate of his dead brother becomes his. If she is not entitled to a share of her late husband's estate, why then is the wife of the dead brother (אשת המת Deut 25:5) not designated as a widow so that she could be entitled at least to a share in the proceeds of the triennial tithes (Deut 14:29)? By carefully avoiding to designate the wife of the dead as a widow, the writers look beyond the immediate interest of the bereaved woman to consider the interest of more destitute widows. As the foodstuffs set apart for the landless is a percentage of the yearly yield (§ 1.1.1), the local community is spared the need to adjust the quantities set apart for the support of its Levite, *ger*, widow and orphan. As the amount of food stored within your gates is not calculated according to the number of beneficiaries, it is in the interest of these beneficiaries to keep their numbers as low as possible and exclude anyone who may find other means to survive.

The surviving brother is expected to be the one who, by either marrying his widowed sister-in-law or, failing that, returning her the dowry she brought into the partnership, will prevent adding another widow to the beneficiaries of the triennial tithes. This second option would be a light burden indeed because the dissolution of the partnership is a boon for him, all the more so in the absence of any other sibling to claim a share of the deceased brother's estate. By turning down his widowed and childless sister-in-law, the surviving brother takes his share of his brother's estate and finds himself the sole beneficiary of a larger capital, up to twice his initial share, if it is not reduced by the shares of other potential heirs. In the latter case, he might still have to find funds to pay off their share in the partnership and return the dowry of the dead brother's wife, if any part of it was tied up in investments or transactions that have not

---

43   Otto, *Deuteronomium 12–34*, 1850.

reached their term. Whatever their complexity, such potential problems in no way diminish the gains that the death of his childless brother entails for he who inherits his estate.

Instead of producing a law to force a fortunate brother to be kind to an unfortunate woman, Deuteronomy 25:4–9 advises on how best to resolve a borderline case by calling the surviving brother to go beyond the call of duty (§6.5–7) and act against his immediate interest. This would be one example of the kind of case that local elders might refer to the *maqom* (§3.2.7), unless these verses provided them with guidelines on how to deal with a textbook case.

The next question is whether the proposed solution implies an indissoluble marriage or only a temporary arrangement until the birth of a first son, as the firstborn (בכיר) in verse 6 suggests. The LXX favors a temporary union because it renders the phrase לקחה לו לאשה in verse 5 as συνοικέω instead of γαμβρεύω in Genesis 38:8. The Alexandrian clearly understood that Onan's liaison with Tamar was supposed to be a proper marital union, while the wife of the deceased merely cohabitates with the surviving partner, a cohabitation likely to end upon the birth of an heir. She may then be free to contract a proper marriage with a man outside (חוצה) the partnership because at that point the problem of a lack of an heir has been solved. For the time being, the partnership survives, the wife of the dead co-administrates it as guardian of her son's share and feeds herself and her son from its proceeds, and the triennial tithes need not be shared with an additional widow and orphan. Ruth 1:15 and Genesis 38:8 are commonly referred to in order to clarify the meaning of the term יבם (Deut 25:5) but it is methodologically unsound to do so as the stories of Ruth and of Tamar could belong to the reception of Deuteronomy 25. These stories introduce blood ties into the Deuteronomic business partnership in order to shift the focus towards an ethnic definition of Israel, which is also one of the burdens of the Deuteronomic frames.

These stories devote much space to the reluctance in performing one's duty. In Ruth 4:6, Polony's reasons to refuse Ruth are not elaborated beyond his fear that it would destroy his estate (אשחית את נחלתי Ruth 4:6). Genesis 38:9 goes further. It explains Onan's stubborn refusal to impregnate Tamar: he knew that the offspring would not be his. Worse, the son he would father would claim the whole of Er's estate, whereas that estate would be his if Tamar remained childless as her marriage to Onan prevented her from marrying an outsider. Onan's "solution" is thus a brilliant legalistic elaboration upon the borderline case of the unwilling brother-partner, but with a crucial difference in outlook. The unwilling brother gains social credit by acting beyond the call of duty and against his immediate personal interest, while Onan is viewed with scorn and is thus punished by YHWH himself.

The grabbing woman of Deuteronomy 25:11 deploys a different strategy to the same aim, without having to wait for the partner's death. Her peculiar gesture targets the reproductive potential of her husband's brother. If perchance that brother has not yet fostered heirs, his estate will eventually go to the children of the grabbing woman. Besides saving her husband from the grip of his brother (הציל Deut 25:11), her grab saves her own children from having to share the assets of the partnership with the heirs of their father's partner, whether they are actual cousins or not. Onan made sure Tamar remained childless, the grabbing woman made sure her husband's brother/partner became sterile.

Whether or not the partners are blood brothers, exploiting an estate in partnership generates tensions, hence the brawl. Blood ties are secondary to the transmission of the assets of the partnership. Therefore, the story of the grabbing wife of Deuteronomy 25 has similar economic implications to the stories of Onan and Ruth—Onan is killed by the Lord, Ruth's reluctant redeemer is shamed at the gate and the grabbing wife is be stoned—because their behavior has negative financial implications for their opponents' progeny.

Warfare has obvious economic implications. Blood ties are irrelevant to the warrior whose fear endangers the zeal of his brothers at arms (Deut 20:8). This is one of the few instances when the brother is more likely to be an ordinary Israelite than an Edomite, though it is also possible that Israelite brothers band with Edomite colleagues to raid a neighboring country.

Finally, the limitation of the corporal punishment of a guilty brother to forty lashes "lest your brother be demeaned in your eyes" (Deut 25:3) supports the understanding of a Deuteronomic brotherhood beyond blood ties but within the narrow brotherhood of the economic elite. Nothing indicates that the case is judged in public, at the gate of the local settlement or at the so-called high court at the *maqom*. The judgment may be an internal affair and the flogging could occur behind closed doors. It is in the interest of the brotherhood to punish the guilty member without shaming him to the point where his honor is beyond recovery. Humanitarian concerns are secondary to the preservation of individual and collective honor. The brotherhood has no interest in airing its dirty linen in public. Whatever the crime committed by the guilty brother, its broadcasting beyond the strict confines of the brotherhood would dent the reputation of the entire association.

The *lex talionis* of Deuteronomy 19:16–21 adds support to a brotherhood conceived as the elite to whom the core addresses it recommendations. Though verse 17 starts with any men (אנשים) involved in a legal dispute, the *lex talionis* is specifically required for the accuser of a brother (Deut 19:18–19). False witness is all the more serious if it occurs from "among you", from within the ranks of the brotherhood (Deut 19:20).

The conclusion at this point is that chapters 15–25 present the full range of meanings entailed by the notion of brotherhood that includes some clearly designated Israelites and Edomites besides a majority of brothers who can be either. All are involved in economic activities between themselves as well as with the other economic agents to be considered now.

2.2 A Levitical brotherhood

Besides the twenty-eight references to the economic and financial brotherhood of the core, two other occurrences of the term brother refer to the Levites (Deut 18:2–7, see Table 2.1 above). They receive no shares of communal land among their brothers (Deut 18:2) and a Levite may travel to the *maqom* to minister there like his fellow Levites (Deut 18:7).

The mention of the tribe of Levi (שבט לוי Deut 18:1) is the sole attestation of a tribal Israel in the Deuteronomic core, which wavers between Levites and Levitical priests, a designation unique to Deuteronomy (17:9.18; 18:1; 24:8). Levites form a brotherhood of their own (Deut 18:7), the only verse in the whole of Deuteronomy where the term brother designates fellow Levites. The blessing of Levi (Deut 33:8–9) uses the term brother for Israelites who are not Levites, an allusion to the episode of the Golden Calf when the sons of Levi slaughtered three thousand Israelites (Exod 32:28).

The allusion to the Exodus episode underlines the lethal potential of the Levitical brotherhood for the rest of Israel. Israel is split into two clearly identified brotherhoods: the brothers addressed as you and the Levitical brotherhood, with little common interest between the two. Israel is a people of two brotherhoods, not a *Volk von Brüdern*.

The first occurrence of Levitical priests (Deut 17:9) is also set at the *maqom*, where they serve as coadjutors at the supreme court, beside a judge whose presence there is textually better attested to than the presence of the priest, Levite or Levitical priest. The other references are not clearly located.

Beside the Levites an appointed priest appears in Deuteronomy 17:12, though he might be a shortened form of the Levitical priest mentioned three verses earlier (Deut 17:9). Appointed priests and judges appear again in the context of legal disputes (Deut 19:17). A priest exhorts the troops before the battle (Deut 20:2). The priests performing the ritual to absolve an unsolved murder are specifically described as "sons of Levi" (Deut 21:5). Therefore, no particular distinctions between priests, Levite in your gates and Levitical priests "emerge from the Deuteronomic text itself".[44]

---

44   Altmann, "Levites in your Gates," 154.

The difference between Levites and Levitical priests may be difficult to pinpoint, but their different economic roles are clear. The Levite in chapter 14 is the counterpart of the most striking feature of the *maqom* economy in Deuteronomy 14:22-26—the consumption of yearly tithes by the tithe payers. The Levite is confined within your gates where he only receives a share of the triennial tithes (Deut 14:28-29). Verse 27 marks the transition between the two kind of tithes with an exhortation not to abandon the Levite who is in your gates because he has no share and *naḥalah* with you. Verse 29 repeats the Levite's deprivation of share and *naḥalah* to justify his access to the proceeds of the triennial tithes besides the *ger*, the orphan, and the widow. One may thus get the impression that the Levite is badly discriminated against and is rightly designated as one of the *personae miserae*. This impression is quickly dispelled considering the revenues attributed to the Levites in chapters 12, 16, 18, and 26 (Table 2.3).

Levi appears already in Deuteronomy 10:8-9, first with a reminder that he has been set apart to carry the ark and to stand in front of YHWH, then with an echo of his deprivation of share and *naḥalah* with his (Israelite) brothers (Deut 14:27 and 29).

Table 2.3 Levitical revenues in Deuteronomy 12; 16; 18 and 26

Deut	
12:12	Rejoice, you, your sons, daughters, slaves, servants, **and the Levite** in your gates because he has no allotment or inheritance
12:18	Eat your tithes before YHWH you, your son, daughter, slave, servant, **and the Levite** who is in your gates
12:19	Beware that you do not abandon the Levite
16:11	You shall rejoice before YHWH, you, your son, daughter, slave, servant, and the Levite who is in your gates **and the *ger*, the orphan and the widow** in your midst at the *maqom*
16:14	You shall rejoice before YHWH—you, your son, daughter, slave, servant, the Levite and the *ger*, the orphan and the widow who are in your gates
18:1	The Levitical priests—all the tribe of Levi—have no allotment with Israel
18:3-5	Priestly portions for him because YHWH has chosen him out of all your tribes
18:6-7	The Levite may leave from one of your gates from all Israel and go to the *maqom* and minister in the name of YHWH like all his brothers the Levites who stand there before YHWH
26:11	You shall rejoice... you, the Levite and the *ger* in your midst...
26:12-13	...once you have completed the third year tithe and given it to the Levite, the *ger*, the orphan and the widow in your gates

The Levite—always singular—appears for the first time in 12:12, which equally echoes chapter 14 with the motif of rejoicing at the *maqom* (Deut 14:26) followed by the deprivation of share and *naḥalah*. No one asks how can anyone rejoice before YHWH while the poor Levite is deprived of share and *naḥalah* because, in stark contrast to the dual tithing system of chapter 14, chapters 12, 16, and 18 royally compensate the Levite and the Levitical priests. Twice, chapter 12 introduces the Levite to the *maqom* festivities beside the farmers' households (verses 12 and 18), with a final admonition not to abandon the Levite, an echo of 14:27. The Levite is not left behind at home anymore. He now seems to be a guest and partakes in the banquets, which ensures that he is not abandoned.

Chapter 16 twice picks up the motif of rejoicing before YHWH (verses 11 and 14) to introduce further measures ensuring that the Levite is not deprived. Every time, the rightful place of the Levite at the gate is recalled (Deut 12:12.18; 16:11.14). The Levite is added to the list of partakers in the banquets according to a subtile accumulative strategy. After chapter 12 where only the Levite shares the *maqom* meals with the tithe-payers families, chapter 16 brings in the *ger*, orphan and widow as well. In verse 11, the Levite is still singled out as the one in your gates, then verse 14 mentions the gates after the widow, thus aligning the four guests with chapter 14 to better disagree with its dual tithing system, which has no place for the Levite at the *maqom*.

The place of the Levite now secure at the Place, chapter 18 goes far beyond the introduction of guests at the *maqom*. After yet another reminder that Levitical priests are deprived of share and *naḥalah* with Israel, verses 3–5 list meat cuts that would represent a large amount of meat (see §1.1.2). It is not clear in these verses whether the meat is collected from carcasses at the *maqom*, but the migrating Levite of the next verses insist that the Levite in your gates has exactly the same rights as the Levites at the *maqom*.

From a single Levite who shares triennial tithes in your gates, the Levitical priesthood ends up commanding significant resources. Even if the triennial tithes were indeed insufficient to satisfy the needs of the so-called *personae miserae*, the priestly dues (משפט הכהנים Deut 18:1–5) turn the Levitical priesthood into a wealthy economic actor in the Deuteronomic economy. Deuteronomy 26:11 repeats the rejoicing motif a fourth time, but this time the Levite has more grounds to rejoice than the addressees whose high value staples—meat and first fleeces—are heavily taxed by the priestly dues collected by the Levitical priests and shared with the Levite when he travels to the *maqom*. Verses 26:12–13 give a polite nod to the prescriptions relative to the triennial tithes (Deut 14:28–29), but at that point of the narrative the means of the Levite are on an entirely different scale. The first-fruits of the grain, wine, and oil may be ignored as negligible quantities. Nevertheless, the Levitical priests collect huge amounts of wool and meat (a shoulder, the jowls, and the stomach of every bovine and caprovid sacrificed by every single Israelite). In this case, the Deuteronomic Levite closely resembles the priesthood portrayed elsewhere in the Pentateuch. Deuteronomy's Levitical priests become a clergy controlling the meat market as was the case in Babylonia.[45]

If the Assyrian *tamkārus* rolled into one bundle the tasks of tax collecting and loan-sharking, as Boer suggests, Deuteronomy splits tax collection and loan-sharking between two separate groups. On the one hand the brothers who grant loans to neighbors and foreigners. On the other hand, it is the Levitical priests who play the role of tax-collectors.

2.3 Non-Brothers

2.3.1 Widows and orphans

Not every woman who survives her spouse is a widow. Naomi Steinberg has proposed several titles to distinguish different categories of widows according to their status.[46] For instance, the wife of the deceased brother who exploited his business in partnership (Deut 25:5) is not deemed a widow because the surviving partner is expected to take her into his own household (§2.1.11). As Deuteronomy 25:5 applies specifically to brothers living together, the duty to take the wife does not apply to blood brothers who do not live together.

Childlessness is an important factor in the determination of the status of a woman who survives her spouse. As most women died before reaching menopause, all adult women were potentially fertile even if they had yet failed to bear children. The status of widowhood, and the concomitant right to a share of the proceeds of triennial tithes is thus determined by the absence of other means, in particular the lack of shares of communal land.

A widow who functions as tutor for her under-aged son might not qualify as widow because she is entitled to the usufruct of her deceased husband's share of communal land. When any son of hers is old enough to receive a share of his own, the care of his mother becomes incumbent on him. Hence, only the wives of deceased men who were deprived of shares of communal land are likely to qualify as widows. The concubines of men who did own such shares might also qualify as widows because

---

45   On Babylonian meat trade, see Jursa, "Eating and Food," 181–98; Waerzeggers, *Ezida Temple*, 268–71.
46   Steinberg, "Romancing the Widow," 327–46. Spinsters are inconceivable.

their partial marital status did not entitle them to the usufruct of their deceased partner's share.

Though fictional, and thus not to be used as evidence of actual practices, the story of Ruth implies that widows can retrieve the usufruct of the land shares of their deceased husband, even if they had left the village for a decade, especially if they returned at the time of the harvest, i.e. before the next reallocation of land shares. Hence, Naomi is entitled to Elimelech's share and Ruth to Chilion's or Mahlon's, depending which of Elimelech's son she had married. The status of the mother of daughters is more uncertain as shares of communal land were often distributed according to the number of male adults.[47] Hence, a Deuteronomic widow would be a sonless woman who survived her latest husband and found no other man to marry her and who had no other family to take care of her.

In the same way, the Deuteronomic orphan is not simply a widow's child. To qualify as an orphan and thus receive a share of the proceeds of the triennial tithes, an orphan would be: an under-aged girl with or without a living mother; an under-aged fatherless *and* motherless son too young to work the land share inherited from his father; and an under-aged boy or girl sired by an unknown father and never adopted. Such a boy probably corresponds to the *mamzer* (Deut 23:3, English verse 2).[48]

The reduction in the number of likely beneficiaries of the proceeds of the triennial tithes appears less humanitarian than many modern readings, though it increases the size of the portions allocated to the widows and orphans who had no other means of survival.

Deuteronomy's core grants widows, orphans, and *gerim*, exclusive and extensive gleaning rights (Deut 24:19–21). Like anyone else, widows and orphans hire themselves out as day laborers during seasonal labor peaks. The prohibition on taking a widow's garment as a pledge (Deut 24:17) confirms that widows are considered creditworthy. Even if they own nothing apart from that one cloak, they can still contract short-term unsecured loans against labor or any other service she might provide. As such, they need no alms.

Steinberg's surprise that "the widow is not mentioned in Deut 15:11 as being among those deserving of economic help" is thus unwarranted.[49] Deuteronomy 15 discusses defaulting brothers, an entirely different circle from widows and orphans who are taken care of by the triennial

---

47 See Guillaume, *Land*, 28.
48 On the *mamzer*, see Otto, *Deuteronomium 12,1–23,15*, 1753–54.
49 Steinberg, "Romancing," note 6.

tithes, a 3.33% tax on all plant produce to support them alongside the Levites and *gerim*.[50]

Though no meat is included in the proceeds of the triennial tithes, widows, and orphans should not be listed as *personae miserae*. They do not linger idly at the gate to receive their share of triennial tithes. They contribute to the pool of day laborers without which agricultural economies cannot function. They thus receive salaries and gleaning rights. Far from being miserable, they are likely to be credit-worthy and receive loans rather than alms.

2.3.2 Slaves

The Deuteronomic core envisaged three sources of chattel slaves: runaway slaves from neighboring areas (Deut 23:15–16), self-indentured Israelites (Deut 15:17) and war captives.

The word love to describe the motivation of the person who asks to remain perpetually at the service of another may well cover hardship, but hardship would be expected to be rare, were the laws delineated in the legal core put in practice. In fact, self-indenture occurs at the end of a period of up to six years during which the future slave reimburses an antichretic loan with his or her work. The point is that self-indenture occurs in a contractual context rather than as the result of hardship when slavery is no more the result of a free choice between at least two options, as is the case with a war captive. The welcome of runaway slaves (Deut 23:15) is presented in a similar way. They chose to escape to Israel, and even if they remain slaves there, their arrival is the result of their choice to escape in the hope of finding better conditions.

The beautiful female war prisoner becomes a legal spouse with all inferential rights and duties. If ever divorced, she is never to be sold in slavery (Deut 21:14). Most other occurrences of the term *'ebed* (עֶבֶד) within Deuteronomy 12–26 are found in references to the Exodus and Egypt as the house of slavery.[51] A few more occur besides mentions of Levites at the *maqom* banquets (Deut 12:12.18; 16:11.14), contrary to Deuteronomy 14:23 where neither Levites nor slaves are listed among the partakers of the banquets in front of YHWH. The inclusion of slaves in the feast makes sense because they belong to the household, but it also increases the number of partakers to make the exclusion of Levites and priests inconceivable.

---

50   Contrary to Deut 10:18–19, the core drives no wedge between the *ger* and the widow and orphan.
51   Egypt: Deut 13:6.11; 15:15; 16:12; 24:18.22; 28:68.

The NRSV mentions a slave in Deuteronomy 15:13, as though this verse introduces a new section devoted to manumission. In the Hebrew text, however, verse 13 is the continuation of verse 12, which introduces a section discussing different labor contracts (Deut 15:12–18). There is no trace of manumission in the entire section because there is no slave to start with. The word slave (עֶבֶד) does occur twice in the passage, in verse 15 as a reminder of Israel's servitude in Egypt and thus as the reason for being dealt with differently, and again in verse 17 as the result of a procedure of self-indenture. Through self-indenture, a particular person may ask to become a permanent slave (עבד עולם), with no requirement for manumission. The question is the identity of the candidate for this voluntary and irrevocable type of slavery.

2.3.3 Hebrews

The whole of Deuteronomy 15:12–18 deals with only one kind of individual. As in the bulk of the Deuteronomic core, the addressee is a brother. Like the previous section dealing with the šemiṭṭah, verses 12–18 focus on dealings between two brothers. Hence verse 12 clearly sets the scene when your brother trades with you (כי ימכר לך אחיך). To simplify, "you" is the buyer and "your brother" the seller, though the situation is more complicated than buying and selling. The object of the transaction is the ʿIbry and the ʿIbryah (העברי או העבריה). This Hebrew man or woman may serve (root עבר used as a verb in verses 12 and 18) the buying brother for a maximum of six years of service (not slavery) after which the buying brother is to send them back to his brother (the seller). The word free (חפשי) occurs twice (Deut 15:12.18), which would suggest manumission, were the word free not immediately followed by "from you" (מעמך). Another element that has wrongly suggested slavery and manumission is the mention of wage in verse 18. The buying brother is urged to send back the ʿIbry and the ʿIbryah with no grudges after six years of service because during six years they have served you for twice the wage of a hireling (כי משנה שכר שכיר עבדך). If twice is correct, the general idea is that the buying brother got a very good deal from these Hebrews who did the work of a hireling at half the cost.

There is, however, another way to render משנה i.e., as "double" in the sense of equivalent.[52] In this case, the release is justified by the simple fact that the Hebrews have fully reimbursed the loan with the exact equivalent of its value in labor. This approach is far more akin to Deuteronomy's sense of justice and fairness than the idea that slaves provide

---

52 See Tsevat, "Hebrew Slave;" 587–95.

twice as much work as hirelings. In any case, these Hebrews are no ordinary hirelings. But are they slaves?

At this point, it is necessary to focus on the *'Ibry* and the *'Ibryah* because Deuteronomy 15:12 has been pivotal in the discussion of their relative standing within the different biblical legal collections.[53] Though this particular issue is beyond the purview of the present inquiry, the status of this Hebrew man or woman and of the brothers is crucial.[54]

Against John van Seters, Levinson uses this passage to argue that the Deuteronomic code reworks the Covenant Code and thus reads the verb ימכר as a reflexive *nip'al* form:

כי ימכר לך אחיך העברי או העבריה

If your <u>Hebrew</u> kinsman <u>sells himself</u> to you, whether male of female... (Deut 15:12)

According to Levinson, "The new formulation, accomplished by technical reworking, realigns the language of the Covenant Code's manumission law and brings it into conformity with Deuteronomy's concentration on the אח as fellow Israelite."[55]

Levinson assumes that Deuteronomy's brother is a fellow Israelite, an assumption based on the notion that the understanding of the term brother as fellow Israelite is a hallmark of Deuteronomy.[56] This assumption is very widespread but, as discussed above (§2.1), it hardly stands the test of evidence.

If the brother in Deuteronomy 15:12 is not any Israelite but the member of a financial elite, Levinson's argument in favor of the priority of Exodus 21:2 and its reworking in Deuteronomy 15:12 loses some of its validity since at least two different stages are required in the production of Deuteronomy. In this case, the question of the priority of the Deuteronomic Code over the Covenant Code becomes more complex. Is it Deuteronomy's older core that reworks Exodus 21, or does the reworking belongs to the framing process(es) of the Deuteronomic core? If the reworking of Exodus 21 is attributed to the framing process of Deuteronomy, and that this framing process involved redactional activity within the Deuteronomic core, the relationship of the Deuteronomic core with

---

53   Stackert, *Rewriting*, 113–65: the legislators of H intended to subvert and replace the earlier D and CC. Bergsma, *Jubilee*, 139 argues that H (Holiness Code) predates D (Deuteronomic law) and denies any literary connection between the two legal corpora. Kaufman, "Deuteronomy 15," 273–76 viewed D as predating Leviticus 25.
54   Rossi and Guillaume, "Alternative Reading," 1–28.
55   Levinson, "Manumission," 304.
56   Levinson, 317; following Perlitt, "Volk von Brüdern".

Exodus 21 may be different from the relation of the framing process of Deuteronomy with Exodus 21. The Deuteronomic frames may know and rework Exodus 21 while the older Deuteronomic core may have been produced in isolation or before Exodus 21, in which case Exodus 21 may even be reworking Deuteronomy 15. These additional options prevent resolving the question of the order of dependence between the legal collections of the Pentateuch in a conclusive way.

A range of other readings of the transaction in Deuteronomy 15:12 is possible, thanks to the different options regarding the parsing of the verb ימכר and the identification of its subject and object.

As Levinson argues, the verb ימכר can be read as a reflexive *nipʻal* form "he sells himself". Or, ימכר can be read as a passive *nipʻal* form "he is sold", as the Septuagint translators understood it.[57] In a non-vocalized text, ימכר can also be a simple *qal* "he sells". The choice between *nipʻal* or *qal* and between passive or reflexive *nipʻal* opens a range of possibilities regarding the different parties involved in the transaction:

1. As argued by Levinson and Van Seters, an Israelite sells her/himself to a fellow Israelite: a reflexive *nipʻal* involving two Israelites in a case of self-indenture.[58] First problem: instead of Israelites, Deuteronomy 15:12 distinguishes between two brothers and a Hebrew man or woman. Second problem: your brother who sells himself can also be a Hebrew *sister* or an *Israelite* sister.
2. As read by Alt and Japhet, ימכר is a passive *nipʻal*: "When your brother, a Hebrew man or a Hebrew woman, is sold to you".[59] Instead of self-indenture, this case is closer to the sale of a Hebrew slave in Exodus 21:2 (עֶבֶד עִבְרִי), except that in Deuteronomy 15 the Hebrew becomes a slave only once the procedure of self-indenture is completed.
3. To avoid the above problems, the brothers and the Hebrews can be dissociated and the verb ימכר parsed as a *qal*: a first brother as subject (the seller), a second brother as the purchaser addressed as לך, and a Hebrew man or woman as the object of the transaction: "When a brother trades with you/sells to you the Hebrew man or the Hebrew woman". Problem: with three nominative cases for ὁ ἀδελφός ὁ Εβραῖος ἢ ἡ Εβραία, the Septuagint takes the article in

---

57 Ἐὰν δὲ πραθῇ σοι ὁ ἀδελφός ὁ Εβραῖος ἢ ἡ Εβραία, where πραθῇ is a passive form of πιπράσκω "to be sold" (BDAG 1666), "But if your brother is sold to you, whether a Hebrew man or a Hebrew woman" (NETS).
58 Van Seters, *Lawbook*, 85.
59 Japhet, "Relationship," 63–69.

העברי או העבריה as the indication that the *'Ibry* or the *'Ibryah* is identical with the immediately preceding term אחיך your brother.

The main objection to reading העברי או העבריה as the direct objects of the verb מכר to sell is the absence of the particle את in front of העברי in order to clearly identify the Hebrew. Yet, with a determined noun את, though very frequent, is rarely necessary.[60] Muraoka mentions שא־נא עיניך (Gen 13:10), תן־לי הנפש (Gen 14:21); ויצא אלהם לוט הפתחה (Gen 19:6); השב אשת־האיש (Gen 20:7). Muraoka mentions the long list in Deuteronomy 14:13–17, where four out of ten animals are not preceded by את.[61]

In sections that are more likely than Deuteronomy 14:13–17 to belong to the same layer as chapter 15, the following examples of the missing particle את in front of a noun determined by the article (as in העברי) can be adduced:

- וצרת הכסף You shall tie the silver (Deut 14:25)
- ונתתה הכסף You shall give the silver (Deut 14:26)
- תאכלנו הטמא והטהור You shall eat the unclean and the clean (Deut 15:22)
- ובערת הרע You shall purge the evil (Deut 17:12; 19:19; 21:9; 22:21–22.24; 24:7)
- לא־ירבה־לו סוסים He shall not multiply for himself horses, followed by ולא־ישיב את־העם מצרימה and he shall not return the people to Egypt (Deut 17:16)
- תכין לך הדרך You shall measure the distance (Deut 19:3)
- ופרשו השמלה They shall spread out the cloth (Deut 22:17)

Other examples of determined nouns could be added since in biblical Hebrew the determination is also indicated by a genetival construct such as לא תגז בכור צאנך You shall not shear the firstling of your flock (Deut 15:19). Yet, for the present purpose, the demonstration should be limited to cases of determination with the article ה־.

The above list shows that with the seven-fold repetition of the formula to purge evil, there are a dozen cases of omissions of the particle את. Hence, in this case at least, the omission is less rare than Joüon and Muraoka's grammar would suggest. Hence, the omission of the particle את in Deuteronomy 15:12 would not be exceptional. There is thus a distinct

---

60 Joüon and Muraoka, *Grammar*, §125f; Muraoka, *Emphatic Words*, 150: "I have read through Gn 12–20 and 1Sm 1–8 [...]. In the former there are found 86 cases of the determined object out of which 22 lack the particle, while in the latter only 8 out of 116 cases lack it". See also Waltke and O'Connor, *Introduction*, §10.3. Bekins and Kirk, "Thorny Text," 360 use the fact that the object marker can be omitted to argue against its use to "add any sort of emphasis".

61 Muraoka, *Emphatic Words*, 153–54.

possibility to distinguish between העברי או העבריה as the objects of the sale and אחיך as the subject of the verb מכר, in spite of the absence of the *nota accusativi* in front of העברי.

Against this dozen cases of direct object without the particle את, the same textual corpus has thirty-four occurrences of the presence of the particle את in front of nouns determined by the article ה- (rather than by a proper name). As ten of these are followed by the demonstrative pronoun, they are less significant because in this case the presence of the article is required.[62] Nevertheless, for the sake of completeness, they are listed with the others and indicated with the demonstrative pronoun in italics in the English translation:

- לעשות את־כל־המצוה הזאת to do all *this* command (Deut 15:5)
- אנכי מצוך את־הבדר הזה I order you *this* thing (Deut 15:15)
- ולקחת את־המרצע you shall take the awl (Deut 15:17)
- אשר יעשה את־הרע who are doing the evil (Deut 17:2)
- והוצאת את־האיש ההוא או את־האשה ההוא you shall bring out *this* man or *this* woman (Deut 17:5)
- ועשית על־פי הדבר you shall do exactly the thing (Deut 17:10)
- ולא ישיב את־העם מצרימה he shall not return the people to Egypt (Deut 17:16)
- וכתב לו את־משנה התורה הזאת he shall write for him a copy of *this* torah (Deut 17:18)
- לשמר את־כל־דברי התורה הזאת to observe all the words of *this* torah (Deut 17:19)
- זה יהיה משפט הכהנים מאת העם מאת הזבחי הזבח this shall be the priests' due from the people, from those offering a sacrifice (Deut 18:3)
- איכה נדע את־הדבר how can I know the thing? (Deut 18:21)
- כי יכרית יהוה את־הגוים when the Lord has cut off the people (Deut 19:1)
- ונתן לך את־כל־הארץ he will give you all the land (Deut 19:8)
- כי תשמר את־כל־המצוה הזות when you observe *this* entire command (Deut 19:9)
- והורדו את־העגלה they shall bring the heifer down (Deut 21:4)
- ידינו לא שפכה את־הדם הזה our hands did not shed *this* blood (Deut 21:7)
- תשלח את־האם send off the mother (Deut 22:7)
- ואמר את־האשה הזות and said, *this* woman (Deut 22:14)
- ולקחו את־האיש they shall take the man (Deut 22:18)
- והוציתם את־הנער they shall bring the woman out (Deut 22:21)
- והוצתים את־שניהם... מתו את־הנער... ואת־האישה you shall bring both... the man and the woman shall die (Deut 22:24)
- ויהפך יהוה את־הקללה the Lord turned the curse (Deut 23:6)

---

62 Joüon and Muraoka, *Grammar*, §143h.

- ולא תחטיא את־הארץ you shall not defile the land (Deut 24:4)
- יוציא אליך את־העבוט to bring/return the pledge (Deut 24:11 + 13)
- לעשׂות את־הדבר הזה to do all *this* thing (Deut 24:18 + 22)
- וצדיקו את הצדיק והרשׁיעו את־הרשׁע they shall justify the just one and condemn the guilty one (Deut 25:1)

The conclusion is that a third of the time the particle את is omitted. With such a significant ratio, its lack in front of העברי cannot be invoked against the suggestion that the Hebrew is distinct from the brother who buys his or her labor.

What argues against reading ימכר as a *qal* despite the absence of את in front of העברי is the ambiguity of the formulation in Deuteronomy 15:12, contrary to the lack of ambiguity that in the other cases of omission of the *nota accusativi* listed above, a lack of ambiguity which renders את dispensable, except in Deuteronomy 15:12 where the verb can be read as *qal* or *nip'al*. At best, the other cases might permit reading a *qal*, but they hardly support it.

Part of the ambiguity in Deuteronomy 15:12 is the result of over twenty centuries of reading this passage in light of the biblical manumission laws. Ever since the Septuagint, ימכר has been read as *nip'al* and modern scholars who grappled with this text only perceived the ambiguity in the possibility of reading the verb as "he is sold", or "he sells himself".

Ambiguity is relative, and there is no telling whether the scribe who first produced Deuteronomy 15 meant a *qal* or a *nip'al* in verse 12. Nor is there any clue that the generations who read and heard this text in isolation from the other books of the Pentateuch perceived Deuteronomy 15:12 as ambiguous and, if they did, whether they hesitated between passive and reflexive *nip'al* or between *qal* and *nip'al*.

It is the relation between the first two sections of Deuteronomy 15 that is decisive. Is Deuteronomy 15:1–18 to be taken as a single whole, describing the relentless spiral of impoverishment of a brother, or are there two distinct sections dealing with different cases?

If a single section, the recommended remedies fail to palliate the situation of the unfortunate brother. Despite the writing-off of his debts and the charitable gifts provided by his brothers, he ends up sold or selling himself to his own brothers.

If, as the *setumah* at the end of verse 11 suggests, verses 12–18 are not the continuation of the previous verses, verse 12 introduces a new case. Instead of suggesting that the *šemiṭṭah* and the generous gifts of the previous verses could not avert slavery, verse 12 regulates the trading of the labor of a Hebrew between brothers. In this case, Deuteronomy 15:12–18 is *not* dealing with the manumission of a slave.

The comparison with parallel laws has led scholarship to view Deuteronomy 15 as dealing with manumission like Exodus 21 and Leviticus 25 in order to jump to conclusions regarding the anteriority of one legal collection over the others.[63] Yet, as the article in front of *'Ibry* and *'Ibryah* (Deut 15:12) does not necessarily imply that these Hebrews must be identical to the brother who is sold or who sells himself, Deuteronomy 15 may deal with an entirely different matter from the purchase of a temporary chattel slave in Exodus 21. Instead of manumission, Deuteronomy 15:12–18 deals with the trading of a Hebrew whose labor reimburses an antichretic loan, or rather two antichretic loans in one go. The deal can be clarified with the help of a biblical example.

Jacob's situation in Paddan-aram is relevant to that of the Hebrew worker (Deut 15:12), except that the Genesis story involves no secondary trading between brothers. For seven years, Jacob works without wages for Laban, his sole means of payment of Rachel's bride-price. Deuteronomy 15 introduces an element of complexity. Imagine Laban has contracted a debt from another herder. Imagine also that Laban has not enough work for Jacob because his sons (Gen 31:1) or his brothers (Gen 31:23) suffice for the job, or because Laban considers it wise to keep Jacob away from Rachel until the bride-price is fully paid in equivalent work-days. To reimburse his own debt, Laban could, as envisaged in Deuteronomy 15:12, hire out Jacob to his creditor for the length of time it would take for Jacob's labor to cover the value of Laban's debt in whatever currency it might have been contracted. While tending the sheep of Laban's creditor rather than Laban's own, Jacob pays back through his labor the loan contracted by Laban while simultaneously contributing to the bride-price for Rachel. The beauty of the arrangement is that no currency changes hands, only an equivalent sum of labor. All liabilities are paid off in workdays. Though Jacob's wives later complained that their father had sold them (מכר) and had eaten the silver (Gen 31:15), Jacob had in fact disbursed no silver to marry them.

Jacob's situation at Paddan-aram has bearings on the male and female Hebrew laborers of Deuteronomy 15:12. Was Jacob ever Laban's slave? Was Jacob a runaway slave when he departed for Canaan without informing Laban (Gen 31:17)? Of course not. Whatever tricks Laban and Jacob pulled on one another, the nature of their economic arrangements was credit, not slavery. They both acted as free men. The younger one had no capital to start with, other than his youth. The older one had plenty of

---

63   Jer 34 does refer to Deut 15 as manumission, but this does not mean that it was what the producers of Deut 15 meant. Smelik, "Inner Cohesion," 239–50 argues that attempts to harmonize Jer 34 with slavery laws in the Torah miss the point.

assets but two marriageable daughters. Each had what the other needed. They were made for each other and it was a good deal for both.

Like Jacob and his wives, the Hebrew male and female traded between brothers are no slaves. The text refers to them as Hebrews. It is only once their ears are pierced that they are designated as slaves (עבד ואמה), their self-indenture having changed their status. As noted by Levinson, Deuteronomy insists that "the female slave falls under the same procedures to be used for a male slave". As most exegetes, however, Levinson considers verses 12 and 17 as slave laws, though self-indenture is only encountered in verse 17. The bearings of this distinction on the relation of Deuteronomy 15 with the slave laws of Exodus 21 and Leviticus 25 need not be discussed here.

A Babylonian promissory note of the year 510 BCE presents a practical illustration of the reimbursement of antichretic loans through the supply of a laborer:

1   21 shekels of silver, white and pure,
2   belonging to Enlil-iqīša, son of Libluṭ, are at the disposal of
3   Ahīqam, son of Rapā'-Yāma.
4   In the 7th month, these 21 shekels of silver, white and pure,
5   he will deliver. Ila'-bih, his slave woman,
6   whose wrist with the name of Kalbâ, son
7   of Ammâ, is inscribed, is pledge
8   before Enlil-iqīša. Another creditor has silver over her
9   no right until Enlil-iqīša this silver
10 got back. Against (her) death and escape
11 Enlil-iqīša does not guarantee. Wage
12 of the slave is not (existent) and interest of the silver is not (existent).
13 Whatever with her hands from the house of Enlil-iqīša
14 she takes, Ahīqam will replace.
15 Witnesses...[64]

Ahīqam borrowed 21 shekels of silver from Enlil-iqīša (= 21 × 50 or 21 × 60). According to Angelika Berlejung, Ahīqam supplies Ila'-bih, a female slave given as a pledge until he [Ahīqam] has paid back his debts.[65] This is possible, but another reading is possible too. The absence of wages for the work of the slave (line 12) suggests that the loan is antichretic. In that

---

64 Quoted from Berlejung, "Social Climbing," 113. The tablet is designated as BaAr 6, no. 9 = MS2610/5 (510), publication forthcoming since 2014 in Wunsch, *Judeans by the Waters of Babylon*. The tablet is listed with date and subjects in Pearce and Wunsch, *Documents*. On the legal, ethical and methodological issues, see Waerzeggars, "Review Article," 179–94.
65 Berlejung, "Climbing," 113.

case, the slave does more than simply secure the loan. The term of the loan (the seventh month in line 4) equals the duration of Ila'-bih's presence at the service of Enlil-iqīša, which can mean that her unpaid labor pays back Ahīqam's loan. Moreover, the mention of another creditor who has silver over her (line 8) reveals that Ahīqam has also pledged Ila'-bih to another one of his creditors, but lines 9–10 stipulate that Ila'-bih will not be transferred to that other creditor until Enlil-iqīša has been paid back in full, either in silver or in work-days provided by Ahīqam's slave. The contract adds that Enlil-iqīša is not liable if Ila'-bih runs away or dies. In such events, Ahīqam would have to supply another slave or pay back the outstanding debt in silver or silver equivalent.

The status of Ila'-bih differs from that of the *'Ibryah* of Deuteronomy 15:12. Ila'-bih is a slave whose wrist is tattooed with a name, Kalbâ son of Ammâ, possibly the name of her original owner. The Hebrews of Deuteronomy 15:12 are not (yet) slaves. At most, they are so-called debt-slaves.[66] Like Ila'-bih, these Hebrews get no wage, not because they are slaves, but because their labor pays their own debts towards the brother who sent them, as well as the debts the same brother contracted from the brother who receives them. This level of imbrication is not possible in Ahīqam's case, where a single debtor (Ahīqam) is indebted to two separate creditors (Enlil-iqīša and an anonymous one). Deuteronomy 15:12 involves two debtors (the sending brother and the Hebrew) and two creditors (the sending and the receiving brothers), the sending brother being both a creditor (the Hebrew's) and a debtor (the receiving brother's).

To recapitulate, the whole of Deuteronomy 15 deals with credit, while Exodus is far more akin to chattel slavery, albeit one limited in time.[67] As Levinson pointed out, the main difference is the lack of any mention of brotherhood in Exodus, while brotherhood is crucial in Deuteronomy. Because brotherhood in Deuteronomy has often a distinct economic sense, which is given its fullest expression in the presence of Edomite brothers in the *qehal-YHWH* (Deut 23:7), it is necessary to argue against Levinson that Deuteronomy 15:12, before the framing material modified its scope, did not deal with the sale of a brother but with the transfer of a laborer belonging—as client, dependent, debtor or self-indentured slave—to the work force of another brother.

It is also necessary to state that if the two brothers are likely to be Israelites, the two Hebrews are not, which is why they are referred to

---

66 As noted by Van Seters, "Law of the Hebrew Slave," 169.
67 Levinson, "Manumission," 305 n. 68 insists that "Deuteronomy never refers to the normal contractual laborer as a slave". Hence the absence of the term אדון in Deut 15, contrary to Exod 21:2–6, as noted by Levinson, "Manumission," 303.

as Hebrews. In other words, one brother sells the labor of one of his Hebrew dependents to another brother in order to reimburse the loan he contracted from that same brother.

The next question is: why insist that the Hebrew is returned to his original employer after a maximum of six years? The answer is that the same logic pertains for the Hebrew laborer as for loans between brothers discussed in the previous section (Deut 15:1–11). The *šemiṭṭah* makes sure that the credit market is regularly purged to prevent debts from snow-balling out of control. The aim of the clean-slate operation of the *šemiṭṭah* is to enable an adequate assessment of the financial standing of each brother. The aim of the return of the Hebrew hireling to its original employer after a maximum of six years of service is the same: to prevent labor contracts and antichretic loans from reaching a level of imbrication which, after a decade, reaches levels of complexity barring any realistic assessment of the actual financial standing and credit-worthiness of potential associates. The Hebrew may indeed decide to stay as a self-indentured slave (Deut 15:16–17), but all slates must be cleaned before this decision takes effect. His labor must have reimbursed his own loan as well as the loan of the brother who sent him.

This reading avoids the unsupported but common inference that in Deuteronomy, brothers are fellow Israelites, one of whom sells her/himself or is sold to the other. If every brother is an Israelite and he is sold/sells her/himself, why specify that he is a Hebrew? Brothers are indeed fellow Israelites in Leviticus 25, where verse 46 specifies that brothers are sons of Israel (אחיכם בני ישׂראל).[68] If Leviticus 25 is a reworking of Deuteronomy 15, the main aim of the modification was the opening of the brotherhood to all Israelites. For this reason, the term Hebrew does not occur in Leviticus 25 because Leviticus insists that all Israelites are brothers and that all Hebrews are Israelites. The expression your Hebrew brother would be redundant in Leviticus 25, but not in Deuteronomy 15 where the Hebrew is the object of a transaction between Israelite brothers.

If, as argued here, the primary audience of the Deuteronomic core is a brother who belongs to a wealthy elite, Deuteronomy 15:1–10 deals with the case of a brother running into grave financial difficulties through the *šemiṭṭah* (§1.1.5). The next verse deals with charity to the poor. As the brother who has run into financial difficulties has already been rescued by the *šemiṭṭah* and by the generosity of his brothers (verse 11), verse 12 deals with the transfer of Hebrew hirelings, not with a brother for whom the previous measures would have proven ineffective. Then, verses

---

68   As noted by Japhet, "Manumission Laws," 76.

12–14 advise marking the return of the same hirelings to their original employer with thank-you gifts for the Hebrew laborer.[69]

This approach to the Hebrew hireling brings to the fore the matter of the wage mentioned as a concluding remark in verse 18: "Do not view it hard to send him away free from you" because according to the NRSV, "for six years they have given you services worth the wages of hired laborers" (כי משנה שכר שכיר עבדך שש שנים). Omitting the notion of double (משנה), the NRSV's rendering loses what made the argument persuasive, as though the promise of a substantial financial benefit was somewhat shameful and contrary to the common view that the biblical laws are motivated by humanitarianism.[70] The generally accepted sense is that during six years, the labor of the Hebrew hireling yielded for the brother who actually employed him a greater return than that which would have been obtained by the labor of an ordinary hireling.[71] The LXX is even more generous. Instead of twice the return, it promises a sixfold return: "for the yearly wage of a salaried worker he has served you for six years".[72] The difference stems from linking the Hebrew משנה to שנה (year) rather than to the root שנה (to repeat).[73]

Whether twofold or sixfold, the two textual traditions agree that the operation greatly benefited the addressee, the brother for whom the Hebrew hirelings actually toiled. Is this a gratuitous claim meant to motivate the parting gifts or is there an economic logic to back the argument? Why would it be more profitable for a member of the *qehal-YHWH* to settle a debt with the supply of a laborer rather than with any other currency? If the transaction involves two brothers, the loan, in whatever currency, is interest-free (Deut 23:20–21), though this hardly explains why a reimbursement in workdays would be more profitable than a reimbursement in silver or in kind, even if workdays represent a particularly valuable asset. In this case, however, there is no reason why the parties involved could not work out the value of any staple in work-day equivalent. Instead of referring to the value of the labor of the Hebrew, the term double can be applied to his labor. With his unpaid labor, the

---

69 Contrary to the NRSV, where verse 13 begins as "When you sent a male slave out" the Hebrew continues dealing with the Hebrew man and woman from the previous verse, with no mention of any slaves.
70 As popularized by Weinfeld, *Deuteronomic School*, 282–97.
71 Or Van Seters, *Law Book*, 58: "because at half the cost of a hired hand he has served you for six years".
72 Influenced by the common understanding of this passage as referring to slavery, NETS renders ἐδούλευσέν σοι as "he was a slave to you" instead of the verbal form "for six years he served you for the annual salary of a hired servant." See Wevers, *Notes*, 264.
73 McCarthy, *Biblia hebraica quinta 5*, 99*–100*.

Hebrew has effected a double reimbursement, two rather than one antichretic loan—his own and the loan contracted by the sending brother from the brother who employed the Hebrew for six years. Hence, rather than stating that the Hebrew served for twice the wage of a hireling (reinterpreted as half),[74] Deut 15:18b explains that the Hebrew has reimbursed a second (משנה as the second Torah in Deut 17:18) loan, the loan contracted by the addressee.

At the end of six years, the Hebrew is free (חפשי). This does not mean that he was a slave and that he is manumitted in the seventh year. He is free from you (מעמך) because his labor has reimbursed the loan contracted by the brother who sent him. Then, and not before, the Hebrew is free to opt for self-indenture and remain permanently at the service of the brother for whom he worked during the last six years (Deut 15:16–17).

Understanding the Hebrew laborer of Deuteronomy 15 as neither a slave nor an Israelite or a brother, but as a rootless outsider who pays back his debt by working for an Israelite brother is fully coherent with the statement that brothers shall lend to many nations (גוים) but will only borrow from other brothers (Deut 15:6). The coherence was lost when the Deuteronomic core was read in light of the other legal collections of the Torah. As is the case with the brother, the Hebrew and Hebrewess were fused into the Israelite melting-pot. Hebrew and brother ended up meaning a fellow Israelite, and eventually a vague member of your community (NRSV). Yet, the Deuteronomic Hebrew is distinct from the hireling (שכיר) who only occurs again in Deuteronomy 24:14–15 as a day laborer whose economic standing is identified as low with the qualifiers poor and needy (עני ואביון), which is why his wages should be paid daily. This hireling is further identified as a local. Like the Hebrew, he is hired by a brother (or a *ger*), but unlike the Hebrew, he is found in your land in your gates (בארצך בשעריך). Their different geographical origin distinguishes the Hebrew from the hireling. From this difference of location ensues different contractual arrangements. The local hireling is contracted daily and paid daily. The Hebrews come from afar.[75] As the text distinguishes them from the *ger*, either the Hebrews do not reside in the land throughout the year or for some other reason they are not considered as *gerim*. Yet, the Hebrews are involved in long labor arrangements for up to six years with brothers who can subcontract them to other brothers.

Besides the coherence with the use of loans to rule over many people (Deut 15:6), the understanding of the *'Ibry* and *'Ibryah* suggested here also

---

74   Van Seters, *Law Book*, 85.
75   See Davies, *Origins*, 176, quoting Lemche, "Hebrew," 1–23 and Beattie, "Hebrew." Davies suggests that the word Hebrew was used as a generic term for the Aramaic-speaking and largely YHWH-worshipping population from '*Abar Naharah*.

displays the same concern as the refusal to return runaway slaves to their owners (Deut 23:17[Eng. 16]). The aim is to secure as much human power as possible: war captives, runaway slaves, self-indentured Hebrews, and the labor provided by free debtors to reimburse antichretic interest-bearing loans.

All being said, this reading of Deuteronomy 15:12–18 does not invalidate the common reading of this passage as the indenture of an Israelite to his brother. The difference between the two approaches lies in the context in which the passage is read. The common reading is informed by manumission laws in Exodus 21, Leviticus 25 and Jeremiah 34, while the transfer of a Hebrew's labor from one brother to another one is based on the Deuteronomic core read in isolation from other biblical books. Moreover, this new reading takes into account the fact that the importance of free wage labor in the ancient world has been under-rated.[76] Slavery was not the most efficient and the most widespread method to draw labor resources from significant segments of society.

At the end of the day, readers are faced with a hermeneutical choice: canonical versus internal coherence, theology versus economics. The portrayal of Deuteronomic brothers as tough businessmen who use their capital to rule over many nations and acquire as many slaves and laborers as possible is less appealing than current humanitarian readings, but it is more faithful to the Deuteronomic text itself, even though Deuteronomy is a multilayered text.

2.3.4 Neighbors

Neighbors may be Israelites or non-Israelites living in Israelite settlements such as *gerim* and foreigners but they are not brothers, despite the translations of the word brother as neighbor (Table 2.1). Derived from the root רעה (to have dealings with),[77] the neighbor (רעה) is someone with whom the addressees interact on a daily basis at the local level in circumstances such as: a fatal accident while felling trees with a neighbor (Deut 19:4–5), the ambush of a neighbor (Deut 19:11), the prohibition of moving a neighbor's boundaries (Deut 19:14), the rape of a neighbor's wife (Deut 22:24), the murder of a neighbor (Deut 22:26), the purloining of produce in a neighbor's vineyard and field (Deut 23:24–25).[78] Despite the odd

---

76 See Wilcke, "Markt und Arbeit," 71–132; Jursa and Tost, "Greek and Roman Slaving," 6 who consider that the amount of free labor in the Graeco-Roman world has been under-rated.
77 *HALOT* 3:1206, 1256.
78 Wells, "Sex Crimes," 294–303.

mention of a neighbor in Deuteronomy 15:2, the *šemiṭṭah* concerns mostly long-term and interest-free loans between brothers. The loans granted to neighbors are secured by a pledge, or paid back by granting the use of the pledge to the lender (Deut 24:10). No such pledges are mentioned for loans between brothers. The addition of a neighbor beside the brother in Deuteronomy 15:2 may suggest that brothers are free to grant brotherly conditions to neighbors at their own expense.

2.3.5 Gerim

The *ger* is the last of the so-called *personae miserae* to be considered. If the others are not miserable, is the *ger* the only miserable category left in the core?

Much effort has been spent on identifying the *ger*. Depending on which parts of the Hebrew Scriptures are considered, the *ger* is a client, a specialized artisan, a soldier, a trader, a seasonal agricultural worker, or a refugee from the Northern Kingdom.[79] In broad terms, the *ger* is "one who does not belong to the circle which the writer has *directly* in view".[80]

As he is listed among the recipients of triennial tithes (Deut 14:29), the *ger* was naturally viewed as particularly vulnerable. He would belong to the weakest social stratum with the other so-called *personae miserae* (see §§2.9 and 2.3.1).[81] Deuteronomy, however, never specifies that the *ger*, contrary to the Levite, has no portion or inheritance (חלק נחלה), an expression I take as signifying the lack of shares of communal land.[82] Would a *ger* necessarily need communal land? In the well-attested to land-for-service system, officials are granted royal land that does not belong to the communal land of the village in which they are stationed.[83] There are other sources of arable land besides the pool of arable land managed by the local community, but as the *ger* is supposed to be poor, he is imagined as a landless laborer as described in Deuteronomy 24:14.

To refute the old hypothesis of the northern origins of Deuteronomy brought to Jerusalem by Israelite refugees flooding into Judah after the Neo-Assyrian conquest of Samaria,[84] Nadav Na'aman argues that the status of the *ger* and of the Levite in Deuteronomy 12–26 reflects not the post-720 BCE era but the ongoing difficulties caused by the large population displacements in the course of Sennacherib's campaign.

---

79 Bibliography in Zehnder, *Umgang*, 279–87. See also Glanville, "Stranger," 7–15.
80 Snijders, *Meaning*, 77.
81 Bultmann, *Fremde*, 35–45.
82 For a similar meaning at Ugarit, see Bultmann, 25.
83 See Edelman, "Different Sources," 441–45.
84 See Welch, *Code of Deuteronomy*.

Summarizing the scholarly consensus, Na'aman viewed the *ger* of Deuteronomy 24:14, like the brother in the same verse, as forced to hire out his services because he had lost his land. The difference, according to Na'aman, was that the brother who had lost his land remained there, while the sojourner had lost his land elsewhere, though not necessarily very far away.[85] For Na'aman, "the sojourners were the offspring of the refugees who fled from the cities that were devastated by Sennacherib's campaign to Judah and found shelter in the intact parts of the kingdom".[86]

Na'aman challenges Abraham Faust's hypothesis that "the kingdoms of Israel and Judah were extraordinarily progressive in their treatment of the lower classes and tackled the problem of the homeless poor by settling them in public housing near the gate."[87] Yet, Na'aman's article equally relies on the notion that the laws of Deuteronomy were designed to aid a class of needy, landless people, which appeared in the Kingdom of Judah in the aftermath of Sennacherib's campaign. The laws of Deuteronomy supposedly sought to protect the *gerim* from the arbitrary conduct of the powerful farmers of the period who had at their disposal a cheap labor force they could employ in their fields and their households, and had the means to exploit the poor and mistreat them.[88]

As Na'aman rejects Alt's hypothesis of a northern *Urdeuteronomium* brought to Jerusalem by refugees and implemented by King Josiah, he does not explain why and who would feel the need to oppose these powerful farmers and produce a set of laws in favor of the lower classes. Theological readings can take YHWH's special love towards the poor in the Psalms as a sufficient reason for Deuteronomy's humanitarian motivations[89]. Economic readings, however, cannot brush this question aside. As the care of the poor is a significant element of royal ideology, the formulation of a set of humanitarian laws could be attributed to a king who had scribes at his service and had the power to edict laws. The Deuteronomic law of the king is, however, hardly conducive to such a view.

Na'aman's article prompted a response by Axel Knauf, who argues that the legal core of Deuteronomy fits the depressed socio-economic context of the Neo-Babylonian province of Yehud.[90] Both authors view the *ger* as a displaced person. The disagreement revolves around the time it would have taken for the displaced persons to relocate and thus terminate their status of landlessness.

---

85 Na'aman, "Sojourners," 249.
86 Na'aman, 259.
87 Na'aman, 279; Faust, *Israelite Society*, 116–22, 247–48.
88 Na'aman, 277.
89 Levin, "Rereading," 56.
90 Knauf, "Observations".

For Na'aman, the *gerim* who fled their homes in the Shephelah in 701 BCE remained a permanent problem in the second half of the seventh century BCE.[91] For Knauf, the displaced persons did not remain displaced for long after 701 BCE. The loss of the land in the Shephelah was soon compensated by the colonization of the Negev and the Judean desert. The situation was radically different after 586 BCE. The only place where the survivors of the plague, hunger and sword could find relief was Benjamin, the sole region that was spared the devastations of the Babylonian armies.

Noting that "Deuteronomy invested a greater effort in the protection of the displaced person than the 'Book of the Covenant' did or the Laws of Leviticus would do", Knauf logically argues that this greater effort reflects a socio-economic situation in which the *gerim* represented a greater challenge than was the case when Exodus 21–23 was written and would represent when Leviticus 17–27 would be produced. To prove that point, Knauf calculates the ratio of occurrences of the word silver (כסף) per number of verses in the three legal collections of the Pentateuch. With only 7 occurrences for 345 verses (= 2%), Deuteronomy displays a less prosperous economy than Exodus (8 occurrences for 85 verses = 9%) and Leviticus (11 occurrences for 323 verses = 3.4%). This statistical approach is a salutary break from the vagaries of the historico-critical method, which revolves entirely around the ability to arrange the different sources in the correct chronological order.[92] Yet, the sample with which Knauf works is very small. Using the same method with the word gold yields the opposite results. Deuteronomy would reflect the most prosperous era because Deuteronomy has the only legal collection of the Pentateuch to mention gold (Deut 17:17). Unfortunately, the statistical samples for silver and gold are too small to measure the prosperity of the periods in which the laws in question arose.

Therefore, the motivation for the production of biblical laws devoted to the protection of the helpless remains open. According to Knauf's scenario, the large number of displaced persons who supposedly fled to Benjamin after 586 BCE posed a far greater problem than was the case in Jerusalem in 701 BCE because that influx of displaced persons occurred in an economically depressed era, in marked contrast to the booming reign of Manasseh that followed Sennacherib's campaign. At this point, Knauf's argumentation is undermined by two contradictory claims: on the one hand he accepts wholesale Na'aman's view that the *gerim* represented a source of cheap labor in Benjamin and, on the other hand, he insists that Benjamin suffered a dramatic depopulation following

---

91 Na'aman, "Sojourners," 276.
92 Na'aman, 257.

migration to coastal cities and to Egypt.⁹³ Depopulation would either increase the value of labor or render it unnecessary. The notion of cheap labor springs from the common view of the *ger* belonging to the lowest rungs of the society because Deuteronomy mentions the *ger* beside the orphan and the widow.

The portrayal of the Deuteronomic *ger* as a *persona misera* does seem correct in light of the gleaning rights held by the *ger* alongside widows and orphans (Deut 24:19-21), of the shares in the proceeds of the triennial tithes the *ger* receives with the Levite, the widow and the orphan (Deut 14:29) and of the carrion given to the *ger* and only to him (Deut 14:21). But are gifts of carrion and the allocation of tithes obvious proofs of poverty?⁹⁴

That potential buyers of carrion are envisaged (Deut 14:21) indicates that in the writers' minds carrion has intrinsic economic value. As much as gleanings, carrion holds some commercial value even when the meat is beyond human consumption. Carrion by-products are recycled by knackers, whose profession still constitutes a thriving industry today. Therefore, gifts of carrion and gleaning rights can reflect privilege rather than utter poverty. In this case, Na'aman's alternative view of the *ger*'s identity must be considered anew.

Rather than one of the poorest elements of society, some of the *gerim* in the Deuteronomic core may be understood in light of the *ubāru* attested to in Amarna letters and at Ugarit. There, the *ubāru* was a residing foreign delegate, a representative of a foreign ruler who resided in the courts of other rulers and of important vassals.⁹⁵ Na'aman argued that these Late Bronze Age ambassadors became redundant in the Iron Age because the hostages Assyria held to guarantee the proper conduct of its vassals made their long stay in foreign courts redundant. Instead, the Neo-Assyrian *ṣērāni* travelled from vassal kingdoms to the court of Assyria to deliver tributes and gifts before returning to their homeland.

Did the Neo-Assyrian *ṣērāni* make residing foreign delegates entirely dispensable? True, the Deuteronomic core has no room for a foreign ruler and hardly any room for a local ruler (Deut 17:15). Who then is expected to rule? Legal systems based upon divine law have never made human rule redundant. Whether vested in a particular individual or in an authoritative assembly, divine law needs to be applied by humans. That a local ruler is optional in Deuteronomy may simply be attributed to the presence of representatives of a distant and absent and thus invisible foreign ruler. Whereas the *ubāru* at the court of Ugarit was housed and fed

---

93 Knauf, "Observations," 3.
94 As most exegetes take it, for instance Bultmann, *Fremde*, 74.
95 Na'aman, "Resident-Alien," 475–78. On *ubāru*, see also Bultmann, *Fremde*, 27–28.

by the elite,⁹⁶ a Deuteronomic *ubāru* would have been granted royal land as part of the land-for-service system. As such, the Deuteronomic *ubāru* would have owned slaves and controlled workers, which could have been hired out during labor peaks. A Deuteronomic *ubāru* identified in the text as a *ger* would have received shares in the proceeds of triennial tithes as extra revenues or bribes from the local population to underline his privileged status as much as the gleaning rights and the pasturing rights that may go with it and the carrion given to him instead of being sold to foreigners, or given to the dogs (Exod 22:31). Instead of ranking him among the *personae miserae,* these gifts rank the *ger* or some *gerim* among the local elite, next to the brothers who dispose of a similar pool of manpower (Deut 24:14). Read in this light, the injunction not to return to collect the forgotten sheaf "so that YHWH will bless you in all the work of your hands" (Deut 24:19) is a warning to the audience that it is in every Israelite's interest to pay his dues and avoid aggravating the powers represented by the *gerim.*

As representatives of an imperial administration at the local level, this *ger* would have generated more resentment than pity among the population. The custom of the orphan *ger* (משפט גר יתום Deut 24:17; 27:19) reflects the ill feelings the Israelite population would harbor toward that kind of *ger*. The orphan *ger* has been corrected in various ways, as "ger *and* orphan" or LXX's "ger and orphan and widow". All are improvements to be rejected as any *lectio facilior* should be. Israelites are warned not to forget the protection due to the orphan of a *ger* precisely because such an orphan would find himself in a precarious position away from relatives and amidst a population that resented his parents.

The untimely death of a *ger* would indeed turn his orphans into *personae miserae.* Hence the insistence on not neglecting the care due to the *ger*'s family following the death of the *ger.* The wrath of the faraway overlord could be expected if his representatives and their dependents were not treated with due respect and honors.

If some *gerim* are be local representatives of an distant overlord, it would be unwise to rank all Deuteronomic *gerim* in this category. Besides the notion of the *ger* as "one who does not belong to the circle which the writer has *directly* in view",⁹⁷ the Deuteronomic *ger* is anyone residing in Israelite settlements whose ancestry is not rooted locally and who is thus unable to relate himself to noble ancestors, which can thus embrace a number of economic conditions and ethnic origins.⁹⁸

---

96   Bodi, "Outraging the Resident-Alien," 29–56.
97   Snijders, *Meaning,* 77.
98   This notion is common in Arabic and Hebrew. See HALOT 1:82 under אצל.

2.3.6 Foreigners

The *zar* (אִישׁ זָר) who should not be allowed to marry a brother's widow who has not yet borne a son (Deut 25:5) is an outsider, someone who has no blood or business ties with the surviving brother, but not necessarily a foreigner (§2.1.11). The foreigner or stranger (נכרי) is someone who does not belong to Israel but who interacts with Israelites in beneficial ways. He cannot be chosen as king (Deut 17:15), but he may pay for carrion (Deut 14:21) and obtain loans that are not subject to the *šemiṭṭah* release (Deut 15:3) and bear interest (Deut 23:21).

Therefore, Crouch's claim that Deuteronomy constructs a distinctive Israelite identity in avoidance of non-Israelites is an overstatement.[99] The Deuteronomic Israel is not expected to live in isolation. Besides Edomite brothers and third generation Egyptians, *gerim* are present in some if not most Israelite settlements. Foreigners are also part of the picture and relations with them are profitable. Threats to an Israelite identity are more perceivable in the framing chapters than in the legal collection in the central part of Deuteronomy.

2.4 Need and toil in the Deuteronomic economy

As already mentioned, Lohfink argued that none of the beneficiaries of the triennial tithes, gleanings and wages is destitute (§2.1.9).[100] The revenues attributed to the four categories that share the proceeds of the triennial tithes confirms this view. It implies that the expression *personae miserae* should be banned when referring to Deuteronomic *gerim*, Levites, widows and orphans. In this case, who is poor in Deuteronomy?

The poor has evinced great interest in ethical readings of Deuteronomy and of the other legal codes of the Hebrew Bible, as they seem to anticipate human rights millennia before the formulation of that notion.[101] Poverty is a convenient ragbag, but too vague a notion to gain a nuanced understanding of the economic standing of the groups designated by the terms עני and אביון.

The systematic erasure of the brotherhood in the NRSV where the term brother (אח) is rendered as a member of your community (Deut 15:7), a neighbor (Deut 15:9.11) or another Israelite (Deut 24:14) is a further complication to the identification of the different levels of want and the recommended solutions. Table 2.4 lists the occurrences of the terms

---

99   Crouch, *Making*, 218.
100 Lohfink, "Deuteronmische Gesetz," 37; Lohfink, "Poverty," 34–50.
101 Tsai, *Human Rights*.

Table 2.4 Need and toil in Deuteronomy 15 and 24

Deut	עני	אביון	LXX, NRSV
15:4		לא יהיה בך אביון	ἐνδεὴς, no one in need among you
15:7		כי יהיה בך אביון מאחד אחיך באחד שעריך בארצך	ἐνδεὴς, anyone in need, a member of your community in any of your towns...
15:9		רעה עינך באחיך האביון	ἐπιδεομένος ἀδελφός, needy neighbor
15:11a		לא יחדל אביון מקרב הארץ	ἐνδεὴς, some in need on the earth
15:11b		תפתח את ידך לאחיך לעניך ולאביונך בארצך	τῷ ἀδελφῷ σου τῷ πένητι, to the poor and...
			καὶ τῷ ἐπιδεομένῳ ἐπὶ τῆς γῆς σου, ...needy neighbor in your land
24:12	אם איש עני הוא לא תשכב בעבטו		ἄνθρωπος πένηται, poor person
24:14		לא תעשק שכיר עני ואביון מאחיך או מגרך	μισθὸν πένης καὶ ἐνδεοῦς ἐκ τῶν ἀδελφῶν σου ἢ ἐκ τῶν προσηλύτων, poor and needy laborers, whether other Israelites or aliens
24:15	לא תבוא עליו השמש כי עני הוא		πένης, they are poor

עני and אביון in the Deuteronomic core and their renderings in the LXX and in the NRSV.

The LXX has systematically rendered אביון with various forms of the verb ἐπιδέω "to be in need", and עני as πένης. The NRSV has followed suit by systematically rendering אביון as need, but עני as poor. In fact, the primary meanings of πένης (from the verb πένομαι) are toil and hard labor. Destitution and misery are secondary meanings.

2.4.1 Toil is no destitution

The NRSV's rendering of עני and πένης as poverty is confusing. Poverty suggests destitution while toil and hard labor do not. Destitution and toil call for different responses. Charity is the only way to alleviate destitution since destitution means the loss of any means of survival. This is not the situation of the poor man of Deuteronomy 24:12 (איש עני, ἄνθρωπος πένηται) who has been granted a loan secured by his garment. The term of the loan is indeed very short, probably only one day since the garment must be returned by sunset (§2.1.9). The fact that this poor man was granted a loan implies that he is not destitute since there is no point in lending anything to the destitute who have no means whatsoever to pay back. By contrast, the poor (רשׁ) of Proverbs 28:27 only receives alms.[102] The LXX renders that destitute person as a beggar (πτωχός).

Deuteronomion never uses the word beggar (πτωχός), except in Deut 24:19 where it lacks textual support. Nevertheless, Muraoka claims that in the Septuagint it is difficult "to establish any distinction between πένης and πτωχός", that is between the poor and the beggar.[103] In Deuteronomy at least, the distinction is clear. Apart from the dubious beggar of Deuteronomy 24:19, *Deuteronomion* has no beggars. The distinction between poverty and begging is discussed by Aristophanes, *Ploutos* 552–54:

> Tis a beggar (πτωχός) alone who has nought of his own, nor even an obol possesses. My *poor* man (πένης), 'tis true, has to scrape and to screw and his work he must never lack in; There'll be no superfluity found in his cot; but then there will nothing be lacking.[104]

Or in a more modern rendering:

> Beggars have no possessions. They have nothing, whereas the poor people are cautious with their money. They work hard and even though they've got nothing to spare, they've got all they need. That's the difference.[105]

In classical Greek, the πένης works hard for his living, he is a day-laborer (*LSJ*, 359). Physical labor was viewed as incompatible with political activities because a life of constant toil did not afford the leisure to perform the duties of a citizen.[106] Hence, the city of Thebes excluded manual workers from its citizenry, as Plato did from his ideal city (Aristotle, *Politics* II, 1278 a25). Ben Sirach equally reserves the access to wisdom to scribes and excludes manual workers (38:24–34).

The disdain of the Greek elites for physical labor is shared by modern lexicographers who derive the word עני from the root ענה II "to be wretched, emaciated, crouched, oppressed" rather than from ענה III "to try hard, to be busily occupied". Hence, Qohelet 1:13; 3:10 are the only references in the entire Hebrew Bible listed as attestations of the sense of

---

102 The text clearly states that these alms benefit first of all the giver: "he who gives to the poor (רשׁ) will not lack".
103 Muraoka, *Lexicon of the Septuagint*, 543 sv πένης.
104 Aristophanes, *Ploutos*, 415.
105 Aristophanes, *Wealth*.
106 Coin-Longeray, "Πενία et πένης," 249–56.

being busy (HALOT II:852–56). In these two passages, the king of Jerusalem deems the aristocratic pursuit of wisdom as an "evil business (עִנְיַן רָע) that God has given to the sons of Adam to keep them busy (לַעֲנוֹת בּוֹ)." The son of David uses the root עמל to designate toil, in particular the labor involved in the economic activities listed in Qohelet 2:4–8. Though Qohelet ends up equating physical and commercial occupations together with the pursuit of wisdom and pleasure as vanity (for instance Qoh 2:15), equating toil and commerce with poverty is unjustified. Even the aristocratic Aristophanes recognized the difference between a beggar and a laborer. The beggar has lost everything, even the pride of eating the bread he earned by the sweat of his brow. The πένης prides himself in lacking nothing. Contrary to the NRSV's renderings, what distinguishes the πένης from the beggar are the toils of the πένης to make ends meet. Rendering πένης and עני as poor misses this crucial distinction.

If there are no beggars in Deuteronomy, is the עני/πένης destitute? To designate him as poor is a convenient way to skirt around the issue of actual levels of wealth or lack of it. Poverty is good enough for theological readings, which merely seek to motivate kindness among readers who have no immediate stake in actual expressions of kindness. By contrast, the Deuteronomic core expects its audience to tackle various situations of need in concrete ways. In this case, each situation has to be analyzed carefully in order to determine an appropriate response. Hence, Deuteronomy 15 and 24 identify different levels of modest economic power.

First of all, there is no evidence that the אביון/ἐπιδεομένος or the עני/πένης are deprived of their share of communal land to produce their own food. That the אִישׁ עָנִי of Deuteronomy 24:12 secured a day-loan with his garment does not imply that he has nothing else to pledge. The garment is an indication of the size and term of the loan, not of the destitution of the borrower. Though this man does not belong to the brothers who grant one another loans over terms as long as six years, the modest borrower of Deuteronomy 24:12 is not destitute. He has the ability to make a profit within a single day and reimburse the loan and the interest by sunset, otherwise no one would risk lending him anything. The day laborer (שָׂכִיר) of Deuteronomy 24:13–14 is not destitute either, though he is both עני and אביון.[107] He may not have the ability to generate profit from day-loans, but he capitalizes upon his physical power and technical know-how by selling his labor. What this laborer needs is his wages, when he happens to work for others besides cultivating his share of communal land.

---

107 Humbert, "Mot biblique *èbyòn*," 187–92 suggests that אביון conveys the idea of begging (requête).

Certainly, the wealth of the borrower of day-loans (Deut 24:12) and of the day-laborer (Deut 24:14–15) is negligible from a narrow view of economics that only measures capital as assets directly convertible into silver. If, however, economics refers to the maximization of welfare and welfare includes non-market behavior, the difference between a beggar and the economic actors in Deuteronomy 24 is substantial.

The modest borrower of Deuteronomy 24:12 needs creditors to grant him day-loans. The laborer of Deuteronomy 24:14–15 needs employers who pay his wages daily. He covers his needs by the sweat of his brow, contrary to a beggar who needs alms to survive. The beggar lives from hand to mouth, depending on charity given in exchange for the benefits charitable gifts entail for the giver, especially when the giving is displayed publicly.[108] In this sense, even the beggar is an economic actor, but in a different way than the borrower of day loans and the day-laborer. It should now be clear that poverty has no heuristic value in an economic reading of Deuteronomy.

Therefore, it is preferable to avoid the blanket designation of poor and understand אביון/ἐπιδεόμενος as someone in want of something, and עני/πένης as someone of modest means.[109]

Yet, recognizing different levels of modest means is but the first step to understand how the Deuteronomic legal collection deals with need. The next step is to clarify the identity of the laborer of Deuteronomy 24:14–15.

2.4.2 A brother or a *ger* among the day-laborer of Deuteronomy 24:14–15?

The two concepts–need and toil–occur together in two verses, in 15:11b and in 24:14 (Table 2.5). The crucial matter of the brother in Deuteronomy 15:11 is discussed below (§2.4.3). Here, the focus is on the relation of the day-laborer of Deuteronomy 24:14, designated as עני and ואביון with a brother or a *ger*:

לא תעשק שכיר עני ואביון מאחיך או מגרך

The laborer in question is designated as a hireling (שכיר). The question is who are your brother or your *ger*? Are they the hirelings themselves? As the Hebrew of Deuteronomy 15:12 is usually viewed as an impoverished brother and the Deuteronomic *ger* as one of the *personae miserae*, the NRSV presents the brother and the *ger* as identical to the poor laborer

---

108   See Van Leeuwen, *Logic of Charity*.
109   Humbert, "Mot biblique *èbyôn*," 187–92 notes that אביון is never put in parallel with the word רש that properly designates destitution.

Table 2.5 Identity and location of the אביון and עני in Deuteronomy 15 and 24

	בך/אחיך	מקרב הארץ	בארצך	איש	שכיר
אביון	15:4.7.9	15:11a	15:11b		24:14–15
עני	15:11b			24:12	24:14–15

who should not be cheated: "You shall not withhold the wages of poor and needy laborers, whether other Israelites or aliens." After the brother sold as slave to another brother (Deut 15:12), here comes a brother and a *ger* as poor laborers.

The word "whether" in the NRSV stands for the two *mems* in front of the words your brother and your *ger*. Rendering the brother as "other Israelites" is acceptable in some cases, but here it is questionable (§2.1.3). The question here is whether the letter *mem* in front of the words brother and *ger* identifies the hireling as a brother or a *ger*, or if it is a reference to the former employers or patrons of the hireling.

According to Lohfink, the *ger*, the widow and the orphan form a group, which is never used in combination with the other group formed by the words עני and אביון.[110] But, what if the *ger* of Deuteronomy 24:14 is identical to the day-laborer who is deemed both עני and אביון?

The problem with interpreting the *mem* in front of the brother (מאחיך), as the indication of the identity of the laborer, is that it turns the claim of Deuteronomy 15:4 into mere wishful thinking. If the poor and needy laborer is a brother himself, it is at loggerheads with the claim that there shall be no need among *you* (לא יהיה בך אביון) because, according to Deuteronomy 15:2, the addressee includes a brother and a neighbor (את רעהו ואת אחיו).

The contradiction between the needy brother of Deuteronomy 24:14 and the eradication of need among brothers in Deuteronomy 15:4 is lifted when the two *mems* are taken as indications of the workforce from which the hireling comes. The brother and the *ger* in this case are the employers, patrons or owners of the hireling they lent or rented out to the addressee.

Though he accepts Lohfink's view that "D imagines a society in which one can be a גר, orphan, or widow without being poor and needy",[111] Awabdy fails to apply this view to the *ger* in Deuteronomy 24:14. Reading this verse as a reference to an impoverished native (the brother) and an impoverished *ger*, Awabdy resolves the tension by arguing that although the גר, orphan and widow do not represent a separate class of the poor,

---

110 Lohfink, "Poverty," 43.
111 Awabdy, *Immigrants*, 109 and 214.

"they have the potential, just as the native does, to become impoverished (see 24:14)."[112]

Opposing the ideal of a poverty-free society by retaining the potential for everyone in this society to become impoverished is a step away from the common relegation of the ger among the personae miserae. Arguing that neither the brother nor the ger in Deuteronomy 24:14 are impoverished hirelings, but that they are employers of hirelings goes a step further to recover Deuteronomy's economy. In this economy, brothers and gerim represent two different segments of the economic elite that work hand in hand in organizing the labor market. A view more practical than ideal.

The example mentioned above (§2.3.3) to clarify the legal status of the Hebrews (Deut 15:12) is relevant to Deuteronomy 24:14. In the same way as Ahīqam transferred his slave Ila'-bih to the service of Enlil-iqīša in order to reimburse part or the totality of the loan Ahīqam had contracted from Enlil-iqīša, the role of the brother and ger of Deuteronomy 24:14 are similar to Ahīqam's position in the deal. The main difference is that the mention of wages to be paid daily indicates that the brother and ger are not the addressee's debtors. They merely send one member of the pool of manpower at their disposal who is hired out to other brothers as a day worker, temporarily or permanently. Hence, the weaker party is the hireling, not the brother or the ger who sent him to work for a colleague. In this case, the supposed contradiction with the claim that there shall never be any poor brothers among you vanishes (Deut 15:4). The brother of Deuteronomy 24:14 remains a member of an affluent elite in control of a number of workers, slaves, clients, debtors, and obligees, through various labor arrangements. This solution is relevant to the status of the ger, who, according to Deuteronomy 24:14 holds a similar position as a potential provider of hirelings.

Before turning to the identity of the ger, it is necessary to ask why any brother or ger would agree to send off one of their laborers to work for a colleague if it is not to reimburse an antichretic loan? It is fairly clear that the wage to be paid daily goes to the hireling and not to the brother or the ger who sent him, because the hireling is not a slave. The short answer is that while the hireling works elsewhere, the brother or ger who sent him does not find the need for him to work on his own estate. The seasonality of labor and the huge variations in labor requirements were a challenge for employers as much as for laborers. Chattel slaves were not a profitable source of agricultural worker because the cost of their upkeep fell all the year round to their owner, even in times of low labor requirements. It was crucial for large estate owners to secure temporary manpower that turned up when needed and departed as soon as the job

[112] Awabdy, 89.

was done. The institutional households of Mesopotamia could mobilize large pools of unskilled mass labor on a temporary basis, something more difficult or less necessary in marginal Levantine contexts.[113]

The problem is compounded by a second one. Besides being seasonal, labor peaks occur at the same time in the same region. In theory, estate owners could split their estates between different regions at different latitudes and altitudes, but then they faced the even greater challenge of supervision. It was easier for ordinary farmers to move from one region to another where sowing and harvesting occurred early, before moving where it occurred later than on their own farm. Besides the additional revenues they obtained as agricultural laborers (by-employment) during idle times, they could also provide part-time "industrial" labor (shearing, weaving, dying, tanning, leather work, ceramic, logging, pressing, mining, rowing, transport...).[114]

The network of the Deuteronomic brotherhood offers a realistic arrangement to limit the impact of the seasonality and simultaneity of labor peaks. With members from distant regions, the Deuteronomic brothers could attract and secure a larger pool of temporary workers by passing their hirelings from one to the other, thus offering longer terms of employment to a volatile source of labor than if each brother hired for the needs of his own estate only. Knowing that his present employer was likely to secure him a place in the work-gang of another brother as soon as the main tasks were accomplished on his own estate, the hireling saved himself the search for his next employer. This benefit was an incentive for the hireling to work well and to return for the next season, accompanied with family and relatives.

This reading to the letter *mem* in Deuteronomy 24:14 (מאחיך) entails considering the *ger* mentioned in this verse in a similar fashion as the brother, i.e. as a large estate owner who might also lend some of his workforce to the addressee. This is coherent with Na'aman's notion of the *ger* as a resident (§2.3.5).

2.4.3 Opening the hand: credit and charity

The expression "open your hand" occurs twice in Deuteronomy 15, first in verse 8 before the *šemiṭṭah*, and again in verse 11 after the *šemiṭṭah*. In verse 8, the call for generosity towards the brother implies to lend (עבט). In verse 11, however, there is no verb to clarify what opening the hand entails. Before the *šemiṭṭah*, brothers are urged to lend to a needy brother,

---

113 See Jursa and Tost, "Slaving."
114 By-employment in economies with a large agricultural sector is not necessarily a problem. Foldvari and Van Leeuwen, "Market Performance," 24.

despite the higher risk of default due to the approaching compulsory release of outstanding debts. After the *šemiṭṭah,* the status of the brother on the credit market has changed. From a brother in need (אביון) of credit, he is now qualified as עני. This does not mean that he is poor and destitute. In fact, the release of his debts reduces his immediate needs. What the change from אביון to עני implies is the lost of credit-worthiness after the *šemiṭṭah.*

Loss of credit-worthiness implies a number of possible options, all of them excluding further loans at preferential brotherly rates. Solidarity between brothers continues, as the second call to open the hand shows, but it now means granting interest-bearing loans, loans secured by pledges or secured and interest-bearing loans, to compensate the higher risk entailed by a borrower whose previous debts had to be wiped out.

In light of the common renderings of the term עני as poor, it would be possible to argue that after the *šemiṭṭah* solidarity between brothers implies charitable gifts to ensure the brother's survival. These alms would save him from begging and the common designation of that brother as poor would be correct.[115] Such understanding is countered by the use of the word עני in chapter 24 to designate the man (איש עני) whose pledge must be returned by sunset as well as the day laborer who should be paid daily (Deut 24:12.14). Neither of these two cases imply alms. Therefore, the second call to generosity implies further loans, albeit not on the same terms.

The claim that Deuteronomy 15:7–11 is an "appeal to make loans available to destitute fellow Israelites",[116] is thus correct if the following two conditions are fulfilled. First, it is necessary to maintain the distinction between unsecured interest-free long-term loans, and secured interest-bearing short-term loans, whether or not they are exempted from cancellation at the next *šemiṭṭah.* Second, instead of destitute fellow Israelites, Deuteronomy 15:7–11 refer either to a fellow member of the *qehal-YHWH* who has lost some creditworthiness or to a brother who has been excluded from the *qehal-YHWH.*

There is no indication that brothers may lose membership, even in case of default, because excluded members would pose a bigger threat to the other members than their default. Hence, the cost of his default is borne by his creditors, while he might still be able to receive loans from the other brothers, but on less favorable terms. His brothers might charge interest and secure the loan.

The second call to open the hand does imply charitable gifts to the needy ones in your land (לאביונך בארצך) mentioned at the end of

---

115 Otto, *Deuteronomium 12,1–23,15,* 1328 uses *Elend* i.e. wretched or destitute.
116 Oosthuizen, "Deuteronomy 15:1–18," 68.

Deuteronomy 15:11. The motivation, however, is not merely a concern for the well-being of the most vulnerable elements in the society.

The distinction between the brother's status before the *šemiṭṭah*, when he is only needy (אביון) and after the *šemiṭṭah* when he has become עני is missed when the last four words of Deuteronomy 15:11 (לאחיך לעניך ולאביונך בארצך) are compounded into a single category of needy persons, *the* poor. Reading these four words as referring to one individual, the poor and needy neighbor in your land (NRSV) eliminates the distinction between brothers and others and takes the words עני and אביון as synonyms for the notion of poverty.

Despite the three *lamed*s in front of לאחיך לעניך ולאביונך and the *kaphs* at the end of these words, the conjunction *waw* between לעניך ולאביונך splits this group of four words into two separate categories: your brother designated as עני, and your needy one in your land (אביונך בארצך). The localization of the needy ones in your land (בארצך) reinforces the distinction between the brother and the non-brothers.

Alternatively, the letter *lamed* in front of the words brother, modest and needy and the pronoun "your" at the end of the same words (-לאחיך לע ניך ולאביונך) argues against the distinction between a modest brother and a general need. In this case, the expression in your land still establishes a distinction, but this time between the needy brother of Deuteronomy 15:9 who belongs to the inner circle of the *qehal-YHWH* and the modest and needy brother of verse 11 who now finds himself in your land following the change of status caused by his default. Needy in your land is thus opposed to the absence of need among you (Deut 15:4).

The difference between the two readings concerns the incidence of default. If default does not mean the loss of the status of brother and admission to the *qehal-YHWH*, default means loss of credit-worthiness and greater difficulty in borrowing at the preferential rates current within the brotherhood, at least for the next seven-year cycle.

There is no indication of alms in Deuteronomy 15:1–11. There would be no point in mentioning the imminence of the *šemiṭṭah* in verses 9–10 if giving implied alms. Were it a matter of gifts to the poor, the *šemiṭṭah* would be irrelevant because the givers of alms expect returns other than the straight reimbursement of the gift.

After the *šemiṭṭah* and despite the forgiving of his debts, the brother remains needy, but he is now designated as עני because his rating on the credit market is akin to that of non-brothers. He is not destitute. He still belongs to the elite. He still owns assets that he now pledges to secure loans. For at least the next seven years, his loans will be different from the interest-free, long term and unsecured loans that are the norm among brothers.

Chapter 3
Three Institutions and their Interplay: Beyond the Temple of Jerusalem

The Israel envisaged in Deuteronomy's core relies on three different institutions: your gates, the *maqom* and the *qehal-YHWH*. Each institution is active in its specific domain to regulate the interaction between the different social groups enumerated in the previous section, and adjust "disequilibriums on a day-to-day basis".[1]

3.1 Your Gates: where Israelites, *gerim* and Levites live

To designate village life, Deuteronomy uses the expression in your gates (בשעריך). The bulk of the occurrences of your gates appear in the core traditionally defined as Deuteronomy 12–26 (26 out of a total of 33 occurrences). All occurrences in the frames deal with theological matters (Deut 5:14 Sabbath; 6:4–9 *Shemaʿ*; 11:20 commandments; 28:52.55.57 curses; 31:12 *gerim* at the seventh-year assembly).

In the core, some occurrences deal with cultic matters: Levites and Levitical priests (Deut 12:12.18) increase the significance of the *maqom* by forbidding the celebration of Passover in your gates (Deut 16:5.11.14). They involve Levitical priests at the supreme court of justice (Deut 17:8). They restrict the scope of the so-called profane slaughter (Deut 12:15.17.21) and consider the case of a Levite moving to the *maqom* (Deut 18:6). Or they introduce the matter of idolatry (Deut 17:2.5).

Other occurrences deal with the administration of justice within your gates: the allocation of triennial tithes (Deut 14:21.27.28.29), of loans for a needy brother (Deut 15:7), the consumption of defective animals (Deut 15:22), setting up judges and officials (Deut 16:18), executing prodigal sons (Deut 21:19), shaming troublesome spouses (Deut 22:15.24; 25:7), protecting runaway slaves (Deut 23:17[16]), and paying wages (Deut 24:14).

---

1   Boer, *Sacred Economy*, 39, quoting Boyer and Saillard, "Summary," 41.

3.1.1 Allocation of food to the landless

Triennial tithes are stored in each Israelite settlement. Assuming that legal sanctions such as biblical laws reflect the interest of "affluent socioeconomic subgroups which have the resources to create regulations that establish their positions of privilege", Bennett reacts against readings of the Deuteronomic tithes as part of a revolutionary social program seeking to alleviate the sufferings of marginal groups. For Bennett, Deuteronomy 14 limits the distribution of tithes for the needy to once every three years, thus contributing to a critical level of deprivation that forced the poor into exploitative relations while claiming that it was the divine will.[2]

Bennett's reaction to rosy readings of biblical laws is legitimate, but its relevance to the Deuteronomic core is far from obvious. Though needs are expected to remain in the land (Deut 15:11), needs do not imply deprivation. Moreover, among the needy ones in the land there is no Levite, *ger*, orphan or widow. To claim that the beneficiaries of the triennial tithes are deprived requires deciding that the proceeds of the triennial tithes are insufficient to cover basic needs. In the absence of the percentage of landless individuals per village, there is no way to evaluate whether 3.33% of the yearly production of a given local community would cover the needs of the Levites, orphans, widows, and *gerim* that community is responsible for. Yet, the actual number of individuals qualifying as widows and orphans is more limited than the modern use of these terms implies (§2.3.1). Nor can the likelihood that the amount of tithes are self-assessed be adduced to argue that farmers will deliver as little as possible at the gates. As much as for the tithes brought to the *maqom*, farmers will tend to set aside more rather than less for the local Levite, orphan, widow, and *ger* because in communities small enough for everyone to know everyone, social pressure is acute. Any farmer delivering or thought to be used to deliver short measures gains an enduring reputation of meanness. Orphans and widows hired as day-laborers to help farmers harvest some of the tithed produces (Deut 24:14–15) would have an accurate idea of the amounts harvested by each family, but even without any direct involvement in the harvest, everyone in the local community has more than a vague inkling of the number of sheaves each family brought to the threshing floor and the size of the winnowed pile of grain. The force of social pressure and the importance of social capital are easily missed by individuals who live in large anonymous cities.

As discussed above (§2.4.1), the term πένης designates someone who earns his food by the sweat of his brow, or a brother who has benefited from the release of his debts. Branding these people as poor implies that the vast majority of human beings were and still are poor, which empties

---

2   Bennett, "Tithes," 7–18.

the term poverty of any value to gauge comparative levels of wealth and welfare.

If the writers were dishonest in implying that triennial tithes would be sufficient, the Levites were not the affluent group that had the resources to create the regulations of the Deuteronomic core, unless they are the ones collecting the meat cuts due to the priests (Deut 18:3–4). The limits of critical exegesis are reached at this point and no clear-cut decision can be reached regarding the status of this passage. If it belonged to the core, the Levites might indeed qualify as an economically affluent group that may be suspected of manipulating social values for their own benefit.[3] Otherwise, the affluent group, which had the resources to create the regulations of the Deuteronomic core to establish its privileges is the brotherhood involved in supra-regional commercial ventures (§3.3).

3.1.2 Waste management

Whether the list of clean and unclean animals (Deut 14:3–20) belongs to the original core or was added later, the mention of the home consumption of defective animals (Deut 15:22–23, repeated in 12:15.22) reflects an economic concern that is rarely found elsewhere. Holocausts are only mentioned in the frame (Deut 12:6–27; 27:6; 33:10), as though the core reflected the point of view of the breeders of the sacrificial animals rather than the point of view of their recipients who collected meat cuts and thus had a vested interest in inflating the number of sacrifices. The recycling of carrion reflects a similar concern to protect the interest of the producers and minimize their losses, even if the Levites collect meat cuts from animals slaughtered at home.

3.1.3 Administration of justice

The Levites are not involved in the condemnation of the stubborn and rebellious son (Deut 21:19–21). It is the local elders who hear the case brought to them by parents who accuse their son. Drunkenness and gluttony threaten hard-won family possessions (Deut 21:20).[4] Divine blessing and prosperity (Deut 15:4.10; 23:20; 24:19) are no reason to squander assets. The stoning of the prodigal son is another example of the core's concern for down-to-earth economical matters.[5]

---

3   Knight, "Whose Agony?" 106.
4   See de Pury, "Steinigt den störrischen Sohn!" 151–60.
5   I could not access Welton, *Glutton and Drunkard*.

Three Institutions and their Interplay: Beyond the Temple of Jerusalem   113

The execution of the drunken son does not mean that human lives are easily dispensable. Human lives are assets too. The core is lenient in the application of the death penalty in unclear cases such as rape and murder without witnesses.[6] As the source of human lives and manpower, female fertility is preserved as much as possible to ensure the birth of the greatest number of children. The public shaming of a commercial partner who refuses to impregnate his dead partner's wife (Deut 25:7) illustrates the awareness that the burden of raising children is offset by the labor they provide. In theory, the more children one fathers, the smaller the share of each heir. In practice, however, a greater number of hands in the field is likely to mean better yields. Of course, this is but a general principal, but on this particular point, the core agrees with Genesis 1:28; 9:1.7.[7]

For this reason, there are no unmarried women in the Deuteronomic Israel and the importance of pre-marital virginity is downplayed. In theory, lack of evidence of pre-marital virginity is condemned by stoning (Deut 22:20-21). In practice, difficulty to garner evidence of the loss of pre-marital virginity, except through pregnancy, protects women.[8] Suspicious husbands are shamed publicly by the presentation of the evidence of defloration. A fine and the loss of the divorce right would be powerful deterrents. The ease with which the conclusive evidence can be produced after the act (Deut 22:13) protects women and underlines the importance of their reproductive potential to the community. Wives and fiancées have to be caught in the act of lying with another man. Otherwise they have the advantage of the benefit of the doubt granted to the young woman deemed victim of rape (Deut 22:28-29). Children are too precious to waste female fertility through celibacy, marital strife and widowhood resulting from sending newly married men to war (Deut 24:5).

3.1.4 Management of the workforce

Children are extra mouths to feed until they become extra hands in the fields.[9] As the food requirements of children increase proportionally with the amount of work they can furnish, populations involved in labor-intensive agricultural production tend to have large families. Before the arrival of farm machinery, the number of hands at one's disposal was a

---

6   See Lipton, "Legal Analogy," 21–38.
7   See Guillaume, "Seventh Year," 123–50.
8   Berlin, "Sex and the Single Girl," 95–112; Fleishman, "Spreading the Cloth," 295–308.
9   Guillaume, "Seventh Year," 123–50.

crucial factor in the production of wealth. Hence the importance of female fertility, the natural source of manpower.

Day laborers (שָׂכִיר) include all valid hands. Brothers and *gerim* have a workforce of dependents (children, slaves, pledges) at their disposal that they hire out to neighbors as day laborers when they are not busy in their own fields. Some day laborers are paid a wage (Deut 24:14), others, including widows, reimburse antichretic loans with their labor (Deut 24:17).

The integration of runaway slaves and war prisoners is another way to increase the availability of manpower (Deut 23:17[16]; 21:10–14). These laws are humanitarian as long as humanitarianism is understood as contributing to economic wealth thanks to a healthy and plentiful pool of manpower.

3.1.5 Recapitulation

The writers accorded a more limited credit to the local community than does Boer, who imagines it as a place where each one lends tools in harmonious solidarity to ensure "the mutual allocation and reallocation of all goods".[10] The solidarity is more likely to result from social pressure and the fear of shame if one sought to deliver less than a fair share of his tithes at the gate under the public gaze, and where *ger*, Levite, widow and orphan have every interest in the identification of potential cheaters.

Rather than a harmonious place, the local community needs elders at the gate to regulate everyday business, arbitrate family conflicts and deal with cases of murder. If, as argued above (§2.3.5), one of the *gerim* is the local representative of a foreign overlord, this *ger* monitors the activities of the Levite and of the elders at the local level. Or, if he only has the status of public guest (*próxenos*), he represented the interests of one community in another one, thus generating diplomatic and economic relations at the local level precisely because the Deuteronomic world is devoid of a capital city.[11] Therefore, the "gates" represent the multitude of political centers that make up Israel.

3.2 The *maqom:* where Israelites are made

For the last century, Josiah's reform has been the backdrop for the vast majority of studies of Deuteronomy. Yet,

---

10   Boer, *Sacred Economy*, 157–58.
11   Welwei, "Proxenia."

scholarly constructs of Josiah's "Deuteronomistic" reform and the role of Deuteronomy in the "project of centralization" create a problem for the production of knowledge. A hypothesis such as the DH [Deuteronomistic History] is quite easily reductive and can quickly lead to overly simplified explanations that overlook many details. Or, because of all of the textual data that do not fit into a simple picture, it produces a body of secondary literature that can become impenetrable in its mass of detail, textual reconstruction, confusion of terminology, and systems of internal referencing between scholars working on the same issues. This impenetrable system blocks the effective transmission of new insights because it so dominates the grounds of the conversation that new voices might not find anyone to listen to them or might find the language too difficult to learn.[12]

As collateral damage, the growing uncertainty over the validity and usefulness of the Deuteronomistic History hypothesis, the *Urdeuteronomium* is gradually unfettered from Josiah's reform and it becomes possible to read Deuteronomy's chosen place without the lens of 2 Kings.[13] Read independently from Josiah, the tenuous hints that the Deuteronomic *maqom* presupposes the temple of Jerusalem vanish into thin air.[14]

With or without Josiah, the twenty-one occurrences of the place that YHWH has chosen or will chose in the so-called centralization formula make the identification of the *maqom* the crucial point for the recovery of the time and milieu of the writers and readers of Deuteronomy.[15] Except for Deuteronomy 31:11, the *maqom* occurs in the core broadly defined as Deuteronomy 12–26 (12:5–26; 14:23–25; 15:20; 16:2–16; 17:8–10; 18:6; 26:2). The other criteria, namely the change of the number of addresses (second person singular or plural) and comparisons with the Covenant Code are insufficient because that code has a history of its own.

3.2.1 A templeless *maqom*

It is difficult to read cultic centralization in Deuteronomy without having 2 Kings 22–23 importing into it the notion of a temple. As neither Deuteronomy or the Torah mention Jerusalem and that the house of YHWH (בית יהוה Deut 23:19[8]) is the sole hint at a temple, that temple would be Bethel's, not Jerusalem's.[16]

12 Thelle, *Approaches*, 208.
13 Thelle, 205; Otto, *Politische Theologie*, 12–14.
14 Against Tigay, "Place His Name," 17–26 who understands placement of the name as inscription of the divine name on his temple.
15 Ben Zvi, "Utopias", 67; Hagedorn, "Placing (a) God," 194.
16 As argued by Adamczewski, *Retelling the Law*, 107–108.

Wherever that temple is supposed to stand, the verses that mention it deprive it from certain revenues without explaining how it could be financed. The opposite is true for the *maqom*. After the initial mention of the *maqom* in Deut 12:5, the next occurrences in chapter 12 list various offerings and sacrifices (verses 11.14.26), mention the Levites as guests at the banquets (verse 18) and discuss profane slaughter (verse 21). None of these elements are found in the most elaborate description of the pilgrimage to the *maqom* in Deut 14:23–25. There, only the addressees are expected to travel to consume their yearly tithes in front of YHWH with their families. At the *maqom* and in the gates, the Levite has no sacrificial functions role. At both places, it is the farmer himself who is ordered to pour the blood on the ground (על הארץ תשפכנו כמים Deut 15:23). The textual history of Deuteronomy 17:9 suggests that the priests operating at the supreme court of the *maqom* are secondary. Therefore, the priest in verse 12 is also likely to belong to a secondary hand that introduced the priesthood and the sacrifices to support it at the *maqom*. The remaining mentions of the *maqom* serve the same purpose. The festival calendar (Deut 16:1–16) introduces Levites (verses 11.14) and excludes families by specifying that only the males are to appear three times a year at the *maqom* (verse 15). The wandering Levite (Deut 18:6) is active both within your gates and at the *maqom*. As Deuteronomy 14:28–29 only grants the Levites a share of triennial tithes, Deuteronomy 18:3–4 and 26:2 add priestly revenues in the form of meat cuts, first fleeces, and first fruits to those serving at the *maqom*.

Therefore, Deuteronomy 12:16–18 and 26 introduce a clergy and its revenues at the *maqom* to overturn the confinement of the Levites to the local communities expressed in chapters 14–15 and align the *maqom* with the portrayal of the priesthood elsewhere in the Pentateuch. Accordingly, the *maqom* in a previous version of the core that ignored the books of Leviticus and Numbers, was where every Israelite family gathered at an unspecified location, and no more. As they eat "in front of YHWH" in order to learn (למד) to fear him (Deut 14:23), the contents of the learning are social interactions with other Israelites from other parts of Israel. That learning became textual when the rules of the core were turned into a text to be read at the *maqom* every seventh year (Deut 31:11).

The only clue Deuteronomy's frame provides about the *maqom* is that Israel first worshipped YHWH at Mount Gerizim/Ebal, a rather odd beginning if Deuteronomy was meant to limit YHWH's worship to Jerusalem only.[17] According to Ancient Near Eastern name theology, all it

---

17   Wenham, "Deuteronomy and the Central Sanctuary," 103 quoting Welch, *Code*, Welch, *Framework to the Code*, Oestreicher, *Grundgesetz*, Wijngaards, *Dramatization*. In this context, Hagedorn, "Placing (a) God," 190 notes the absence in the

would take to have YHWH's name placed somewhere is to inscribe it upon a monument, statue or stela—or on the plastered stones mentioned in Deuteronomy 27:1–3.[18] Hence, even according to the frame, the Deuteronomic *maqom* need no temple.[19]

The altar built solely with undressed field stones mentioned in the frames or in passages within the core that are likely to belong to later additions (Deut 12:27; 16:21; 26:4; 27:5–6) does not evoke much of a temple complex either.[20] Therefore, the temptation to read Deuteronomy's *maqom* as the cipher for any temple should be resisted if Deuteronomy is to be understood on its own terms. The temple complexes eventually built at Jerusalem and on Mount Gerizim were presented as fulfilling Moses' orders concerning the Place. This development belongs to the earliest recoverable step in Deuteronomy's *Wirkungsgeschichte* that should not be confused with the thrust of Deuteronomy's core. The mirror image of Deuteronomy's world in Nehemiah 9:36–37 belongs to a later phase of Deuteronomy's influence on later biblical literature.[21]

If, according to the core, the *maqom* is not a temple, could it nevertheless be a sanctuary? Temporary sanctuaries are known from Mesopotamian sources. Before the repair of a temple, a brick was removed and taken, together with the divine images held in the temple, to a temporary site during the repairs and then sent to a workshop for refurbishing before they were brought back to a new temple.[22] Such temporary arrangements suggest that the notion of a mobile and temporary *maqom* is not fanciful. The problem, however, is that Deuteronomy identifies a single holy sphere, heaven (Deut 26:15), but also ascribes holiness to Israel as a whole (Deut 7:6; 14:2; 26:19). In this case, no particular level of holiness is ascribed to the *maqom*.[23] Deuteronomy has neither holy land nor a holy site. Therefore, the common designation of the *maqom* as the central sanctuary misses Deuteronomy's idiosyncratic concepts of holiness and of the *maqom*. Cultic centralization is too influenced by 2 Kings 23. Centralization of worship better renders how Deuteronomy conceives the *maqom*, but one must be clear that Deuteronomic worship means big

entire Pentateuch of a term to convey the notion of centre such as "navel" (טבור).
18 See Richter, "Placing the Name," 64–78.
19 Bedford, "Temple Funding," 336 nevertheless quotes Deuteronomy to argue that though tithes for the central Jerusalem temple should be construed as voluntary donations, "there were attempts to make their payment obligatory through divine sanction".
20 Hagedorn, "Placing (a) God," 203.
21 See Sulzbach, "Building Castles," 312; Davies, "Authority," 37–38.
22 Hurowitz, "Temporary Temples," 37–50.
23 Rütersworden, "Purity," 419.

parties with lots of food and drink in front of YHWH, but not necessarily in a temple.[24]

Ritual meals in the open are attested by communal ritual picnics in Elamite groves that involved the consumption of fairly large quantities of meat. Little is known about these rituals, but at least they indicate that rituals could occur away from temples and sanctuaries.[25]

3.2.2 The location of the *maqom*

If communal worship of YHWH at the *maqom* requires no temple and no sanctuary, does it require the same location year after year? According to Deuteronomy 12:5, the first occurrence of the centralization formula, the location of the *maqom* is to be sought (דרש). The search concludes with the choice of Mount Ebal (or Gerizim[26]) as the location of the initial gathering (Deut 27:4). There, an altar is built and stones bearing the name of YHWH are set up.[27]

Deuteronomy maintains a total blackout over the location of the *maqom*. One possible explanation for the silence is that the location of the *maqom* was expected to change. Referring to this understanding as the distributive meaning of the centralization formula, Stefan Schorch convincingly rejects Baruch Halpern's notion of the synchronic existence of a number of chosen places, a view explicit in Exodus 20:24 but not in Deuteronomy.[28]

Less convincing is Schorch's rejection of Gerhard von Rad's view of several places chosen in succession rather than coexisting with one another.[29] The argument that the "Deuteronomic concept that Israel's entry into the chosen land is the end of wandering and the beginning of a period of general rest" is hardly relevant to a sequence of chosen places

---

24 The expression is used in Hagedorn, "Placing (a) God," 189 and in Pitkänen, *Central Sanctuary*, 95–109.
25 Henkelman, *Other Gods Who Are*, 441–51; Henkelman, "Parnakka's Feast," 125.
26 See Schenker, "Seigneur," 339–51. Schorch, "Samaritan Version," 23–37.
27 See Richter, "Place of the Name," 342–66.
28 Halpern, "Centralization Formula," 20–38. Morrow, *Scribing the Center*, 52–54 rejects this view in favor of a single site, but not necessarily Jerusalem. Greenspahn, "Deuteronomy and Centralization," 227–35 favors the distributive view, Arnold, "Deuteronomy and the Law," 236–48 assessed the arguments against a single shrine as insufficient to resolve the ambiguity of Deut 12. Halpern, "What does Deuteronomy Centralize," views the ambiguity as intentional and uses it in a new reconstruction of Deuteronomy's origins.
29 Von Rad, *Fünfte Buch Mose*, 67; Von Rad, *Deuteronomy*, 94; Richter, "Place of the Name," 366; Lundbom, *Deuteronomy*, 426.

in succession.[30] Rather than implying sitting under one's own fig tree forever after, rest in Deuteronomy entails traveling to the *maqom* every year, a journey that is expected to become longer as YHWH's blessing extends the confines of Israel (Deut 14:24). Deuteronomy clearly implies one place at a time, but not necessarily the same one all the time. The distributive meaning is indeed excluded in terms of space, but not in terms of time.[31]

To Deuteronomy's silence over the location of the *maqom* corresponds the core's silence of tribal divisions, except in chapters 27 and 33. The aim of gathering every Israelite family at one unspecified place is to forge an Israel in which tribal divisions become secondary. Pilgrimage to the *maqom* "undermines familial, local and traditional ways of belonging".[32] Yet, advocates of the Deuteronomistic History insist that the place YHWH will chose/has chosen is set "in one of your tribes" (באחד שבטיך Deut 12:14), which supposedly implies that one tribe and one tribe only is favored over the others and that this tribe is obviously Judah because, as the hypothesis goes, the *maqom* can only refer to Jerusalem.[33] In fact, the one tribe Deuteronomy favors is Levi, not Judah.

Instead of pointing to Jerusalem, the term tribe (Deut 12:14) underlines the difference between the core that uses gates and its reworking. It reflects the tribes in Deuteronomy 27 and 33, and thus anticipates the rivalry between Jerusalem and Gerizim once Deuteronomy became a part of the Torah of Moses. Nevertheless, in the core as much as in the frames, there is no clue that the *maqom* is an obvious reference to Jerusalem. Jerusalem is a city, not a tribe.

3.2.3 YHWH has chosen and will continue to choose the place

A corollary of Deuteronomy's silence over the location of the *maqom* is the different forms of the verb to choose in the centralization formula in the Masoretic and the Samaritan texts. It was long believed that the Samaritans changed the verb "He will choose" (יבחר), referring to YHWH's choice for the location of the Deuteronomic *maqom*, into "He has chosen" (בהר) in order to contest the legitimacy of the temple of Jerusalem and to claim instead that YHWH had chosen Gerizim from the beginning once and for all, as is the case in Deuteronomy 27:12.

---

30 Schorch, "Samaritan Version," 25.
31 Against Schorch, 25.
32 Houston, *Contending for Justice*, 176.
33 See Römer, "Cult Centralization," 169–70, but Pyschny, "From Core to Centre," 305 notes that "Deuteronomy is far more interested in the activities linked to the makom than its exact location."

Adrian Schenker's recent demonstration that the accomplished form "He has chosen" in the Samaritan Pentateuch is not a Samaritan correction implies that it is Jerusalem that replaced the accomplished form with an unaccomplished one (from בהר to יבחר) to open up the possibility that Jerusalem would be YHWH's future choice.[34]

That the accomplished form of the verb בחר ("He has chosen") is probably older than the unaccomplished one found in MT יבחר ("He will chose") is no impediment to a mobile *maqom*. Schorch convincingly argues, on the basis of the accomplished form בחרתי in Nehemiah 1:8–9, that Judahite readers had no difficulty in reading a reference to Jerusalem in Deuteronomy despite the mention of Gerizim/Ebal as the location of the first gatherings.[35] Schorch even quotes 2 Kings 23:27, Jeremiah 7:14.16, and Psalm 78:60–68 to show that the concept of a succession of chosen places is broadly attested to and that "Following this succession theory, Judeans could accept that Mount Gerizim was one of the chosen places of the past, while Jerusalem was the chosen place of the present and the future."[36]

That Judeans concluded that Jerusalem would remain the only chosen place in the future does not imply that it is what the Deuteronomic writers envisaged. A yearly succession of chosen places is as likely. In fact, claiming that Deuteronomy's *maqom* was constantly relocated and that Judean readers accepted such a view saves postulating an earlier version of Deuteronomy 27 with no mention of Gerizim or Ebal.[37] That Jerusalem qualified as one possible location of the *maqom* would have been the main concern of the Judahite readership while it did not disqualify other sites and allowed the Samaritans to continue arguing that Gerizim is the place YHWH chose once and for all.

Wondering how it was possible for Jews and Samaritans to read the same set of scriptures and yet understand them differently, Knoppers states that there was more at stake than the difference between בחר and יבחר. Each community construed the centralization legislation in its own way. Hence, "deciding upon the priority of one reading is insufficient by itself to prove the validity of one sanctuary over against the other."[38] It is even possible to read the *qatal* form בחר as a future perfect: "He will have chosen".[39] Before the tensions between Jerusalem and Shechem,

---

34 Schenker, "Seigneur," 339–51; Schenker, "Textgeschichtliches," 105–21.
35 Schorch, "Samaritan Version," 32.
36 Schorch, 33.
37 As suggested by Gallagher, "Cult Centralization," 561–72 who follows Ulrich, "4QJoshua^a" 89–104.
38 Knoppers, *Jews and Samaritans*, 195.
39 Himbaza, "Lieu," 115–34.

the main thrust of the single place of worship in the frame and the reworking of the core was the avoidance of Canaanite altars (Deut 12:2–5). The changes from "He has chosen" to "He will choose" and from Gerizim to Ebal as the place of the first altar (Deut 27:4) did not occur before the middle of the second century BCE.[40] In that context, the change had more to do with Deuteronomy 17:15 and the legitimization of a future king from Jerusalem than with the location of a temple.[41]

The silence over the location of the *maqom* has been read as "a sign that the Pentateuch is fundamentally a compromise document."[42] If, however, the location of the centralized sanctuary was subject to change year after year, the centralization formula is an expression of the mobility of the *maqom* rather than of a compromise between Samaritan and Judahite priests. It does not reveal the location of the *maqom* because only the location of the forthcoming gathering was known. The location of the gathering of the following year was most likely determined at the forthcoming meeting. Hence, notions of compromise arise from the failure to conceive a mobile *maqom*.

Had Deuteronomy belonged to a Pentateuch understood as a compromise document, the changes introduced in Exodus 20:24 (SP במקום but MT בכל המקום) and in Deuteronomy would have been irrelevant.

If, as argued here, the absence of location is the result of the mobility of the *maqom*, there is no compromise to talk about. Each side reworked the text to fit its agenda and counter the agenda of its opponent. Gerizim and Zion claimed to be *the* site of the *maqom*. According to the mobile *maqom* of Deuteronomy 14–15, Gerizim and Zion could indeed be selected, but temporarily so and never to the exclusion of other candidates within Israel. When and where it was composed, the Pentateuch was oblivious to the tensions that arose between Zion and Gerizim when the Achaemenids set up a Yahwistic centre in each place. Therefore, identifying a precise historical context from the absence of location for the *maqom* is best avoided.[43]

---

40 Schorch, "Samaritan Version," 34.
41 Schorch, "Construction of Samari(t)an Identity," 145–46.
42 Knoppers, *Jews and Samaritans*, 196.
43 Contrary to newer suggestions such as Sargon's campaign against Samaria, Sennacherib's 701 BCE campaign, or that of Psammeticus II in Palestine (592 BCE), Albertz, "Possible *terminus ad quem*," 271–96 holds on the traditional dating of the Deuteronomic legislation during the reign of Josiah with post-Josianic developments during the reigns of Jehoiakim and Zedekiah.

3.2.4 Regulation of the *maqom* market through mobility

Why a mobile *maqom*? The reason the Israelites should gather at a different place each year is stated explicitly in Deuteronomy 14:24: as a consequence of YHWH's blessing, the distance to the place will increase to the point at which the cost of the transport of the yearly tithes there would become prohibitive for the Israelites living at the periphery. Were these tithes earmarked to feed the priests of a central sanctuary, the problem would concern these priests more than the producers, who would be tempted to deduct transport costs from the quantities delivered until they found a closer sanctuary. Or they might decide to built an "altar of great size" on their side of the Jordan (Josh 22:10–11). Territorial expansion would consequently be a curse rather than a blessing, as it would split Israel up rather than uniting it.

Yet, the option offered to the distant farmers to change the value of their yearly tithes against silver is not sufficient on its own to ensure that the *maqom* gatherings are the nexus that holds together the entire Israelite population. The loss of up to 20% of the purchasing value of the silver incurred by the farmers who convert their tithes are gains for the farmers who live close enough to sell their surpluses to the colleagues who arrive with silver (§1.1.5).

That the tithes are dedicated entirely to the enjoyment of the tithe payers themselves has been deemed a magnanimous gesture on Moses' part that "makes it as convenient as possible for people who live far from the central sanctuary".[44] In fact, the main beneficiaries of Moses' magnanimity are the farmers who live close to the *maqom*. They are at the receiving end of the flow of silver while the farmers who live afar and decide to exchange their produce against silver retain none of that silver.

The text is silent over the origin of the food available for purchase at the *maqom*. One likely source is the farmers who brought their tithes in kind. Farmers who bore minimal transport costs were in the best position to sell foodstuffs to their distant colleagues, whether the food they sold came from their tithes or from their surplus. *De jure*, it is only surplus that could be sold, but the aim of the festival is that everyone throws a big party, which renders the strict distinction between what is earmarked as tithes and what was available for retail irrelevant.

Overabundance is an essential element of the banqueting spirit. It is attested to in Ugaritic by the word ʿšr, a cognate of the Hebrew word for tithe (עשׂר מעשׂר).[45] The festive spirit transpires in the invitation of Deut

---

[44] Block, *Gospel according to Moses*, 98.
[45] Olmo Lete and Sanmartín, *Dictionary*, 1.188; see discussion in Altmann, *Festive Meals*, 221–26.

14:26 for every tithe payer to enjoy all the meats and drinks they might desire. Yet, however much the festive meals increased ordinary consumption levels, the system requires an excess of supply in kind to make up for the loss of purchasing power incurred during the exchange of tithes into silver. The *maqom* would generate a disparity between the farmers that would soon turn the joyful spirit of the feast into resentment.

If the same half of the population bears the extra costs year after year while the other half gains from the losses of the other half, the only way to ensure fairness is to rotate the venue of the banquets. Farmers would accept bearing the extra cost when they had to travel a long way to the *maqom* if they know that once in a while they will find themselves close enough to profit from windfalls generated by the festivities. The mobility of the *maqom* is thus crucial. It ensures fairness and explains Deuteronomy's silence over its location that should ideally change every year.

3.2.5 A flexible system

The description of the *maqom* festivities in chapter 14 does not specify the duration of a festival because the number of days spent there varies in proportion to harvest output, which can fluctuate considerably from one year to the next. As tithes, the victuals represent a theoretical tenth of the actual yield. The quantities set aside for feasting vary and the time spent at the *maqom* adjusts accordingly.

As such a flexibility is at loggerheads with the festive calendar of chapter 16, scholars are tempted to fit the banquets of chapter 14 into the festivals of chapter 16. Ignoring the great variability of actual yields, Maimonides claimed that "Inasmuch as the man and his household would not be likely to consume the whole of the tithe, he would be compelled to give part away in charity."[46] On the basis of Deuteronomy 16:1–17, Tigay calculates a maximum of nine days of presence at the central sanctuary and thus considers that it would be impossible for the farmers to dispose of over a month's worth of food and drink during these nine days, even if they doubled their normal level of consumption during festivals.[47] Hence, Tigay increases the number of mouths to feed at the *maqom*. Inviting many Levites and poor to partake of the banquet (see Deut 12:12.18; 16:11–14) would help disposing of that month's worth of food and drink.[48] Lundbom takes another approach. Instead of increasing the number of

---

46 Hertz, *Pentateuch and Haftorahs*.
47 Tigay, *Deuteronomy*, 143.
48 Tigay, 143. For Kline, *Treaty of the Great King*, 93, the tents are the ones erected near the central place for or by the pilgrims.

mouths to feed, he equates Deuteronomy's *maqom* with the temple of Jerusalem. The rooms around the temple described in 1 Kings, Nehemiah, and 1 Chronicles 31:11–12 can thus serve to store the annual tithes that were not consumed during the pilgrimage.[49]

There is no clue in Deuteronomy that it was ever intended that the *maqom* should hoard tithes and silver, as would have been the case with a temple. Rather than shoring up the rights of a priesthood to treasure silver, the Deuteronomic writers conceived the pilgrimage to the *maqom* as a means of ensuring the movement of partakers from the periphery towards a centre, albeit a centre that is constantly shifting to prevent the rise of a group privileged by its closeness to a fixed meeting place. Nevertheless, the banquets at the *maqom* represent an economic system based on the flow of silver.

The beauty of the *maqom* is the combination of geographical mobility with the flexibility of the duration of the feast and the balance between kind and silver. The silence over the location of the *maqom* goes hand in hand with the silence over the number of days spent there. As a theoretical tenth of the yearly yield, the amount of victuals set apart for the feast would inevitably vary.

When the rains were sufficient and came at the right time, households would spend more days at the *maqom* to consume their tithes than in lean years. During lean years, the scarcity of produce available at the *maqom* would reduce the purchasing power of silver, thus offsetting the higher price obtained at home. During good years, the greater amount of foodstuffs available at the *maqom* required less silver per unit of quantity, thus compensating for the lower prices obtained for the tithes and firstlings at home.

Hence, all the variables, i.e., distance to the *maqom*, yearly yield, duration of the festival, prices in silver equivalents, and the number of consumers tend to balance out one another without external intervention, as long as all farmers are given the option between tithes in kind or in silver.

As the demand created by distant farmers at the *maqom* generates revenues for those who bring their tithes in kind, every farmer figures out the distance that separates him from the *maqom* in order to decide whether he should offset the cost of transport of his tithes by selling some of them to more distant colleagues or save that cost by traveling with silver.

Hence, the *maqom* economy establishes an invisible line that divides Israel between kind and silver. In any given year, the choice between kind and silver would be obvious, both for those Israelites living close and

---

49 Lundbom, *Deuteronomy*, 484.

those living far from the place of the feast. Those farmers living in between would have to decide on which side of the line they find themselves. They would base their decision on an estimate of the number of their colleagues living closer than them to the *maqom*, and on the number of those living further away. As the ability to generate income by selling tithes in kind at the *maqom* hinges on the correctness of the estimate, the *maqom* economy is an incentive for every farmer to use his best knowledge of geography and of the current levels of surplus in the land.

3.2.6 The *maqom* as a distribution centre?

According to Bennett, the centralization of the cult "worked to the disadvantage of the poor by forcing them to travel the great distance to the distribution centre, returning from this site with grain, wine, and meat", which put these persons at the mercy of murderers, rapists, robbers, kidnappers, and other nefarious individuals.[50] As is often the case in Deuteronomic studies, Bennett's reading relies on a vague definition of poverty. The storage of foodstuffs set aside for the Levites, *gerim*, orphans, and widows within your gates rather than at the *maqom* saves them the dangers Bennett imagines as they return from the distant distribution center. The widow dodging wayfarers with a sack of grain on her back and an orphan hanging at her skirts makes a great story, but Deut 14:28–29 makes sure that all women granted the status of widow need not return from a distant distribution center with "grain and wine". Moreover, there would be nothing to distribute and take back home if the annual tithes are entirely consumed at the *maqom* during festivals of unspecified duration. In good years, households extend their stay until only the provisions for the return journey are left. During bad years, they return home earlier.

Indeed, the rations received within your gates do not specify meat, which is hardly surprising as meat consumption occurred mostly in festive occasions. Yet, even if the triennial tithes do not mention meat, their beneficiaries need not be vegetarians. The list of revelers in front of YHWH ignores the Levite, *ger*, orphan, and widow (Deut 14:26), but it does not forbid inviting them as special guests to the feast. Inviting those who are not required to be present are public displays of generosity. Compared to alms (Deut 15:11) and loans granted against insignificant pledges (Deut 22:10–13.17), the *maqom* festivities are unique occasions for wealthy brothers to broadcast their generosity Israel-wide and thus convert tithed products into social capital.

---

50   Bennett, "Tithes," 14–15.

3.2.7 Arbitration of difficult cases

A judge is mentioned at the *maqom* to decide cases that could not be arbitrated at the local level (Deut 17:8). The transfer of the case to the *maqom* court is expressed with two verbs וקמת ועלית, which the NRSV renders as "then you shall immediately go up". There is, however, no evidence for a supreme court active throughout the year. In fact, the next verse mentions Levitical priests besides the judge in those days (יהיה בימים ההם Deut 17:9). What are those days if they are not those spent at the *maqom* to eat and drink yearly tithes in front of YHWH? "You shall rise and go up" does not specify that arbitrations occur *then*, but it does specify that they occur *there*. If the *maqom* is a place where farmers sacrifice their own firstlings and eat the tithe of their annual yield, a central court operating year round presupposes that the *maqom* is a temple with clergy and storage facilities.

"These days" during which a judge is present at the *maqom* can of course refer to an entire year. Yet, arbitrating difficult cases during the festival when every household that considers itself Israelite gathers at the *maqom* to prove its allegiance to YHWH allows all to witness the proceedings and hear the verdict. The verdicts pronounced in front of the entire people (כל העם Deut 17:13) are presented as parts of the substance of the learning (למד) taking place at the *maqom* (Deut 14:23). The disclosure of the decisions of the court to the entire people (כל העם Deut 17:13) thus presupposes that it occurs when every one gathers at the *maqom* for the pilgrimage. Without further ado, the practical aspects of customary law (משפט) are known to all concerned. Petty squabbles are dealt with at the local level, but the arbitration of new cases establishes precedents that update the customs while all Israelites are kept updated in real time. The NRSV's "you shall immediately go up" is coherent with the king copying "this Torah" under the supervision of Levitical priests (Deut 17:18) who store it in the ark and read it publicly only once every seven year (Deut 31:9–13; Neh 8). This elaborate scenario presupposes the notion of the *maqom* as a large temple institution and the rivalry that arises inevitably from the control of revenues generated by such an institution.[51] The question at this point is whether the public arbitration of cases at the *maqom* during the festivals was a reaction to other types of arbitration the writers deemed unfair for whatever reason—in this case the *maqom* court belongs to an utopian vision—or does it simply delineate a practical approach to the exercise of justice in a world where kings and priests exist but grant much leeway to autonomous bodies?

---

51   See Rossi, "Not by Bread Alone".

3.2.8 Production and maintenance of a common identity

The *maqom* gatherings would be an awesome experience and a powerful means of building a common identity.[52] Regular social interaction and festive meals are essential to develop a tight network of families.[53] To be successful, the production of Israel's corporate identity presupposes the presence of most if not all households at the *maqom*. For practical reasons, a few people would remain behind to care for the farm. Apart from that, the self-consumption of yearly tithes would be the most powerful incentive to secure the broadest attendance at the *maqom* banquets. Moreover, social pressure would effectively minimize reluctance: positive pressure in the form of additional prestige gained by the invitation of guests (Levites, *gerim*, widows and orphans), and negative pressure because anyone staying behind would automatically be suspect of anti-Israelite sentiments and irreverence towards YHWH. Private suggestions not to attend (Deut 13:7) would be liable to ostracism if not the listed penalties that chapter 13 delineates for idolaters. Attendance need not be mandatory for anyone in his right mind to make the trip to the *maqom* and join the fun.

In such circumstances, very few would even consider missing the festivities and the socializing that occurred alongside YHWH worship: exchange of news, match-making, marriages, labor contracts, and loans.

As groups from all corners of the Israelite territory arrived, the size and contents of the caravans of those bringing tithes in kind were commented upon. Each household paraded its best calf and lamb before the slaughter. The prestige of herders was at stake. A breeder's reputation was made there and then, and broadcast Israel-wide immediately, with consequences for the value of the surplus animals to be sold to colleagues who came with tied silver, as well as the animals left behind at the farm, which might interest other breeders for reproductive purposes. Men would roam around each others' stands, comparing animals and products while slaves prepared meals and women displayed children. The *maqom* gatherings functioned as any modern agricultural show. They were the highlight of the year, eagerly anticipated. They established a yearly ranking based on the actual amount of yearly tithes displayed and consumed, which provided a measure of the net value of one's asset. This rating had direct consequences on credit, trade, self-indenture, hire of labor, election for public offices such as judge and officer, admission in the *qehal-YHWH*.

---

52 Yu, "Tithes and Firstlings," 69; Altmann, *Festive Meals*, 227–40. Crouch, *Making*, 132–37.
53 Davies, "Authority," 35.

The economic activities generated by eating in front of YHWH at the *maqom* are no different from the market designated at Bronze Age Ebla by the term KI:LAM$_7$ that associates economic activities with a divine name and religious festivities.[54]

Yearly gatherings at the *maqom* are a realistic means of constructing the new Israel. Modern examples confirm the capacity of such gatherings to build identities around invented traditions. For instance, the Ottomans restored the *maqam* of the Nabi Musa shrine south-west of Jericho to promote a week-long pilgrimage to the site that coincides with the Orthodox Easter so that Muslims can celebrate at the same time as their Christian neighbors. The pilgrimage drew huge crowds in nineteenth and twentieth century CE Palestine.[55]

3.2.9 Recapitulation

Worship, according to Deuteronomy 14–15, involves the sacrifice of the year's firstborns by the breeders themselves, and their consumption with 10% of the yield of the fields and orchards by each family in front of YHWH, thus dispensing with the services of priests and other specialists associated with sanctuaries (Deut 23:17–18). Of course, it is difficult not to read these *maqom* banquets in light of the sacrificial economy attested to elsewhere in the Torah and in the Prophets. Yet, Deuteronomy itself is torn between two irreconcilable views regarding religious personnel. On the one hand, chapters 14–15 confine the Levite to your gates with the *ger*, widow, and orphan, who are not *personae miserae* any more than the Levite (Deut 14:22–29). On the other hand, chapter-long passages within the core prescribe priestly dues for the Levites (Deut 18:1–5; 26) and insist on their presence at the *maqom* where sacrifices are to take place (Deut 12:6.11–15; 16:11.14; 18:6–8). Chapter 16 aligns the core's gatherings of entire families to the *maqom* into three-yearly gatherings of males according to the calendar of Leviticus 23, a far cry from what is prescribed in Deuteronomy 14:22–29.

At this point, the reader reaches a crossroads at which a decision on Deuteronomy's origins has to be made between two irreconcilable views. Either Deuteronomy was imagined from the start with the *maqom* as a temple, or the *maqom* was first conceived to render a temple as dispensable as the king is in Deuteronomy 17. In both cases, the *maqom* is the

---

54 Biga "Feste e fiere a Ebla", 55–68.
55 Halabi, "Nabi Musa Festival"; Friedland and Hecht, "Nebi Musa Pilgrimage," 89–118.

main (but not the sole) hub of exchange,[56] but the similarity between the two approaches stops there.

The first approach—essentially a single-phase model—views the *maqom* in light of Leviticus and Numbers where the Aaronites functioned as priestly families did in Mesopotamian temples, except that their involvement in the redistributive mode of exchange of Mesopotamian temples is far from obvious.[57] The distinction between ordinary brothers and the Levitical brotherhood must be ignored to view Israel as a *Volk von Brüdern*. A major weakness of this approach is that it downplays one economic actor attested to in first millennium BCE Mesopotamia besides priestly families, i.e., private entrepreneurs.[58] This second group is present in Deuteronomy as much as in first millennium BCE Mesopotamia, but Leviticus and Numbers ignore it. Hence the question: should Deuteronomy be read in light of the preceding Torah scrolls, or should it first be read on its own? Reading Deuteronomy on its own would lead to recognizing the internal tension between the frames that do consider Israel as a *Volk von Brüdern*, and the bulk of the legal core that focuses on a brotherhood that meets with the entire Israel at the *maqom* to display its wealth, albeit wealth that stems from commercial activities besides the production of agricultural surplus. Deuteronomy sets the seat of this second element of the urban economy at the *qehal-YHWH*.

3.3 The *qehal-YHWH:* where brothers make deals

3.3.1 The *qehal-YHWH* outside Deuteronomy

Among the various assemblies mentioned in the Hebrew Bible, the assembly of the Lord (קהל יהוה *qehal-YHWH*) is rare. It is mentioned in passing in Numbers 16:3; 20:4; Micah 2:5; and 1 Chronicles 28:9, which does not necessarily imply that such mentions refer to the same kind of assembly as that at the Deuteronomic *qehal-YHWH*. If so, reading the Deuteronomic *qehal-YHWH* in light of the references to a *qehal-YHWH* outside Deuteronomy is suspect, though it is a temptation hard to resist considering the minimal information regarding this assembly.

The eight verses dealing with the *qehal-YHWH* (Deut 23:2–9[1–8]) are devoted entirely to who can and cannot enter it. Four categories are barred entry: the emasculated man, the one born of illicit unions, the

---

56   See Jursa, *Aspects*, 32.
57   Jursa, 54–55. In favor of a single phase Deuteronomy, see Edelman, "Deuteronomy as Instructions."
58   Jursa, 29–31.

Ammonite, and the Moabite. No reason is stated why the first two are barred, while three verses justify the exclusion of the Ammonite and the Moabite with references to the Exodus. Nehemiah 13:1–2 quotes these verses to justify the expulsion of the Tobiads from the *qehal-haElohim*. Given the stress on ethnic purity in this chapter, Nehemiah 13 omits the next two verses (Deut 23:8–9[7–8]) that urge not to abhor an Edomite or an Egyptian. The omission of these verses in Nehemiah 13 and the change from YHWH to Elohim in the designation of this assembly reveals in the clearest possible way the *scandalon* of the presence of the Edomite in the Deuteronomic *qehal-YHWH* because he is your brother and of the sons of an Egyptian because you were a *ger* in his land (Deut 23:9[8]).

There is no clue in Numbers that its *qehal-YHWH* includes Edomites. This is even less likely for 1 Chron 28:4 where the mention of the *qehal-YHWH* is preceded by the words all Israel (כל ישׂראל), as though the writer was aware of the Deuteronomic *qehal-YHWH* and insisted that the assembly in front of which Solomon stood was strictly Israelite. The assembly involved in the distribution of land lots in Micah 2:5 would be the sole reference to the *qehal-YHWH* outside Deuteronomy that could possibly include non Israelites, though no Edomite ever appears in Micah. Therefore, the analysis of the Deuteronomic *qehal-YHWH* has to be based on Deuteronomy itself.

3.3.2 *qehal-YHWH* and other *qehals* in Deuteronomy

Deuteronomy refers to Israel in the wilderness as an assembly *tout court* (Deut 5:22; 9:10; 10:4; 18:16; 31:30). The difference between the wilderness *qehal* and the *qehal-YHWH* is usually ignored and the rules regarding the camp in Deuteronomy 23:9–14 are used to describe the *qehal-YHWH* as a military and cultic institution.[59] The presence of sons of Edomites and Egyptians in an assembly that bears the name of Israel's god is admitted as a crux.[60] Or it is downplayed as a mere expression of a friendly attitude towards the Edomites that reflects the coexistence of Jewish and Edomite villages in southern *Yehud*.[61] Why Egyptians are included besides Edomites remains unexplained. Do they reflect the existence of a Jewish Diaspora in Egypt or the presence of Egyptians in southern Yehud? In this case, the integration of third generation Edomites and Egyptians would cohere with the expected expansion of Israel that would

---

59   See Otto, *Deuteronomium 12,1–23,15*, 1736–48. Or the *qehal-YHWH* is confused with Israel itself: see Hensel, *Juda*, 395.
60   Otto, 1738–48.
61   Römer, *So-Called Deuteronomistic History*, 171.

eventually require an additional three cities of refuge (Deut 19:8–9). Yet, why exclude Ammonites and Moabites who are at least as close neighbors as Edomites and who are just as likely to mingle with Israelites?

If no Ammonite and Moabite is ever to enter the *qehal-YHWH* because they did not meet Israel with food and water (Deut 23:4–6), one would expect an even deeper abhorrence towards Egyptians.[62] The decisive criterion for admittance in the *qehal-YHWH* cannot be the attitude towards Israel during the Exodus, nor should the fact that Israel was a *ger* in Egypt (Deut 23:7) justify a more friendly attitude towards the Egyptian than towards the Ammonite and the Moabite whose welfare or prosperity must never be promoted (Deut 23:7[6]). Once again, the reason for the acceptance of Edomites as members of a guild-like *qehal-YHWH* is economic.

3.3.3 The Deuteronomic you as a Pan-Israelite brotherhood?

Ever since Perlitt portrayed the original Deuteronomic audience as a people of brothers, the Deuteronomic Israel has been understood as just that.[63] Politically correct as it is, this consensual view is misleading. It reflects the burden of the producers of the framing chapters, but the brothers in the core of Deuteronomy—the singular "you" of the addressee—is *not* commensurate to Israel as a whole.

Frank Crüsemann listed eight socio-economic categories that did not belong to the Deuteronomic you: slaves, day laborers, foreigners, levites, widows, orphans, king, and *personae miserae*.[64] Yet, Crüsemann included the women among the brothers, while considering that the Mosaic law implies some sort of democracy, despite the absence of any indication of how the various officials mentioned in Deuteronomy were nominated.[65] As Greek democrats excluded women as much as slaves and metics (equivalent to the biblical *gerim*?) from their democratic constitutions,

---

62 Anderson, *Brotherhood and Inheritance*, 173. These references to the Exodus support the suggestion in the BHS to delete the words גם דור עשירי לא יבוא להם בקהל יהוה from verse 4 on the basis of their absence in verse 3.
63 Perlitt, "Volk von Brüdern".
64 Crüsemann, "Theokratie als Demokratie," 204.
65 Crüsemann, 214: "Dagegen kann ich nicht sehen, dass wegen einer dem Volk selbst entzogenen Grundlage im Form eines mosaischen Gesetzes grundsätzlich nicht von einer Art „Demokratie" gesprochen werden könnte. Es gibt in der Gegenwart des Israel, für das das deuteronomische Gesetz entworfen wurde, keine institutionalisierte Macht, die über dem hier angeredeten „Du" steht. Prophetie wie Zentralgericht sind zwar dem Volk nicht unterworfen, sie haben aber auch nur sehr begrenzte Möglichkeiten der Wirkung und gar keine Macht. Das Deuteronomische Gesetz ist ja nicht nur dem Volk, es ist zunächst und vor allem dem König selbst und der assyrischen Besatzungsmacht entzo-

broad definitions of the Deuteronomic you as equivalent to the entire Israel are suspect.

3.3.4 The Deuteronomic *qehal*-YHWH as *ekklesia kyriou*?

Some of the confusion regarding the social composition of the Deuteronomic you goes back at least to the Alexandrian translators who rendered the Deuteronomic *qehal*-YHWH as ἐκκλησία κυρίου.[66] As the *ekklēsia* in Classical Greece was the assembly of the *demos*, it was logical to conceive Deuteronomy as a democratic constitution. This view, however, entailed equating the Deuteronomic *qehal*-YHWH (ἐκκλησία κυρίου) with the *maqom* gatherings including slaves and Levites (Deut 12:12), plus the *gerim* according to Deut 12:18.

Were Greek parallels at all legitimate, the Israelite *demos* would assemble at the *maqom* and the Deuteronomic *maqom* would correspond to the Athenian *ekklēsia*, the popular assembly of the entire citizenry (*polis, dēmos, eliaia*), in which was vested the fundamental authority of the *polis*.[67] In this sense, the Deuteronomic constitution would appear far more democratic than any Greek constitution because it includes women, slaves, levites and *gerim* in the *ekklēsia*. The differences between chapters 12 and 14 reveal the presence of a debate over the composition of the revelers who were to congregate at the Deuteronomic *maqom*.

Deuteronomy keeps the *qehal*-YHWH apart from the *maqom*. The *qehal*-YHWH is only mentioned in Deuteronomy 23:1–8. Instead of listing the activities of this *qehal*, these verses are entirely dedicated to a restrictive definition of its membership with no clue whatsoever about slaves, *gerim*, Levites or women. Were the Greek analogy carried a little further, the *qehal*-YHWH would be a better fit for the *boulē*, the council attested to in both democratic and oligarchic constitutions, for instance the Athenian Council of the Four Hundred (later Five Hundred) that set the agenda of the assembly.[68] The Edomite brother as a member of the *qehal*-YHWH besides Israelite brothers who belong to a financial elite points, however, towards a narrower kind of assembly.

gen (was später die Grundlage der Autonomie im Rahmen der Möglichkeiten des Perserreiches bilden wird)."

66 Rütersworden, *Politischen Gemeinschaft*, 105.
67 See Blok, "Citizenship," 161–75.
68 See Wallace, "Councils," 191–204.

3.3.5 Deuteronomy's *qehal-YHWH* and oligarchic assemblies

In Classical Greece and elsewhere, oligarchy is the rule of the more affluent few. The parallel with the Deuteronomic brotherhood is fairly obvious. Brothers have financial means to borrow within the brotherhood and to lend to foreigners (Deut 15:6).

A major weakness of oligarchies is the temptation of one oligarch to side with groups outside the circle of oligarchs in the hope of greater gains that are not foreseen by remaining loyal to fellow oligarchs. Breaches of honor and shaming by rival oligarchs were likely to push the offended oligarch in the arms of the *demos* to set up a democratic regime, perceived by the offended oligarch as a way to obtain revenge from his peers.[69]

Contrary to democratic regimes that admit adult male citizens without discrimination, oligarchic regimes shut out most adult males and reduce the number of deciders. In other words, democracy is an arithmetical form of equality, oligarchy a geometrical one.[70] Democratic regimes dilute political power among a large segment of the adult male population. Oligarchic regimes concentrate political power in the hands of a small group, "with the result that each oligarch possessed comparatively greater influence."[71]

To counterbalance its restricted membership, the assembly practices strict *isonomia* between its members because strife between oligarchs represents a far greater danger to the oligarchy than is the case in democratic regimes where the power of each member is diluted in the mass of the overall membership. As oligarchies concentrated power in the hands of those who had the greatest capacity for aggression, equal power had to be matched with equal honor. Designating one another as brothers underlines the honor shared among equals. The question at this point is whether or not the call not to abhor (תעב) the Edomite and the third generation Egyptian because they belong to the *qehal-YHWH* (Deut 23:8) is a clue in favor of viewing the *qehal-YHWH* as an oligarchy practicing *isonomia* within its ranks.

The presence of Edomites and third generation Egyptians in the *qehal-YHWH* is problematic if it functions as a political body in addition to its commercial and financial activities. Were third generation Egyptians designated as *gerim*, the *qehal-YHWH* may be imagined as a sovereign assembly with powers similar to those of Greek oligarchies. While *gerim* are indeed present at the *maqom*, Deuteronomy 23 mentions no *gerim* in the

---

69   Simonton, *Oligarchy*, 268–69.
70   Simonton, 76.
71   Simonton, 77.

qehal-YHWH. It would be unwise to equate the *maqom* assemblies with the *qehal-YHWH*. Therefore, the Deuteronomic Israel is no oligarchic regime. Nevertheless, Greek oligarchies are not entirely irrelevant.

Secrecy was a crucial component of the domination of the oligarchic minority, and secrecy accounts for the limited space devoted to the *qehal-YHWH* in Deuteronomy. The need for secrecy explains why none of the eight verses Deuteronomy devotes to the *qehal-YHWH* lift the veil over the activities of this assembly.

Instead of explaining the function of this assembly, the text underlies the need of sexual and genealogical integrity (*mamzer*) to justify the exclusion of rival elites. Crushed testicles and severed penis (Deut 23:2) may refer to eunuchs as high ranking officials belonging to an imperial elite. The *mamzer* is someone of dubious ancestry. Like the eunuchs, they are rivals and should not be treated as brothers with all the privileges and duties pertaining to members of the *qehal-YHWH*.

The presence of non-Israelites brothers within an assembly designated in reference to the god of Israel places the activities of the *qehal-YHWH* under the auspices of the Israelite god to enforce high levels of accountability required of its members.

3.3.6 The *qehal-YHWH* guild

A Deuteronomic *qehal-YHWH* as a group of commercial partners fits the rise of Arabian centers such as Teima and Hindanu to cater for the specific needs of large camel caravans traveling between Yemen, Egypt and Mesopotamia from the ninth century BCE onwards.[72] The Edomite and Egyptian members of the *qehal-YHWH* could reflect trade between Arabia and Egypt. Sustained Assyrian efforts to foster this commercial network underline its importance. Tiglath-pilezer opened a *kāru* at Gaza in the wake of his 734 BCE campaign.[73] The same *kāru* was reopened by Sargon after an interruption caused by local entities, among them Jerusalem. In 701 BCE, it is the turn of Sennacherib to intervene to protect Assyrian trade with Egypt.[74] The presence of Edomite and third generation Egyp-

---

72 Caravan trade between Yemen and Babylonia is already attested in 890 BCE: Liverani, "Early Caravan Trade," 110–15; Lawson Younger, Jr., "Ninurta-Kudurrī-uṣur," 281–82.
73 See Elat, "Economic Relations," 34. Elat, "*Tamkāru*," 254 on the mina of the merchants.
74 Van der Brugge, "Production, Profit and Destruction," 292–335 notes that 2 Kgs 18:8 presents Hezekiah's intervention in Gaza as rebellion against Assyria.

tian brothers in the the *qehal-YHWH* is thus coherent with its understanding as a guild-like association dedicated to long distance trade.[75]

The challenges caused by distance had to be compensated by high levels of trust between traders whose opportunities to meet face to face were limited. A much later report from Theophrastus explains the organization of the frankincense and myrrh trade:

> ... the myrrh and frankincense from everywhere were deposited in the Temple of the Sun. This temple was by far the most sacred possession of the Sabaioi of the region, and was guarded by certain armed Arabs. When they bring it in, each man piles up his own produce of frankincense and myrrh, and leaves it with those on guard. On the pile he puts a tablet with a statement of the number of measures and of the price at which each measure should be sold, and when the merchants come, they look at the tablets, measure out the price of whichever pile pleases them, and leave the payment at the place whence they have taken the goods. Then the priest comes, takes one third of the price for the god, and leaves the rest safe for the proprietors when they come to collect it. (Theophrastus, *History of Plants* 9.4.6)

The Temple of the Sun mentioned here served as a safe place of deposit and transactions between producers and merchants. Storing precious staples under divine auspices offered some warrant trust between the different parties without which no trade can be conducted.[76] The House of YHWH in Deuteronomy 23:19 may be a lone echo of an actual building, as long as this House of YHWH is not confused with the *maqom*, but related to the activities of the the *qehal-YHWH*.

Deuteronomy's notion of brotherhood includes the particular duties and privileges entailed by fictive kinship to express special ties of solidarity.[77]

Fictive brotherly ties between Israelite and Edomite traders would aptly underline the kind of trust expected between associates in joint ventures.

However disturbing the Edomite brother is for today's scholarship, his presence was accepted by the producers of the frames who underlined it with a double mention of the sons of Esau designated as "your brothers" and "our brothers" (Deut 2:4.8). If Edom is your brother, the term brother is broader than Israeliteness. As there are Edomites among brothers, it

---

75 On brothers as a commercial elite in Late Bronze Syria, see Démare-Lafont, "Frères," 129–41.
76 Late Bronze Age Mycenean commercial transactions were also carried out with little use of written contracts: Liverani, "La ceramic e I testi," 105–412.
77 Waerzeggers, *Ezida Temple*, 85–87.

was necessary to stipulate that the potential king is to be chosen among brothers and that he must also not be a foreigner (Deut 17:15). Otherwise, an Edomite brother would be qualified as Israelite king. Hence, the Deuteronomic brother is not necessarily an Israelite, and when he is, he is not any Israelite.

The presence of Edomite brothers is the key to designations of the Deuteronomic brother that are otherwise awkward or outright tautological if the brotherhood includes all Israelites or Judahites and only them. The tribes to be supported by their Transjordan brothers are "sons of Israel" (Deut 3:18) because the mention of sons of Esau (Deut 2:4.8 אחי־כם בני עשו) renders the meaning of the word brother ambiguous.

The status of brother granted to the Edomite is likely to have exacerbated the debate over the beneficiaries of the šemiṭṭah revealed by the complicated textual history of Deuteronomy 15:2. Shifting the focus from brothers to neighbors turned the šemiṭṭah into an internal Israelite affair, to express "the special relationship obtaining among members of God's people".[78]

The presence of Edomites within the brotherhood explains the two conditions for the choice of a king: he must be both a brother and not a foreigner (Deut 17:15), otherwise an Edomite brother would qualify as king of Israel. The expression "his brother from the sons of Israel" to designate the victim of kidnapping in Deuteronomy 24:7 equally presupposes the existence of non-Israelite brothers.

In his oft quoted study of the biblical concept of brotherhood, Perlitt attributes most of the plural forms of אח to the *brüderliche Organisation der Israelitischen* (Deut 1:28; 10:9; 13:18.20; 33:9.16.24), except those referring to Edom (Deut 2:4.8), which he considered as echoes of the pre-state nomadic tribal organization based on blood relationships when Edomites were some kind of related tribe. Therefore, the Edomite brothers are not *Dtn-spezifisch* and can thus be safely ignored, though they are a unique feature in Deuteronomy.

Yet, there are ten plural forms and nineteen singular ones in the Deuteronomic core (12–26), a ratio that prevents a simple attribution of all plural forms to pre-Deuteronomic traditions and leaves singular ones as typical Deuteronomic traits. Moreover, "your brother" (אחיך) in Deuteronomy 23:8 is a singular form found within what Perlitt considers the historical core of Deuteronomy. The Edomite brother has thus every qualification to become a hallmark of Deuteronomy, except of course that he does not fit the portrayal of Israel as a *Volk von einzelnen Brüdern*. Therefore, a footnote erases "your brother the Edomite" with the argument

---

78 Levin, "Rereading," 67.

that "Your brother" in Deuteronomy 23:8 is a *gentilicium*, a singular form standing pars pro toto for a plural form. As such, "Your brother the Edomite" means "your brothers the Edomites", the single form אָחִיךָ belongs with the plural forms to the non-Deuteronomic material, though it is a singular form within the legal core.[79]

Instead of dispatching the Edomite brother into a pre-monarchic limbo, recent exegetes attribute the Edomite brother to a post-exilic elaboration to the same aim. Pre-Deuteronomic or post-Deuteronomic, the Edomite brother has no more place in true Deuteronomic thinking than the Ammonites and Moabites.[80] The admission of Edomites in the *qehal-YHWH* supposedly reflects a time when Edomite and Jewish villages may have coexisted in the Negev around Hebron in the first part of the Persian period.[81] If so, the brotherhood of the sons of Esau in chapter 2 and of the Edomite in chapter 23 is highly relevant to the understanding of Deuteronomy, except of course that Perlitt wrote that they are not. As for the third generation Egyptian, whom Deuteronomy 23:8 places on an equal footing with the Edomite brother, he must reflect an undefined time when Egypt was no threat any more.[82]

For argument's sake, let us accept as factual that, in the Persian or early Hellenistic period, that is before the Torah became an authoritative document, the Edomite brother was the result of the historical circumstance that part of the territory of monarchic Judah became Edom/Idumea. In this case, the writers wanted to emphasize that YHWH worshippers in that territory could be part of the pilgrimage celebrations and be eligible for business and marriage arrangements.

The problem is that no Edomites are ever mentioned in relation to pilgrimage celebrations at the *maqom*, the prime venue for business and marriage arrangements and for the assimilation of Israelite norms (see §3.2.8). Deuteronomy only mentions Edomite brothers and Egyptians in relation to the mysterious *qehal-YHWH*. Therefore, the introduction of Idumeans in the purported historical circumstance requires equating the *qehal-YHWH* with Israel gathered at the *maqom* as well as ignoring the third generation Egyptian.

Another problem is that the relevance of the Idumean factor loses much of its value if the bulk of the Deuteronomic core was produced in Israel rather than in Jerusalem. The Idumean factor presupposes de Wette's notion of a *Urdeuteronomium* crafted in Jerusalem, even though it dates the insertion of the Edomite brother much later than Josiah's reign.

79   Perlitt, "Volk von Brüdern" 36 n. 28.
80   Otto, *Deuteronomium 12,1–23,15*, 1752–61.
81   Römer, *So-Called Deuteronomistic History*, 171.
82   Otto, *Deuteronomium 12,1–23,15*, 1743.

The exclusion of Ammonites and Moabites in Deuteronomy 23:2–7 could be explained as intra-biblical exegesis in light of the story of Lot's daughter in Genesis 19:30–38, and historically as reflections of Tobiah and Sanballat's opposition to Nehemiah's activities. The echoes of Deuteronomy 23:2–7 in Nehemiah 13:1–2 recall the exclusion of Ammon and Moab and avoid any mention of the favorable attitude to Edom and Egypt. In the biblical meta-narrative, Edomites and Egyptians who had wanted to join Israel have done so long ago. Jeremiah 49, however, adopts a different strategy against the Deuteronomic Edomite brother. A series of judgments on Edom follows those on Egypt, Ammon, and Moab. Instead of ignoring the Edomite brother, Jeremiah 49:7–13 equates Edom with Arabia thanks to references to Teman, Dedan, and Bosrah.

If the presence of Idumeans in southern Jewish villages was the cause of the admission of Edomites in the *qehal-YHWH*, why insert Edomite brothers in Deuteronomy rather than in Nehemiah, a work more likely produced when the presence of Edomites in Southern Judah was significant?

Indeed, Deuteronomy 23:8–9 is one among other passages in which the "brother language appeals to the idea of Israel as a large extended family and draws on the affective power of such language in efforts to motivate certain kinds of behavior within the community".[83] Edomites and Egyptians could be part of the Israelite extended family, except of course that the expected brotherly behavior would apply well beyond what is usually defined as the Israelite community.

Therefore, Deuteronomic scholarship tends to be more Deuteronomistic than Deuteronomy. As the plural "sons born to them" (Deut 23:9a) is followed by a singular "he will enter" (Deut 23:9b), the Egyptian is considered secondary and only the Edomite is to be treated (תעב) as an Israelite.[84] After all, "if the Egyptian can enter the assembly of YHWH, then the whole process of Israel's separation from Egypt is brought full circle back to its beginnings."[85] Exit the Egyptian, can the Edomite remain in the Israelite extended family?

In fact, he can but only in the third generation, which once the Egyptian is deemed secondary, applies to the Edomite whose admission into the *qehal-YHWH* implies that he has been resident long enough to assimilate Israelite norms.[86] The Edomite brotherhood can now belong to the Israelite family because he has in fact become an Israelite. The "use of familial language in Deuteronomy 23:8 to articulate the Edomite's unusual

---

83 Crouch, *Israel*, 117.
84 Crouch, *Making*, 197.
85 Greifenhagen, *Egypt*, 195.
86 Crouch, *Making*, 198 n. 240.

potential as a future Israelite makes sense in an identity framework in which significant weight can be given to traditions of common descent, provoked by notions of just such a familial relationship with Edom".[87] In other words, after living among Israelites for three generations these Edomites have become quasi-Israelites, or at least "semi-foreigners or half brothers".[88] In fact, there are no half brothers or semi-foreigners in Deuteronomy.

Were admission into the *qehal-YHWH* conditioned by the assimilation of Israelite norms, this principle would apply to Egyptians as much as to Edomites and even more to the *ger* who resides within your gates. This is not the case. The principle of assimilation is not explicit in the text. What is explicit is that Deuteronomy 23 grants a special status to some Edomites and Egyptians—while Moabites and Ammonites are, like the eunuchs and the *mamzer*, forever barred from the *qahal-YHWH*.

The rejection of the Ammonite and Moabite may echo the story of Lot's daughters in Genesis 19:30–38. This genealogical argument would neatly explain the exclusion of Ammonite and Moabite and the admission of Edomites, but it fails to account for the very positive attitude towards the Edomite and the Egyptian. Were genealogical factors the guiding principle for the selection of brothers, Arameans would have an even stronger claim to admission in the *qahal-YHWH* than Edomites, but Deuteronomy ignores the Arameans. Moreover, this kind of reasoning attributes much weight to genealogical stories and ethnicity, which usually result from political and economic circumstances, which they justify. Arguing that actual genealogical ties are the cause of the admission of the Edomite and third generation Egyptian is counter-intuitive.

It is hard to avoid the conclusion that the various strategies deployed to ignore the Edomite brother are cases of special pleading. The Edomite brother is a crux, complicated by the absence of indications relative to the nature and activities of the mysterious *qahal-YHWH* into which they are admitted.

The inclusion of Edomites and Egyptians in the *qahal-YHWH* remains a crux, until Edomite brotherhood is considered outside the confines of familial, genealogical and ethnic ties. To be sure, the redefinition of the Edomite brother of Deuteronomy 23:8 along ethnic lines is the burden of the references to your brother Esau in Deuteronomy 2:2.8. In the process, however, the Egyptian of Deuteronomy 23:8 is ignored because he does not fit the context of the Exodus, the baseline of which is the escape from the Egyptian house of slavery.

---

87   Crouch, 199.
88   Stulman, "Encroachment," 615 n. 8.

The easy way out is to argue that these references to Esau/Edom as brother are later redactional additions aimed at harmonizing the Pentateuch, the Hexateuch, or the Enneateuch into a single meta-narrative through the addition of internal cross-referencing among the individual books. This may well be the case for brother Esau in Deuteronomy 2:2.8, but it is less likely that later redactors insisted that at least some Edomites and even some Egyptians could enter the *qehal-YHWH*. It is even less likely when the *qehal-YHWH* is assumed to be equivalent to Israel. Given the definition of this assembly outside Deuteronomy, Deuteronomy 23:8–9 is a crux that harmonizes nothing. A late redactor who produced a crux that has to be explained away would be a poor harmonizer. The Edomite and Egyptian members of the *qahal-YHWH* are the cause rather than the result of the harmonizing redaction of Deuteronomy 2:2–8. They represent the kind of *lectio difficilior* that must be faced squarely.

Theological readings reduce the significance of the Edomite brother and insist instead on integrating the socially and economically marginals within Israel.[89] An economic reading takes the opposite stance and views the *qehal-YHWH* brotherhood with its Edomites and Egyptian partners as the backbone upon which a new Israel is built. Thanks to its close connections with traders from neighboring countries, the *qehal-YHWH* is expected to generate enough wealth to eradicate poverty among its ranks (Deut 15:4).

A focus on economics recovers the significance of the *qehal-YHWH* that otherwise remains a vague gathering for cultic and military activities.[90] Brotherhood with Edom takes on concrete meaning when read in light of the interest-free loans granted between brothers (Deut 23:20[19]). Interest-free loans are the hallmark of dealings between brothers and interest-bearing loans are the hallmark of dealings with foreigners. Admission into the *qehal-YHWH* has significant financial implications.

The economic implications associated with the status of brother designate the *qehal-YHWH* as some kind of guild, though this term is used *faute de mieux*. It would correspond to the Late Achaemenid *kiništu*, professional assemblies representing the interest of particular professional groups, each having its own "guild house".[91] The Deuteronomic *qehal-YHWH* is a circle restricted to influential Israelites, Edomites and Egyptians. As such, the *qehal-YHWH* represents the economic elite, a kind of biblical Rotary club.[92] The raison-d'être of any guild is the control over entry and over

---

89   Crouch, *Making*, 218.
90   Anderson, *Brotherhood*, 169.
91   See Hackl, "Esangila," 175–177.
92   Bultmann, *Fremde*, 118.

the supply of services.⁹³ The first six verses of Deuteronomy 23 do just that. Eunuchs, *mamzers*, Ammonites, and Moabites are barred entry outright. The justification for the exclusion of the Ammonites and Moabites could be secondary as it recalls an episode of the Exodus (Deut 23:4). The cultic concerns for the exclusion of the eunuch and of the *mamzer* is coherent with the commercial activities of the *qehal-YHWH*, because, as argued above on the basis of the incense trade reported by Theophrastus, commercial activities are conducted under divine auspices. Israelite, Edomite and Egyptian partners may address their god under different names, but what matters most is the fear the god inspires in the devotees, and the implausibility of perjury on their part. Honesty is sacred and is a crucial component of each partner's social capital.⁹⁴

Though they would not address their god as YHWH in their dealings with Israelite brothers, Edomite and Egyptian partners are not abhorrent, contrary to the eunuch and the *mamzer*. Hence, cultic requirements are relevant when partners of different origins meet for business and for bonding at a *marzeaḥ* or a symposium.⁹⁵ The economic sustainability of the *qehal-YHWH* rests on restricted entrance, confidence in one another's honesty sustained by divine auspices, and a knowledge of one another's financial standing that reduces transaction costs.

The *qehal-YHWH* brotherhood implies a brotherhood that differs significantly from the fictional wilderness *qehal*. Were the *qehal-YHWH* merely a cultic assembly, the Edomites admitted into the *qehal-YHWH* would be YHWH worshippers. Nothing of the like is suggested in the text, though 1 Chronicles 15:17 mentions Kushaiah (קושיהו), a man with a name compounding the main Edomite (*qws*) and Israelite deities reflects close Israelite-Edomite connections. In this context, the presence of Edomites in the *qehal-YHWH* is hardly surprising, nor is the use of the term *qehal* for such a guild.⁹⁶

---

93 Jones, *Economic Theory*, 356–57 takes as examples labor unions and the American Medical Association, "which has substantial influence over licensing of doctors and medical facilities. Such organizations invariably refer to their activities benignly as providing quality control and hence improving the wellbeing of customers, but their control over the supply of services is inescapable. Not to act in their self-interest, taking advantage of their control over entry to raise their own incomes – would be unexpected."

94 Liverani, "Influence," 126–27. On Ptolemaic and Roman guilds, see Kloppenborg, "New Institutional Economics," 117–29.

95 Lynch, "Hellenistic Symposium," 233–56; Miralles Maciá, *Marzeaḥ y thíassos*; Na'aman, "Four Notes," 215–22.

96 Gottheil, "קושיהו and קישי."

3.3.7 Regulation of commercial credit through the *qehal-YHWH* network

The designation of Edomites and third generation Egyptians as brothers throws light on the matter of the *šemiṭṭah* in Deuteronomy 15 where the practical implications of membership in the *qehal-YHWH* are exposed. The divine economy in which some Edomites and Egyptians are included can be taken in a far more literal sense than is usually the case.[97] Despite the prevalence of the term brother and its range of meanings, the terms of the loans granted between brothers, the absence of interest and of security indicate that the *qehal-YHWH* is involved in commercial activities that exceed the scope of ordinary agricultural finance. This means that the debt release benefits every brother, even those who are not Israelite, while not every Israelite benefits from it, only those who are brothers.

This view of the Deuteronomic brotherhood has been resisted as early as the turn of the era, as the differences between the Masoretic text and the Septuagint in the first part of Deuteronomy 15 show. Modern translations further muddle the issue with inconsistent renderings of the Hebrew terms for brother and neighbor. Though the issue has already been discussed above (§2.4.3), the translation of Deuteronomy 15:2–11 in the New Revised Standard Version is given below with the corresponding Hebrew term in parenthesis:

> ²And this is the manner of the remission: every creditor shall remit the claim that is held against a neighbor (רעהו), not exacting it of a neighbor who is a member of the community (את רעהו ואת אחיו) because the LORD's remission has been proclaimed. ³Of a foreigner you may exact it, but you must remit your claim on whatever any member of your community (אחיך) owes you. ⁴There will, however, be no one in need (אביון) among you, because the LORD is sure to bless you in the land that the LORD your God is giving you.... ⁶When the LORD your God has blessed you, as he promised you, you will lend to many nations, but you will not borrow; you will rule over many nations, but they will not rule over you. ⁷If there is among you any one in need (אביון), a member of your community (מאחד אחיך) in any of your towns within the land that the LORD your God is giving you, do not be hard-hearted or tight-fisted toward your needy neighbor (מאחיך האביון)...
>
> ⁹Be careful that you do not entertain a mean thought, thinking, "The seventh year, the year of remission, is near," and therefore view your needy neighbor (אחיך) with hostility and give nothing; your neighbor (—) might cry to the LORD against you, and you would incur guilt...

---

97 The expression "divine economy" is borrowed from Anderson, *Brotherhood*, 176.

¹⁰Give liberally and be ungrudging when you do so, for on this account the LORD your God will bless you in all your work and in all that you undertake. ¹¹Since there will never cease to be some in need on the earth, I therefore command you, "Open your hand to the poor and needy neighbor (אחיך) in your land." ¹²If a member of your community (אחיך), whether a Hebrew man or a Hebrew woman, is sold to you and works for you six years, in the seventh year you shall set that person free.

The translators were uneasy with a narrow notion of brotherhood. Admittedly, rendering the brother as a "member of the community" is supported by the double mention of a neighbor besides the brother in verse 2. Apparently they both benefit from the remission of debt at the end of the seventh year. Does this justify turning the brother into a neighbor or a member of your community in the rest of the passage?

The problem has a long history as the critical apparatus of the BHS shows. One Hebrew manuscript and some Samaritan ones read את אחיך instead of ואת אחיך, ignoring the conjunction between neighbor and brother: "do not exact (payment) of your neighbor your brother". This *lectio difficilior* is to be preferred to the easier reading in the MT "your neighbor *and* your brother". The omission of the second neighbor by the Septuagint in verse 2b is also a *lectio facilior*.[98] Ignoring the MT and the LXX, the instructions concerning the *šemiṭṭah* begin with a mention of the debts of a neighbor in verse 2a followed by a neighbor/brother in verse 2b and six references to brothers (verses 3–12) with no further mention of any neighbor. Hence, this sequence shifts the focus away from the neighbor towards the brother.

One may ask why neighbors are mentioned at all in verse 2 if only brothers are meant to benefit from the *šemiṭṭah* release. Shemaryahu Talmon took Deuteronomy 15:2 MT as an example of a scribal technique modeled after the "syntactical co-ordination of two synonymous readings, achieved inadvertently when one of the components happened to be in the construct state".[99] Talmon explains that this model "apparently served the scribes as a model on which they patterned their attempts to combine synonymous readings by transforming them from the absolute to the construct state."[100] According to Talmon, the juxtaposition of brother and neighbor in Deuteronomy 15:2b is one such instance of a pair of synonymous expressions appearing side by side. The question is whether or not the two terms in question were considered synonymous.

---

98 Against Fabry, "Deuteronomium 15," 104 n. 35.
99 Talmon, "Double Readings," 167.
100 Talmon, 167.

Lundbom considers that they are synonymous though recognizing that the brother is mentioned five times in the following verses.[101]

The word brother occurs *seven* times in Deuteronomy 15, in relation to the remission of a brother's debt and the release of pledges (Deut 15:2, 3, 7, 7, 9, 11, 12). Rather than synonymity, the juxtaposition of the neighbor and the brother in verse 2b is a case of redefinition. The neighbor is redefined as brother and brothers only benefit from the release of their debts and of their pledges. Whether of not the neighbors in verse 2 belong to a pre-deuteronomistic version of the law,[102] there is no evidence to support their erasure from the core because the *lectio difficilior* neighbor/brother is attested to by the Samaritan Pentateuch and the Samaritan Targum without any connective *waw*. Translators and exegetes are only too happy to follow the improved reading of the MT because splitting Israelites between neighbors and brothers has undesired implications, especially when Edomite brothers lurk in the background. Yet, the term אח (brother) remains "one of the most distinctive features" of Deuteronomy.[103]

Adding neighbors to the beneficiaries of debt remissions otherwise reserved for brothers is the collateral damage caused by the moral appeal of the command to love one's neighbor as oneself (Lev 19:18).[104] In the NRSV, the needy brother who is to benefit from a loan during the seventh year becomes a neighbor (Deut 15:9) so that this verse echoes the neighbor in verse 1. The same needy brother becomes a neighbor when he turns out to be insolvent and in need of charity (Deut 15:11). Modern translators recoil from the idea that an Israelite may abstain from appropriating lost property only if it belongs to a brother (Deut 22:1–3), or that only a brother benefits from the limitation of corporal punishment to forty lashes (Deut 25:3).

Strictly speaking, Deuteronomy only requires the release of a brother's debt at the end of the seventh year. Nothing forbids the extension of the release to a neighbor who is not a brother but this would be a matter of personal appreciation, not a requirement stemming from the status of brother and the solidarity expected between members of the *qehal-YHWH* guild. In fact, the *šemiṭṭah* release is irrelevant to neighbors and ordinary Israelite farmers whose credit requirements involve smaller amounts over shorter terms than the seven-year cycle of the *šemiṭṭah*. Were they in need of a release of debts, waiting until the end of the seventh year

---

101 Lundbom, *Deuteronomy*, 488.
102 As claimed by Hamilton, *Social Justice*, 35–36.
103 Nicholson, *Judaean Diaspora*, 30.
104 See Akiyama, *Love of Neighbour*.

could be catastrophic. Within a few years the debt would spiral beyond all possible return to solvency.[105]

The brotherhood of the *qehal-YHWH* guild identifies an inner-circle of equal business partners endowed with privileges and responsibilities not shared by women, children, slaves, Levites, *gerim*, widows, orphans, neighbors, foreigners, ordinary Israelites and ordinary Edomites, but potentially shared with the sons of Edomites and Egyptians—or fellow YHWH worshippers identified as Edomites and Egyptians due to the geographical sphere of their activities. The release of all outstanding debts held within their circle at the end of every seventh year holds the promise of having the means to lend to many outsiders (גוים רבים) but to borrow from none (Deut 15:6 עבט). The rationale is that lending to many people will enable the brotherhood to rule over its debtors. It is a question of dominating in order not to be dominated, a situation bewailed by Nehemiah 9:36–37. It would, however, be mistaken to read this as implying a negative view of borrowing as is common in exegetical literature that considers every loan as the beginning of an irresistible spiral of destitution (see §2.4). The aim of the *qehal-YHWH* guild is that brothers borrow from brothers on preferential terms.

Loans between brothers are interest-free. Pledges are not mentioned, possibly because there is no point securing loans if outstanding sums have to be cancelled at the end of the seventh year. Loans granted to foreigners bear interest (Deut 23:20). They are to be recovered by any means (Deut 15:3), by confiscation of the pledge if any. This leaves open the matter of loans granted to neighbors. Such loans are mentioned in Deuteronomy 24:10, forbidding the lender to enter the borrower's house to seize the pledge that secures the loan. As the matter of interest is not considered, it is left to the discretion of the lender. As for the release of a neighbor's debt on the day of the *šemiṭṭah,* it can only be argued on the basis of Deuteronomy 15:2.

Therefore, despite the occurrence of a neighbor alongside a brother in Deuteronomy 15:2, Deuteronomy's core distinguishes loans between brothers (interest-free, unsecured and subject to debt release) and loans to neighbors that may or may not bear interest and that are not subject to release.

It is therefore doubtful that the Deuteronomic writers considered that poverty was not a condition that ought to be overcome on the grounds that it is supposedly "the mark of a religious group characterized by its special closeness to God."[106] As stated by Levin, such theological rationalizations are indeed found in Psalm 37:11 (and Matt 5.5), but to find them in

---

105   For a simulation of credit see Guillaume, *Land*, 130–34.
106   Against Levin, "Rereading," 59.

Deuteronomy springs from a misunderstanding of ancient credit transactions. Deuteronomy's concerns for the establishment of a healthy credit market reflect the interest of the lenders as much as that of borrowers. Contrary to the sacralization of poverty in the Psalms, the aim of Deuteronomy's core is the preservation of creditworthiness within the members of the *qehal-YHWH*. Such preservation has a price. To ensure that every need in terms of credit is taken care of among brothers (Deut 15:4), the defaulting brother must be identified and isolated. As credit rating agencies would do today, the brother who has benefited from the *šemiṭṭah* sees his rating degraded. He still has access to credit but on less advantageous terms because he represents a greater risk to the system.

Despite the many claims to the contrary, in real life a regular *šemiṭṭah* occurring at predictable intervals of seven years does not quench credit.[107] On the contrary, it sustains the credit market by eliminating defaulting debtors for the duration of the next cycle. The small print of the *šemiṭṭah* is that the size of any loan is proportional to the time left before the next release. Instead of drying up credit, the knowledge of the date of the next release enables the calibration of the loan according to the revenues the lender could expect to obtain from the work of the pledge or from the investment of the loan.[108] The minimal amounts lent in the seventh year are compensated for by larger amounts lent the day after the *šemiṭṭah*, the *šemiṭṭah* being the last day of the seventh year or a day during the festivities at the *maqom*. The extinction of all outstanding loans on that day would be followed by the granting of new loans the next day. The purpose of the release is to purge the market of all outstanding debts by setting a time when all loans are extinguished before the next round of lending and borrowing. Insolvent borrowers are identified and removed from the market of commercial credit before their debts snowball to the point where their bankruptcy threatens the entire system.

The release of a brother's debt represents an "extreme example of indebtedness",[109] because it represents a loss of reputation that is as devastating as the financial consequences of the loss of access on the preferential terms current within the *qehal-YHWH*. Once again, Becker's broadening of the notion of wealth beyond mere matters of financial standing to understand the economy as the maximization of welfare

---

107 See Guillaume, *Land*, 217–19; Villard, "(an)darāru," 121; against Soss, "Old Testament Law," 334; Otto, "Programme," 41.
108 See Lipínski, "Esclave hébreu," 120–24. Kessler, "Debt and the Decalogue," 1–9 argues that the prohibition to covet the neighbor's wife (Exod 20:17; Deut 5:21) relates to debt slavery rather than sexual relations. In the framework of antichretic loans, it is the wife's labor that the lender would covet.
109 Against Crouch, *Making*, 208.

(§1.4) provides an alternative to spiritualizing notions of poverty. The practical implications of such readings are calls to lend to the poor (an obvious aberration), lending indiscriminately after the *šemiṭṭah* on the same terms as before (which makes the entire procedure irrelevant) or pouring loans into a bottomless basket of poverty. Deuteronomy's careful distinction between loans within the *qehal-YHWH* brotherhood and loans to neighbors and foreigners deserves better than the kind of readings reflected in the rendering of these passages in the NRSV.

3.3.8 Recapitulation

To conclude this section on the *qehal-YHWH*, a rendering of Deuteronomy 15:2–12 based on the NRSV with corrections integrating the different points discussed above is provided:

> ²And this is the manner of the remission: every creditor shall remit the claim that is held against his neighbor (רעהו), not exacting it of his neighbor-brother (רעהו אחיו) because the LORD's remission has been proclaimed. ³Of a foreigner you may exact it, but you must remit your claim on whatever your brother (אחיך) owes you. ⁴There will, however, be no one in need (אביון) among you, because the LORD will bless you in the land that the LORD your God is giving you as holding, ⁵as long as you cling closely to the voice of the Lord your God, making sure you put fully into practice the counsel that I am giving you today. ⁶When the LORD your God has blessed you, as he promised you, you will lend to many nations, but you will not borrow; you will rule over many nations, but they will not rule over you. ⁷When there is among you anyone in need (אביון) from a single one of your brothers (מאחד אחיך) in any of your towns in the land that the LORD your God is giving you, do not be hard-hearted or tight-fisted with your needy brother (מאחיך האביון).

> ⁸Instead, open your hand for him and lend him enough to cover the shortfall he is deficient of. ⁹Be careful that you do not entertain a mean thought, thinking, "The seventh year, the year of remission, is near," and hence view your needy brother (באחיך האביון) with hostility and give him nothing; he might cry to the LORD against you, and you would incur guilt. ¹⁰Give liberally and be ungrudging when you do so, for on this account the LORD your God will bless you in all your activity and on everything you put your hand to, ¹¹because need (אביון) never decreases in the land. Therefore I urge you, "Open your hand to your brothers of modest means (לאחיך לעניך) and to your needy ones (ולא־ביונך) in your land." ¹²When your brother sells you the *'Ibry* or the *'Ibryah* (כי ימכר לך אחיך העברי או העבריה) and serves you six years, in the seventh year you shall set him free.

The presence of sons of Edomites (and possibly Egyptians as well) within the *qehal-YHWH* is a litmus test for any reading of Deuteronomy. It can be ignored entirely, or painfully downplayed.[110] Equally, the presence of a non-Israelite elite within the *qehal-YHWH* is one significant characteristic of Deuteronomy's core, next to the yearly tithes dedicated for the sole consumption of the tithe payers themselves and the confinement of the Levites to the local settlements.

Compared with the storage and distribution of triennial tithes at the local level, and to the yearly banquets at the *maqom*, the *qehal-YHWH* is invisible. Nothing is written about where and when it meets, if it ever does meet. The *qehal-YHWH* remains a blind motif, until the brotherhood of the Edomite is read in light of the difference between loans granted to a brother and loans granted to a foreigner discussed in Deuteronomy 23:19–20. The intervening verses (Deut 23:10–19 [Eng. 9–18]) introduce miscellaneous matters that are more at home in Leviticus than in Deuteronomy: holiness threatened by nocturnal emissions and latrines, prostitutes and a house of YHWH. These rules separate the section on the membership of the *qehal-YHWH* from the verses that give some substance to the brotherhood. Most likely, these verses were inserted there purposefully by the framers to sever the link between the Edomite brother and the practical implications of membership to the *qehal-YHWH*. True to the aim of the framers, modern translations continue the process initiated in Deuteronomy 15 by rendering the brother in Deuteronomy 23:20–21[19–20] as another Israelite, a countryman or a fellow Israelite.

Entry into the *qehal-YHWH* means access to commercial credit on advantageous terms, but this privilege implies responsibilities as well. For instance, the death penalty in case of stealing applies specifically to kidnappers when the abducted person is or belongs to a brother (Deut 24:7). That his brother must also be from the sons of Israel (מאחיו מבני ישראל) does not condone the abduction of an Edomite brother or of a dependent of an Edomite brother. This case is not considered because geographic distance makes it less likely than abduction between residents of neighboring localities.

The rules concerning the return of lost property reflect a code of honor between members of the *qehal-YHWH*. The contrast between Deuteronomy 22:1–4, which deals with a brother's animals and garment and Exodus 23:4–5, which requires the return of stray or fallen animals of one's enemy can hardly be greater, though it hardly helps decide which version depends on the other.[111] The use of the term 'brother' instead of 'son of Israel' to designate the owner of stray or fallen animals is shocking

---

110 As does Crouch, *Making*, 195–99.
111 Pace Otto, *Deuteronomium 12,1–23,15*, 1684–86.1694–96.

to modern sensitivities. Hence, the NRSV takes again the liberty to broaden the application of that 'law' by rendering את as 'neighbor'. Yet, apart from the garment mentioned in verse 3, it is mostly the members of an inner circle of wealthy owners who are likely to suffer the loss of livestock and other kinds of property from the simple fact that they own more assets than ordinary farmers who are not members of the *qehal-YHWH*, and are thus unable to supervise them as closely as the owners of smaller flocks would.

Finally, the code of honor that regulates interaction within the *qehal-YHWH* is illustrated by the limitation of physical punishment of a brother (Deut 25:3). Unless the brother in question is any Israelite, forty lashes only indicates that a member of the guild may not be treated like a commoner, even when found guilty.

3.4 Purpose of the three levels

To conclude Part I, the three institutions delineated above present what appears to be a functional society. The yearly tithes finance the yearly pilgrimage to maintain the social cohesion of the Deuteronomic Israel. Preferential credit facilities within the *qehal-YHWH* "guild" finance supra-regional trade in close collaboration with certain Edomite and Egyptian brothers/partners. An Israelite elite of traders is thus able to grant loans to their neighbors and to foreigners to ensure the independence and prosperity of Deuteronomic Israel.

3.4.1 Confinement of the Levite to the local level

If the original core did confine the Levite to the local level and ignored priests, the Levite was involved in the administration of daily life and agricultural production at the local level in particular managing the needs of the landless, including the *gerim*. The limitation of the revenues of the Levite to a quarter of 3.33% of annual plant produced at the settlement he belonged to shows that the core was not conceived by priests or Levites, whose functions are never explained.[112] This silence, however, is no evidence of absence. The systematic pairing of a Levite and a *ger* at the

---

112 It would be interesting to articulate the Chronicler's insistence on inserting the Levites "into every possible situation" with their confinement away from the *maqom* in the Deuteronomic core of the core. Levin, "Lists," 630–31 argues that throughout the Second Temple period the Levites had little or no function in the temple cult. Presumably Levin refers to the temple at Jerusalem. See also Levin, "Role of the Levites in Chronicles," 146.

local level simply reflects how cultic and administrative tasks were interwoven in daily practice.¹¹³

If, on the contrary, the Levites and/or the Levitical priests collect meat cuts, first fruits, first fleeces and are involved at the *maqom* as well, the brother may refer to any fellow Israelite, and the words אביון, עני and גר can all be rendered as "poor" in order to justify the prerogatives of the Levites and Levitical priests. Seen in this way, the core does not stand out from the chapters that frame it. The identification of an original core conceived independently from the rest of the Pentateuch becomes irrelevant. The strong men are the Levites, the Levitical priests, and the odd priest encountered once in a while in Deuteronomy. In this case, the *raison d'être* of Deuteronomy is beyond recovery. Why produce such a book when Leviticus does a far better job at justifying the extraction of revenues as priestly dues in the form of an intractable variety of sacrifices? Why interpret previous law codes and write up a second or third one if the aim is similar to the others? Such a re-writing effort is more likely to occur in reaction to a core that dispensed almost entirely with any priesthood. This option is more coherent with the presentation of the *maqom* in chapter 14.

3.4.2 *maqom* mobility to prevent centralization

The constant shift of the location of the mobile *maqom* prevents the rise of a central sanctuary thanks to a coalition of producers residing close to it and a clergy collecting offerings. A mobile *maqom* is thus the opposite of the central sanctuary encountered in exegetical writings, which find it hard not to read the Deuteronomic *maqom* in light of 2 Kings 23. A temple-less Israel united around its god thanks to yearly banquets held in front of YHWH and financed by 10% of the yearly yields consumed by the tithe payers themselves resists the rise of a clergy, but would nevertheless be a most efficient tool to forge a collective identity around joy and abundance. It is through banquets rather than through the remission of mutual debts that Israel is expected to become conscious of being YHWH's people.¹¹⁴

3.4.3 *Regular purge of the commercial credit market*
Though almost invisible, the *qehal-YHWH* brotherhood is conceived as the heart of the Deuteronomic Israel, a point obscured by the Zion-centrism of the bulk of the Hebrew Bible in which the centre of *Eretz-Israel*

---

113 For the Achaemenid era, see Henkelman, "Practice of Worship," chapter 86.
114 Against Mukenge, "Toutefois," 69–86.

can only be Jerusalem. The šemiṭṭah purges the market from large commercial debts between brothers that would threaten the source of credit to every sector of Israel if the debts were left to snowball indefinitely.

Throughout history, the economic success of guilds relied on trust between members in whose interest it was to retain their good reputation by honoring their debts towards other members and towards the tax administration.[115] That trust reduces transaction costs and delays to minimal levels, ensuring the efficient circulation of capital. Thanks to the trust that prevails within the membership, each brother is likely to find himself both creditor and debtor in a network of credit that requires no other security than a handshake.[116] Instead of justifying the extraction of revenues, YHWH guarantees the trust between the members of a guild that includes Edomites and possibly Egyptians too, as intermediaries involved in North-Arabian trade.

3.5 Results of the economic reading

It is time to take stock of the harvest gathered so far by reading Deuteronomy's laws economically. The basic approach was to put the matter of dates on hold to seek the purpose of the laws and to avoid equating the *maqom* with Jerusalem and its temple. As a result, a concern to preserve the interest of the producers of wealth comes to the fore. In short, the bulk of Deuteronomic Code focuses on production while the books of Exodus, Leviticus and Numbers focus on the extraction of foodstuffs to finance a priesthood. Simply put, the Torah reflects the inevitable conflict of interest between producers and consumers—farmers versus priests. Tariffs and priestly dues are presented before the central chapters of Deuteronomy focus on the production of flour, oil, wine, sheep and cattle. But it is not that simple.

Deuteronomy itself transmits "two narrative voices which do not necessarily present the same perspective, the one of the narrator, the other of Moses."[117] The perspectives of these two voices are not only different, they present conflicting interests. The narrator's voice reflects the

---

115 Kloppenborg, "New Institutional Economics," 113; quoting Monson, "Ethics and Economic," 221–38 and Tilly, *Trust and Rule*, 13.
116 On striking the hand see Frymer-Kensky, "Israel," 256–57 and Prov 6:1;11:15; 22:26. The sacredness of the given word characterizes the Babylonian merchant in the *Elegies mourning the death of Tammuz*: "The agent, the Babylonian merchant, who gave his word, has left behind his donkeys!" See Livingstone, *Court Poetry*, 39.
117 Lohfink, "Destruction," 103.

interests of the producers. Moses' voice reflects the interests of a priesthood that extracts revenues from the producers. Therefore, putting on hold the matter of dates to identify the purpose of the Deuteronomic laws ends up identify *two* antagonistic purposes.

While the bulk of Deuteronomy 12–26 is devoted to the production, preservation and increase of wealth in the interest of the farmers and traders it addresses, about a third of it (§5) is concerned with the revenues of the priesthood. The threats, commands and curses that frame the legal collection echo the previous Torah scrolls and give Deuteronomy the same authorship as the Covenant and Holiness Codes. Moses is Israel's sole law-giver though he himself appears only indirectly in the central chapters in reference to "a prophet like me/you" (Deut 18:15–18). In this way, it is Moses' voice that one hears warning "you" twice not to abandon (עזב) the Levite (Deut 12:19; 14:27). Why this double warning?

Chapter 12 presents a comprehensive list of sacrifices, tithes and offerings delivered at the *maqom* and Deuteronomy 14:28–29 grants a share of triennial tithes for the Levite in your gates. Chapter 12 does mention the Levite besides the households rejoicing in the presence of YHWH (12:12.18), but does not state what and how much the Levite is entitled to collect. Hence the warning makes sense as the corollary of the silence over the Levite's share of the offerings brought at the *maqom*. The warning makes even more sense in light of chapter 14 that only grants the Levite a share of the triennial tithes delivered in your gates with no mention of his presence at the *maqom*. The second call not to abandon the Levite is found in 14:27 at the transition between the description of yearly tithes (14:22–26) and triennial tithes (14:28–29). As verses 22–26 mention no Levite at the *maqom*—contrary to chapter 12—the warning not to abandon him in verse 27 introduces the triennial tithes in verses 28–29 as the solution to the Levite's predicament: he is taken care of in your gates and is thus not abandoned. Hence, chapters 12 and 14 agree that the Levite is in danger of being abandoned, but they differ on how to avoid it. The mention of the Levite at the *maqom* in chapter 12 anticipates the solution provided in 14:28–29. Chapter 12 implies that triennial tithes are insufficient, and thus introduces the Levite at the *maqom*, though without explaining why he is there. Therefore, his presence at the *maqom* reads as a first concession to the exclusion of the Levite from the *maqom* in chapter 14.

Obviously, synchronic readings perceive no "exclusion" of the Levite because his presence at the *maqom* feast is stated in chapter 12 and repeated in chapter 18. The question is whether chapter 12 smoothens in advance the failure of chapter 14 to include the Levite at the *maqom*.

Taking the economics into account supports the contention that chapters 12 and 18 correct the exclusion of the Levite from the *maqom* feast.

Compared to all the different offerings that must be delivered at the *maqom* (12:11), the theoretical fourth of 3.33% of the yearly yield the Levite is entitled to at your gates (§1.1.1) seems disproportionally small. Having him share the festive meals reads as a compensation, which in turn underlines the oddity of the tithing system of chapter 14.

Scholars, however, perceive no oddity. If the *maqom* is the temple of Jerusalem, the priests are fed from the sacrifices, offerings and tithes listed comprehensively in chapter 12. If Deuteronomy reflects Josiah's cultic centralization, the Levites are also fed from the offerings in chapter 12. That chapter 12 fails to specify the Levite's share at the *maqom,* and that Deuteronomy 14 only grants the Levite a share of the triennial tithes is ignored, though it remains a lingering issue. Part II thus focuses on the scholarly discussion about the allocation of Deuteronomic tithes.

PART II

FOCUSING ON TITHES

The economic reading of Deuteronomy's laws in Part I ends up noting the coherence of the tithing system in Deuteronomy 14:22–29 with the bulk of the legal collection as well as the oddity of this tithing system with the presentation of the *maqom* in chapter 12. A cursory survey of how recent scholarship deals with Deuteronomy's tithes is revealing.

Chapter 4
Yearly Tithes for Whom and How Much?

4.1 Georg Braulik: threat of orgiastic exultation

In 1980, Georg Braulik OSB produced a study focusing on Deuteronomy's concept of joy for the construction of a theory of the feast to renew Catholic liturgy in the context of the Second Vatican Council. This study underlined Deuteronomy's unique approach to the worship of YHWH: eating before YHWH with joy:

> Indeed, it is only in Deuteronomy that joy is mentioned. In a world in which sacrifices were frequent and important, and in which the centralization of the cult into a single sanctuary was therefore experienced as a restriction and an impoverishment, it is now made certain that every meal at this site will be a joyful one.[1]

Braulik did not challenge the Josianic hypothesis. Nevertheless, he went further than most biblical scholars to consider the centralization of the cult from the vantage point of the farmers rather than from that of the disenfranchised Levites of de Wette's theory. Ordinary Israelites would have experienced the closure of local sanctuaries and the obligation to worship their god at a single sanctuary as a restriction and an impoverishment. For this reason, Braulik understood the insistence on the joyful tone of the meal at the central sanctuary as a compensation for the restrictions the centralization entailed.

The promise of a joyful occasion at the central sanctuary was meant as an appeal to the farming population to compensate for the restrictions of the centralized cult, but a cult that had to be different from what prophetic texts ascribe to Baalism, pagan orgies that supposedly characterized the "native fertility rites" that "had always exercised a magic fascination on the farming population".[2] The satisfaction of human desires had to be included in the cultic joy, without "the intoxicating experiences provided by the cultic revels, and the intoxicating excesses of sexual intercourse in the service of fertility" made it difficult "to distinguish

[1] Braulik, "Joy," 59.
[2] Braulik, 30.

between a Canaanized YHWH cult and a yahwistically influenced Baal cult."³

For Braulik, Canaanite fertility rites were times when man and god drank together and experienced union through sexual and alcoholic intoxication.⁴ To pinpoint the differences with Canaanite cults, Braulik noted that cultic joy is induced by eating before YHWH. But he also noted that no common meal is explicitly mentioned during the Feast of Weeks and of Booths in chapter 16 and in connection with the presentation of the first fruits at the *maqom* (Deut 26:11). Yet, it is "impossible to imagine that the Feast of Weeks, the feast of joy par excellence, was kept by a seven day long fast!"⁵ Therefore, Braulik took the mentions of joy when nothing is said about eating precisely when a meal would be most expected as Deuteronomy's way to underline the difference from the cultic meals of the Canaanite fertility rites. In this way, joy is not equated with the consumption of wine and the satisfaction of human desires.⁶

As Deuteronomy 14:22–27 does mention the festive consumption of wine, Braulik noted that "Deuteronomy allows the farmers to sell the produce at their place of residence and then spend the money on a meal in common at the Temple of Jerusalem".⁷

Of course, there is neither temple or Jerusalem in Deuteronomy, but there is food and wine aplenty, and more of it than for a single meal. Baalism and Canaanite practices are no issue in Deuteronomy 14:22–27, but scholars remain uneasy with the consumption of tithes at the *maqom*.

4.2 Timo Veijola: a fraction only

In his commentary of Deuteronomy, Timo Veijola noted that the yearly tithes as Deuteronomy presents them could be an issue. So Veijola skirted the problem by stating it was so obvious that Deuteronomy 14 intends the tithes for the sanctuary and only a fraction of the tithes for consumption by the tithe-payers that it needed no telling. Chapter 14 could not expect families to squander in one trip to Jerusalem a tenth of their hard-won yearly production.⁸ The Levites would certainly concur, but would the tithe payers agree? From their point of view, would squandering a tenth of their hard-won yearly production in one trip to the *maqom* be

---

3 Braulik, 33. See also Humbert, "*Laetari et Exultare*," 133.
4 Braulik, 60, quoting Stolz, *Strukturen*, 227–28.
5 Braulik, 59.
6 Braulik, 60.
7 Braulik, 50.
8 Veijola, *5. Buch*, 306.

preferable to the use of only a fraction of these tithes for a meal and hurry back home in order not to deplete the Levite's share? This is more or less what Benjamin Kilchör suggests.

4.3 Benjamin Kilchör: only one meal

In an impressive comparison of the legal collections of the Pentateuch, Kilchör identifies 180 verses as Deuteronomic *Sondergut*, i.e. almost 53% of the literary material in Deuteronomy 12:2–26:15, against 32% that he views as dependent upon the Covenant Code and/or the Holiness Code. The remaining cases in which he could not determine the direction of dependence amount to almost 15%, though Kilchör himself warns that the difference between reversible and irreversible dependence is not always clear and that the limit between Deuteronomic *Sondergut* and dependence can equally be difficult to identify.[9]

Kilchör does not break down the 32% of non-reversible material between what he considers dependent upon Exodus and what is dependent on Leviticus because he concludes that "the laws in Exodus, Leviticus and Numbers were available more or less in their present form when the Deuteronomic law was composed, and they had a quasi-canonical status."[10] Given the number of instances when Deuteronomy displays similarities with laws in Exodus, Leviticus, and Numbers, this is certainly correct, but it does not help probe the genesis of the Deuteronomic legal collection.

More relevant for the present study is the second by-product of Kilchör's analyses, that Leviticus 19 and Exodus 34 "are important precursors for the Deuteronomic law."[11] Even more significant, "Exod. 34 is likely to be behind Deut. 12 in particular, which in turn is the introductory chapter of the Deuteronomic law and as such serves as orientation for the entire law."[12] Therefore, the Deuteronomic Code that begins with chapter 12 presupposes the existence of some parts of Exodus and of Leviticus since Leviticus 3:17b is quoted in Deuteronomy 12:16a.[13]

This provides some clues about Deuteronomy 12–26, the traditional delimitation of the Deuteronomic Code, but it has no bearings on the possible existence of a previous less extensive version of the Deuteronomic legal collection. Kilchör identifies no subversion in the hermeneutical principle of Deuteronomic innovation. This is stating the obvious if

---

9   Kilchör, *Mosetora*, 333.
10 Kilchör, 340.
11 Kilchör, 340.
12 Kilchör, 340.
13 Kilchör, 339.

Deuteronomy 12 indeed aligns the Deuteronomic legal collection with the other collections to fit it into the Mosaic Torah, but it begs the questions of the existence of a Deuteronomic law that had to be aligned, why it had to be aligned and where in Deuteronomy the non-aligned version began.

Keen as he is to discount the notion of an older Deuteronomic code that would have been modified with borrowings from the other codes, Kilchör claims that the tithing system of Deuteronomy 14:22–29 presupposes the other tithe-related texts in Leviticus 27:30–33 and Numbers 18:21–32.

To argue that Deuteronomy 14:22–29 knows the other two texts, Kilchör lists similar words—tithe, eating, yield, animals, silver, place, Levite—that can be expected from texts dealing with the same theme.[14] For instance, Kilchör uses the fact that the words תבואה "yield" and זרע "seed" occur in Deuteronomy 14:22 as evidence for the dependence of Deuteronomy 14 upon the other two tithe passages because תבואה is attested to in Number 18:30 and זרע in Leviticus 27:30.[15]

As literary arguments are easily reversed, Kilchör then embarks in a lengthy discussion to placate Stackert's opposite view that Leviticus 27 and Numbers 18 presuppose Deuteronomy 14.[16]

To argue that Deuteronomy 14 depends on Leviticus 27 and Numbers 18, Kilchör claims that Deuteronomy's notion of families eating and drinking the whole of their yearly tithes at the *maqom* is unrealistic because tithes are *per definitionem* destined for the Levites.[17] Tithes in Leviticus and Numbers are indeed destined for the priesthood, but instead of proving that the Deuteronomic tithes know and depend on Leviticus 27 and Numbers 18, it underlines the uniqueness of Deuteronomy 14:22–29 where the tithes are victuals to be disposed of by the tithes payers at will. Realistic or not, Deuteronomy's tithing system sticks out of the Pentateuch like a sore thumb, which hardly confirms its dependance upon Leviticus 27 and Numbers 18.

To fit the yearly tithes of Deuteronomy 14:22–29 into the tithes destined for the Levites, Kilchör imagines that the pilgrims are entitled to deduct the expenses incurred during the pilgrimage from the tithes they bring to the *maqom*. The Levites' actual share is thus what is left of the tithes after the pilgrims ate some as provisions for the journey. If tithes are *per definitionem* destined for the Levites (as per Leviticus and Numbers) the deductions ought to be minimal, but Kilchör is aware that this

---

14   Kilchör, 117–19.
15   Kilchör, 121.
16   Stackert, *Rewriting*, 165–208.
17   Kilchör, *Mosetora*, 120, quoting Eissfeldt, *Erstlinge*, 49–50.

hardly fits the generosity expressed in Deuteronomy 14:26: eat and drink in the presence of YHWH as much as you like. Therefore, Kilchör adds that the tithe payers ought to look after themselves and be allowed to make a second deduction from their tithes, i.e. everything needed for a festive meal.[18] Kilchör's attempt to reconcile two irreconcilable conceptions of the tithes is strained.

In fact, Deuteronomy has no place for such parochial calculations. The entire proceeds of the yearly tithes are dedicated to the banquets in front of YHWH. Of course there are travel costs as well as major inherent costs in silver exchange (§§1.1.4), but these costs are shared between all tithe-payers if the feasts are organized at a different place each year (§3.2.4). In any case, these costs are part and parcel of the celebrations. This is far more realistic than Kilchör's imagined scheme, which implies that tithes payers would have good reasons to stay at the *maqom* as long as the food and drink they brought lasted. The aim of the call to eat as much as they wish (כל אשר תאוה נפשך) is to learn to fear God zealously (Deut 14:23). Piety would be enhanced and stores at home preserved, at the expense of the Levite's share of the tithes. By comparison, the mere fraction of the yearly tithes of Deuteronomy 14 Kilchör allows to the tithe payers is miserly.[19] Yet, this scheme is the only crutch to support the notion that the *maqom* is the central store for the tithes.[20]

4.4 Jeffrey Stackert: for the Levite too

Contrary to Kilchör, Jeffrey Stackert considers that Leviticus 27 and Numbers 18 presuppose Deuteronomy 14.[21] Yet, his discussion of the revision of Deuteronomy 14:22–29 in Numbers 18:20–32 is a good example of the difficulty of retrieving the originality of Deuteronomy's tithing system. Stackert summarizes it as follows:

---

18 "Einfach gesagt: Die „Spesen" der Reise zum Zentralheiligtum dürfen vom Zehnten abgezogen werden, d.h., die Pilger dürfen sich auf der Pilgerreise vom Zehnten verpflegen. Die Leviten erhalten dann netto den Zehnten minus die Wegzehrung. Und hierbei dürfen es sich die Israeliten gut gehen lassen, sie dürfen sich vom Zehnten, den sie abgeben, alles herausnehmen, was zu einem Festessen gehört, alles was das Herz begehrt (Dtn 14:26: כל אשר תאוה נפשך)." (Kilchör, *Mosetora*, 120)

19 Kilchör, 123: "der Zehnten in Dtn 14,22f selbstverständlich auch an die Priesterschaft geht und lediglich ein Bruchteil davon vom Geber gemäss Dtn 14,23 konsumiert wird…"

20 "die zentrale Sammelstelle des Zehnten": Kilchör, *Mosetora*, 122.

21 Stackert, *Rewriting*, 165–208.

The Deuteronomic tithe law (Deut 14:22–29) requires a yearly tithe on all agricultural produce, defined further as a tithe of grain, wine, and oil. Two out of every three years, Israelite families must bring this agricultural tithe, as well as their firstborn animals from herd and flock, to the central sanctuary, where they are to feast before YHWH. Israelite families must also include any local Levite in this festal journey, for he has no ancestral heritage (and thus no tithe) like other Israelites.[22]

In fact, the inclusion of the local Levite in this festal journey is stipulated in chapters 12 and 16, *not* in chapter 14. Stackert has simply interpreted verse 27 "as for the Levite who is in your gates, do not leave him behind…" as the indication that the Levite travels with the Israelite families to the *maqom*. In fact, the text warns its audience not to *abandon* the Levite (לא תעזבנו), which may be understood as the justification for his joining the families at the *maqom* banquets or in exactly the opposite way. Instead of justifying the presence of the Levite at the *maqom*, it justifies the share of triennial tithes he receives at the gates. With some stretching, "do not abandon the Levite" might function in both ways—in favor of the *maqom* meals and of the share at the gate as well—but whichever option is chosen it is necessary to explain why one is preferred over the other.

Stackert simply takes the journey of the Levite with the families for granted, which blinds him to the differences between chapter 14 and chapters 12 and 16 to the point that he can write that "In D, Levites share in every tithe, just as in H."[23] Yet, Stackert is aware of the tension and notes that "Num 18:21 may represent a response to the Levites' limited rights to the tithe".[24] Unfortunately, this crucial point gets lost in comparisons with Leviticus, Numbers, and Ezekiel. The main conclusion Stackert draws from his analysis of the Deuteronomic tithes is based on Deuteronomy 18:7: the Deuteronomic author allows the "Levites who do not normally serve in the central sanctuary to assume cultic functions there."[25] As is the case with Kilchör, Deuteronomy 14 and 15 are read in light of chapters 12, 16, and 18.

4.5 James Wilson: let my Levite go

Contrary to Stackert, James Wilson is aware that Deuteronomy 14:27 might be read differently, i.e. that he should be granted a share of the

---

22 Stackert, 171.
23 Stackert, 175.
24 Stackert, 182.
25 Stackert, 206.

triennial tithes because he receives no proceeds from the annual tithes.[26] Against this reading, Wilson argues that, as in at least 65 out of 214 occurrences, the verb *'azab* in Deuteronomy 12:19 and 14:27 can be read locatively, i.e. indicating that the Levite should not be left behind at home.[27] On this basis, Wilson argues that the Levites could function at the *maqom* as back-up ritual specialists for overburdened priests. This is certainly the case for the ritual activity implied in chapter 12—though no priests are mentioned there—but it can only apply to Deuteronomy 14 too if the dual tithing system is read in light of chapter 12 and 16:9–15. Wilson imagines a sore lack of infrastructure as a consequence of the centralization of the cult, a situation that the presence of Levites would help remediate.[28] It is necessary to refer back to the Tetrateuch to postulate that heads of family would not be allowed to sacrifice their own firstlings and would need priests and Levites to do it for them.

4.6 Kevin Mattison: perhaps for the Levites too

Contrary to Wilson, Kevin Mattison readily admits that the urge not to abandon the Levite concerns his share of the proceeds of the triennial tithes, but he adds that *perhaps* they concern the annual tithes too and that it *seems* that the Levite is invited to the annual tithe and firstling meal.[29]

---

26 Wilson, *Roles of Rural Levites*. I thank the author for sharing his work in advance of publication.
27 Wilson, *Roles*, 94 n. 53: Gen 2:24; 39:6–18; 44:22; 50:8; Exod 2:20; 9:21; Lev 19:10; 23:22; 26:43; Num 10:31; Deut 12:19; 14:27; 32:36; Josh 1:5; 8:17; Judg 2:21; 1 Sam 30:13; 31:7; 2 Sam 5:21; 15:16; 1 Kgs 19:20; 2 Kgs 2:2, 4, 6; 4:30; 7:7; 8:6; Isa 6:12; 7:16; 10:3, 14; 17:2. 9; 18:6; 27:10; 32:14; Jer 4:29; 9:18; 12:7; 14:5; 25:38; 48:28; 49:11, 25; Ezek 24:21; 36:4; Zeph 2:4; Zech 11:17; Ps 16:10; 27:9; Job 18:4; Ruth 1:16; 2:11,16; Neh 9:19; 1 Chron 10:7; 14:12; 16:37; 2 Chron 11:14; 24:25; 28:14. Out of a total of nine occurrences of the verb *'azab* in Deuteronomy, only the first and last (Deut 12:19; 32:36) belong to Wilson's list of locative usages and would support reading 14:27 locatively too. Note, however, that in Deut 32:34 עזוב is in parallel with עצור and the pair "bound or free" is not the strongest case of locative usage.
28 Wilson, 97.
29 Mattison, *Rewriting and Revision*, 90 and 126.

4.7 Peter Altmann: for the Levite, implicitly

As far as I know, Peter Altmann comes closest to the recognition that the Levite in Deuteronomy 14 has no place at the *maqom* banquets. According to him, Deuteronomy

> overthrows the typical nature of the tithe and tithe feast. Since, as seems to have been the case in Israel and Judah as much as elsewhere in the ancient Near East, the tithe in Israel generally benefited the palace and temple, then the DC meal that benefits those bringing the tribute goes against the fundamental idea of those feasts since tribute functioned as a sign of a submissive bond towards the monarch. Therefore, missing payment amounted to breaking the contract.[30]

Yet, Altmann wonders whether the Levites, the resident aliens, the widows and the orphans may nevertheless be "somehow implicitly" treated as special guests to the *maqom* celebrations.[31] This is indeed the case in Deuteronomy 16:11–14, and if, for argument's sake, one admits that it is implicitly the case also in chapter 14, the presence of the tithe payers, *gerim*, widows, and orphans besides the Levites is still far removed from the notion of tithes collected for the benefit of palace and temple.

This cursory overview of the allocation of Deuteronomy's tithes reveals a growing awareness in recent scholarship of the problem the yearly tithes of Deuteronomy 14 represents. Yet, ever since Robertson Smith recognized that the Deuteronomic tithing system involves the mere collection of 10% every third year, no one seems to have accepted the notion that Deuteronomy 14 dedicates the whole of the triennial tithes delivered at the *maqom* for self-consumption.[32]

4.8 Tax-free tithes without orgies

The above sample of Deuteronomic scholarship is an indicator of the resistance to the presentation of Deuteronomy's *maqom* in chapter 14 as the site of a huge picnic in front of YHWH where entire households learn to fear YHWH by eating and drinking a tenth of their yearly production.

Braulik did recognize that the first-mentioned consumers of the tithes and firstlings are the tithe payers themselves with their households, but Deuteronomy 14:22–29 is secondary in his definition of the Deuteronomic festal theory because it ignores the Levite and because the banquets

---

30   Altmann, *Festive Meals*, 231.
31   Altmann, 236.
32   Smith, *Religion*, 251.

are reminiscent of Canaanite celebrations that prophetic fulminations fantasize as orgiastic (Isa 22:13; Hos 9:1). Hence, Braulik reformulated the tithes and firstlings of chapter 14 as stipulations "connected with the yearly offering of gifts at the sanctuary, which—it was not even necessary to mention—was, of course, to be deducted from the tithes and firstlings."[33] Recent studies avoid arguing from silence but accept uncritically the notion that priests and Levites collect food from the tithes brought at the *maqom* and ignore the fact that Deuteronomy 14:29 only grants the Levite a share of the triennial tithes stored in your gates, as though this would leave the Levite disenfranchised.

The dual tithing system of Deuteronomy 14 is indeed at loggerheads with the Torah's overall presentation of the cult, but it is coherent with itself: yearly tithes for the households at the *maqom*, triennial tithes at the gates for the Levite and others. Households may invite the Levite and others to share the joyful *maqom* meals, but their presence there is the consequence of the joy of being together, not the cause of the joy. The festive consumption of meat and wine with family and friends is the high point of the pilgrimage.[34] Scholars would rather have them fasting joyfully (Zech 8:19) to steer clear of Canaanite temptations. In fact, the presence of parents, wives and children ensures dignified behavior and prevents the feast from degenerating into an orgy. The supervision of priests and Levites is unnecessary because Deuteronomy 21:20 punishes drunken behavior with the death penalty. A drunkard would publicly dishonor himself and his household in front of the entire Israel gathered at the *maqom*.

Recent studies have given up the threat of Canaanite orgies at the *maqom* but continue to consider the presence of priests or Levites at the *maqom* to collect tithes there as essential to YHWH worship. Hence, the presentation of the *maqom* feast in Deuteronomy 14 is read in light of four pericopes that are placed strategically within the legal core.

---

33 Braulik, 55. See also Veijola, *5. Buch*; Von Rad, *Fünfte Buch Moses*, 73.
34 Lohfink, "Destruction," 104.

Chapter 5
Claiming a Greater Share of Deuteronomic Tithes

As much as Deuteronomy 1–11 and 27–34 form a parenetic frame for the Deuteronomic Code, chapters 12 and 26 introduce and conclude the legal collection proper. The burden of these two chapters differs from the concern of the laws that focus overwhelmingly on matters of agricultural production, credit, war, marriage and inheritance. Deuteronomy 12 and 26 are devoted to cultic matters at the *maqom*, what should be delivered there and what may be consumed at home. Two additional passages within the code deal specifically with cultic matters at the *maqom* (chapter 16) and with priestly dues (18:1–8). Together, these 76 verses alter the significance of the eight verses tucked at the end of chapter 14.[1] The dual tithing system of Deuteronomy 14:22–29 is now a mere appendix that scholars interpret in light of the data provided in chapter 12, 16, 18 and 26, because the oddity of these eight verses does not fit the overall Torah narrative that gives primacy to the priesthood. On the contrary, Deuteronomy 14:22–29 does not involve the Levite in the *maqom* festivities, but he is not abandoned. He is taken care of at home. The dual tithing system is a glitch in the cogs of the grand Torah narrative and in current Deuteronomic scholarship.

5.1 Whose joy?

More than other the studies considered in chapter 4, Braulik's study delved into the function of joy as the specificity of Deuteronomy's cultic theory (§4.1). Braulik perceived that without the promise of rejoicing, the Israelites would experience the centralization of the cult into a single sanctuary as a restriction and an impoverishment.[2] Unless every meal at the *maqom* was an occasion for reveling before YHWH, Israel would have no incentives to bring their tithes there.

---

1 32 verses of chapter 12 + 17 verses of chapter 16 + 8 verses of chapter 18 + 19 verses of chapter 26 = 97 verses.
2 Braulik, "Joy," 59.

As stated above (§4.8), Israelites have every reason to rejoice when they consume a tenth of the yearly yield, including meat and wine at the *maqom* with family and friend (Deut 14:22-26). Joy is already mentioned in 12:7.12.18, but this time the Levite (but the *ger* in 12.18 LXX!) has reasons to rejoice too if the priestly dues in 18:3 apply to the sacrifices listed in chapter 12.

A complicating factor is that Deuteronomy 18:1-3 does not grant these priestly dues to the Levite but to Levitical priests. These priests belong to the tribe of Levi but they are distinguished from the Levite who can only tap into the meat cuts and first fruit collected by the Levitical priests when he travels to the *maqom*. The tribe of Levi, Levitical priests and priests' dues—or customary priestly revenues (משפט הכהנים)—are foreign bodies in the world depicted in Deuteronomy's laws, contrary to the Levite who is literally at home in your gates, even though his functions there are never described.

The presence of the Levitical priests at the *maqom* and the list of priests' dues is coherent with Leviticus, but is not coherent with Deuteronomy 14:22-26. The joyful spirit of the feast does not exclude inviting the Levite and others to share the banquets, but the difference between invitation and taxation can only be ignored when the point of view of the tithe producers is deemed irrelevant.

As Moses views the Israelites as stiff-necked and rebellious (Exod 32:9; 33:3.5; 34:9), Torah readers easily pass over the farmers' point of view. Worse, the *maqom* banquets described in Deuteronomy 14 could evoke the reveling in Exodus 32, without the infamous golden calf. Moses duly recalls the episode in Deuteronomy 9:15-21 to indict Aaron more than is the case in Exodus 32, thus preparing the audience to accept the introduction of Levitical priests at the *maqom* and the collection of priestly prebends there. The implicit exclusion of women in the requirement to meet three times a year at the *maqom* (Deut 16:16) is another awkward element after 14:22-26. The warning not to present oneself empty-handed before YHWH in the same verse underlines the gap between the joyful banquets with family and friends and the liturgies of the festal calendar of chapter 16.

If what is celebrated at the *maqom* is not "the mere consumption of gifts",[3] meat, wine and women contribute to the joy, while the warning not to present oneself empty-handed in chapter 16 reads like a joy killer. It seems to exclude women and mentions neither meat nor wine. On the basis of the presupposition that the *maqom* is a temple and that the bulk of the yearly tithes delivered at the *maqom* are for the temple personnel,

---

3   Braulik, 58.

it is obvious that not presenting oneself before YHWH empty-handed (Deut 16:16) presupposes the tithes and offerings mentioned previously in chapters 12 and 14.

Scholarship recognizes the danger of presuppositions and arguments from silence. As Deuteronomy systematically addresses the tithe payers rather than the Levite or the Levitical priests, the point of view of those who produce those tithes should not be ignored. It is the produce of their labor that the tribe of Levi collects (משלח ידך, מעשה ידיך Deut 12:7.18; 16:15). Ultimately, the yield is the result of YHWH's blessing, but nowhere does Deuteronomy state that the presence of Levitical priests is necessary to express gratitude for YHWH's blessing. Deuteronomy 14 mentions neither Levite or Levitical priest at the *maqom*. Only in chapter 26 is a priest involved. All he takes for his service is a basket of first-fruits, a far cry from the meat cuts, first fruits and first fleeces levied by the Levitical priests (Deut 18:3).

5.2 Joy without women?

The requirement that all males meet three times a year at the *maqom* (Deut 16:16) makes a restrictive reading of the non-mention of wives besides sons, daughters and slaves (12:12.18; 16:11.14). The focus on males renders the presence of daughters and females slaves (אמה) optional. Such a reading is hardly possible with chapter 14 because verse 26 simply mentions your household (ביתך also 26:11), thus presupposing the presence of wives and female slaves. Therefore, the expression "All you males" (כל זכורך Deut 16:16) reformulates the description of the *maqom* feast in Deuteronomy 14:22–26 by making the presence of women dispensable, thus halving the number of partakers and preparing the introduction of Levites, Levitical priests and priestly dues in chapter 18. To the same aim, the expression "three times a year" (Deut 16:16) increases the frequency of gatherings at the *maqom*, and consequently the revenues collected there by the priesthood. Whereas chapter 14 may imply a yearly pilgrimage, chapter 16 specifies three yearly pilgrimages to the *maqom*.

For practical reasons, the consumption of the tithes of wheat, wine and oil together with the firstlings of that year (14:23) would occur at the end of the agricultural season. Once the olives have been pressed and the oil decanted, the household is in possession of the tithable products and in a position to decide how much to set apart for the feast. On this basis it can decide whether to bring its tithes in kind or in silver equivalent (§§3.2.4–5). The festival need not occur right then. Taking meteorological conditions and work load into account, a pilgrimage after the winter months, around the spring Near Year and before the next harvest would be a most convenient time.

If chapter 16 increases the frequency of *maqom* festivities and reduces the number of partakers by excluding women, are chapters 12-13 giving a similar twist to the *maqom* festivities?

5.3 Chapters 12-13 as introduction to a cultic reformulation

As discussed in the previous paragraph, increasing the frequency of pilgrimage would be advantageous for the priests who draw revenues from the *maqom* festivities. Chapter 14 provides no hint to such revenues. Despite the comprehensive list of sacrifices, offerings and tithes in chapter 12, nothing in this long chapter identifies what and how much priests may collect for themselves. A priest appears first in the Deuteronomic Code only in 17:12, and the reader has to wait for the priestly dues in chapter 18 to know that chapter 12 implies the deduction of priestly shares from the offerings and tithes delivered at the sanctuary.

By all means, chapter 12 is "the cornerstone of the legal core" understood as the whole of Deuteronomy 12-26.[4] Yet, it is the parallels with Exodus 20:24b; 23:20-24 (esp. v. 24), 34:12-14 and Leviticus 17:13-14 that render chapter 12 intelligible.

The "warning against heresies" (12:29-31), a parallel to 12:1-4 in inverse sequence, may also introduce the laws of sedition in Deuteronomy 13.[5] The focus on prophecy and idolatry in chapter 13 is more akin to the themes of the theological frames of the book. The total ban on taking spoils from a town found guilty of idolatry is in sharp contrast with the taking of spoils in Deuteronomy 20:14 where they are an incentive to wage war. The mentions of Egypt (Deut 13:5.10) as the land of slavery also mark a sharp contrast with the surprisingly favorable view of the Egyptian who can enter the *qehal-YHWH* in the third generation (Deut 23:8). As is the case with chapter 16 (§5.2), chapters 12-13 participate to a broad effort of reformulation of laws in chapters 14-25. De Wette perceived this reformulation and ascribed it to Josiah's cultic reformation.

5.4 Dietary laws in Deuteronomy 14:1-21

Kilchör considers that the list of clean and unclean animals in Deuteronomy 14 depends upon Leviticus 11 because abbreviation is not common

---

4   Arnold, "Innovations," 165.
5   McConville, *Deuteronomy*, 64.

in Deuteronomy.⁶ Christophe Nihan's claim that both lists depend on a common source is an argument *ex silentio*.⁷ Otto's approach is more convincing because it introduces Deuteronomy 12 in the discussion of the relationship between chapter 14 and Leviticus 11:

> The list of clean and unclean animals in Lev 11:2–23 is taken up in Deuteronomy 14:4–20 and supplemented by a list of unclean birds. The key to understanding the re-interpretation of Lev 11 in Deuteronomy 14 is the law of Deuteronomy 12, which is, indeed, the hermeneutical key not only for Deuteronomy 14, but for the entire Deuteronomic Code (Deut 12–26).⁸

This broader view is relevant to the present purpose. Deuteronomy 12:1–14:21 are the key to the reinterpretation of the dual tithing system of 14:22–29 and of the rest of the Deuteronomic code. Deuteronomy 12:1–14:21 (and 16; 18:1–8; 26) align Deuteronomy with the Tetrateuch and serve the interests of the priesthood, not those of the ordinary Israelites.

The validity of Otto's bird's-eye view is confirmed by the results it yields when applied to details such as the *lectio difficilior* of Deuteronomy 15:22 that grants the home consumption of clean and unclean meats as if it was game (§1.2.6). The repetition of Deuteronomy 15:22 in 12:15.22 succeeded in turning the license to eat at home what is deemed unfit at the *maqom* through the lens of the *kashrut*. The list of clean and unclean meats in chapter 14 tightens the knot that links Deuteronomy to the Torah. Torah readers become impervious to any part of Deuteronomy that may curtail priestly involvement at the *maqom*. To ancient Torah readers as much as to modern biblical scholars, it is inconceivable that farming families could sacrifice their firstborns and revel in front of YHWH without the involvement of priestly personnel.

5.5 Festal calendar in Deuteronomy 16:1–17

Otto's understanding of the function of Deuteronomy 12 as the hermeneutical key for the re-interpretation of chapter 14 can be broadened to chapter 16.⁹ If chapter 12 reinterprets the dual tithing system of chapter 14, the festal calendar of chapter 16 equally modifies a previous version of the *maqom* feast (§5.2). The parallels with Exodus 12:1–28; 13:1–16; 23:14–17; 34:18–25; Leviticus 23 and Numbers 28–29 show that

---

6   Kilchör, *Mosetora*, 102.
7   Nihan, "Laws," 401–404.
8   Otto, "Legal Completion," 181.
9   Otto, "Legal Completion," 162–201.

Deuteronomy 16 presupposes all the festival laws of the Tetrateuch.[10] Torah readers become oblivious to the inconsistency between the joyful consumption of yearly tithes with entire households at the *maqom* and the compulsory pilgrimages of males to the *maqom* three times a year (Deut 16:16). After the first step in chapters 12–13, Deuteronomy 16 is the second step in the alignment of Deuteronomy with the Tetrateuch. The third step is in Deuteronomy 18.

5.6 Priestly portions in Deuteronomy 18:1–8

The statement that the Levitical priests have no allotment or inheritance within Israel (Deut 18:1) repeats Deuteronomy 14:27.29 before introducing priestly dues that deconstruct the dual tithing system.

The list of priestly portions (Deut 18:1–8) is a far cry from the portrayal of the *maqom* festivities in Deuteronomy 14:22–15:23 where households (ביתך) consume the whole of their tithes and firstlings. In addition to sizable priestly dues (Deut 18:3–4, see §1.1.2), verses 6–8 turn the Levite's share of triennial tithes (Deut 14:28–29) into the privilege of collecting dues both in the local village and at the *maqom* in blatant contradiction of the dual tithing system of Deuteronomy 14.

Moreover, Deuteronomy 18:1.5 identifies the Levitical priesthood, which up to this point was somewhat ambiguous, with the tribe of Levi, the only references to a specific tribe in the Deuteronomic core that has little room for the portrayal of Israel as an aggregation of tribes (Deut 12:5.14; 16:18). The promise mentioned in Deuteronomy 18:2 refers back to Numbers 18.[11] Instead of an Israel conceived as a dozen tribes, Deuteronomy 18:1–5 echoes Numbers 18:2–6 by substituting the financial hegemony of the *qehal-YHWH* brotherhood (§3.3) with the hegemony of a Levitical brotherhood set apart by YHWH himself from the midst of the sons of Israel (Num 18:2–6). To align the Deuteronomic core with the Tetrateuch, Deuteronomy 18:1–8 replaces the brother/neighbor distinction with a Levite/non-Levite distinction.

5.7 Melting pot of chapter 26

The insertion of secondary material in Deuteronomy 12–26 culminates with an entire chapter that crowns the alignment of the original theme of the Deuteronomic core with the Torah.

10   Kilchör, *Mosetora*, 102.
11   Kilchör, *Mosetora*, 216; Milgrom, "Profane Slaughter," 3–13.

While chapter 14 focuses on tithes, first fruits are listed as priestly dues in 18:4, an echo of Deuteronomy 12:11 and Numbers 28:26. Chapter 26 begins with the graphic scene of the delivery of a basket of first fruits to the priest at the *maqom* who presents them at the altar of YHWH (Deut 12:27; 16:21) thus completing the reinterpretation of the *maqom* feast in Deuteronomy 14:22–26. While the word "all" (כל) to qualify the contents of the basket is not well attested to, it extends the first fruits from the wheat, wine, oil, and wool listed in 18:4 to any kind of produce of the land for the benefit of the priest.

The contrast with the *maqom* festivities presented in chapters 14 and 15 cannot be greater. Instead of a joyful occasion when families show off their best tithes and firstlings before consuming them in front of YHWH, the priest requires a sworn oath from each producer who must testify before YHWH that triennial tithes have been duly delivered at the gate for the Levite, *ger*, widow, and orphan (Deut 26:12–13). Apart from the mention of commandments, verses 12–13 follow Deuteronomy 14:22–23. Not so the oath that none were eaten in a state of impurity or offered to the dead (26:14).

That the oath is taken at the *maqom* but concerns specifically the triennial tithes reveals the awareness of the writers that the yearly tithes as they are presented in chapter 14 are entirely destined for the sole consumption of the tithe payers (see §1.2.1). Instead of openly contradicting chapter 14 and reserving the bulk of these tithes for the priesthood, as does the present scholarly consensus (§§4.1–7), the framers used subtle devices to reinterpret the dual tithing system. They gathered the various changes introduced so far into the single scene of chapter 26.

Once the priest receives a the basket of first fruits (26:4), the Levite appears together with the *ger* in 26:11 as partaker of the first fruits, though 12:12.18 only have the Levite as a guest at the *maqom* banquets. Yet, the Septuagint mentions the *ger* rather than the Levite in Deuteronomy 12:18.[12] Were the writers aware of the difference? This would explain why they appended the *ger* to the Levite, but not the orphan and the widow, the other beneficiaries of the triennial tithes stored at the gate of the local settlement. Then, verse 12 refers to the triennial tithes to complete the integration of first fruits, yearly tithes, and triennial tithes into a comprehensive tax system supervised by a priest. This rare occurrence of a priest without the qualifier Levitical (also in Deut 17:12; 20:2) adds a layer of ambiguity to the identity of the cultic personnel in the different parts of Deuteronomy.[13] The aim is not to clarify the difference between

---

12 See Graber, "גר (gēr)," 372.
13 On ambiguity as rhetorical strategy in Deuteronomy, see Halpern, "What does Deuteronomy Centralize?" 104.

Levites, Levitical priests and priests. Fuzziness is the aim, fuzziness that conveniently increases the number of priestly partakers in parallel to the reduction of the number of non-priestly partakers, in particular women (§§5.2, 5.5). The lengthy confession of verses 3–11 with two additional references to Egypt (Deut 26:5.8) generates background noise that prevents the audience from noticing the tension with the dual tithing system described ten chapters earlier. The *maqom* is imagined as a sanctuary with priests officiating in turn, as is the case in Deuteronomy 17:9; 19:17.

More secondary material could be identified within the Deuteronomic core besides the four passages discussed so far. Egyptian slavery (Deut 15:15), sacred poles (Deut 16:21), the king's Torah (Deut 17:14) and Amalek (Deut 25:17–19) are obvious references to episodes and concepts from the previous books of the Pentateuch. The systematic identification of all the secondary material in Deuteronomy 15–25 is well beyond the purview of this study, which is limited to demonstrating the presence of two antagonistic purposes in the Deuteronomic Code: the interest of Israelites who produce wealth and the interest of priests who lay claim to greater shares of revenue than the portion of triennial tithes Deuteronomy 14:27–29 sets apart for the Levite.

Chapter 6
Outlines of an Older Deuteronomic Core

If Deuteronomy 12, 16, 18 and 26 operate a systematic reinterpretation of the dual tithing system of 14:22–29 by inflating priestly revenues, these chapters presuppose the existence of a previous version of Deuteronomy's laws, which merely granted the Levite a share of triennial tithes at the local level. In this case, the exclusion of the Levites from the *maqom* is the grain of truth in the old notion of the Levites as a disenfranchised clergy.[1]

The Levites receive their share of the triennial tithes, but contrary to the *ger*, widow and orphan, he has no gleaning rights. The incompatibility of such a view with the economy of Exodus, Numbers and Leviticus is striking. To fit the Exodus epic, it had to be more generous towards Levites and to involve priests as well. The matter of dates comes to the fore. Do Deuteronomy 12, 16, 18 and 26 belong to a (late) process of Torah formation or to an earlier phase of the literary growth of Deuteronomy itself, a process less directly influenced by Leviticus and Numbers?

Any serious attempt to answer these legitimate questions is beyond the purview of this volume. At this point, it is only possible to pinpoint the inconsistency of the economic role of the Levites and priests in Deuteronomy 12, 16, 18 and 26 with the bulk of Deuteronomy 14–25; an inconsistency that current readings of Deuteronomy 14:22–29 perceive but downplay because the influence of de Wette's hypothesis is still too pervasive to admit that yearly tithes are set apart for the exclusive consumption of the tithe payers.

6.1 Priestless or priestly utopia?

Torah readers are preconditioned to conceive that tithes belong to priests and not for tithe payers to revel before YHWH. Indeed, in any given society priests probably tend to collect a greater share of produce than that

---

1 Cook, "Stubborn Levites," 155–70; Stackert, "Cultic Status," 199–214; Samuel, *Priestern*, 146.

which Deuteronomy 14:28–29 allows. That farmers in any real world indeed relinquish a greater amount of their productions as taxes does not mean, however, that Deuteronomy accepts it as a fatality. On the contrary, the exclusive consumption of yearly tithes by the farmers themselves may represent a reaction to a state of affairs that was sufficiently resented to generate the elaboration of a utopia in which Levites provided ritual services at the local level but drew no revenues from a great annual feast when all Israelite households ate and drank their tithes before YHWH in gratitude for his blessings on the previous agricultural cycle.

Deuteronomic scholarship tends to use two different measures when dealing with the dual tithing system, something Deuteronomy 25:13–16 condemns: the heavy shekel of economic realism to consider the consumption of yearly tithes as squandering precious resources, but a light shekel to weigh out substantial priestly dues that are not perceived as squandering precious resources. As a result, priestly dues feel a lighter burden for the family budget than the self-consumption of yearly tithes, a paradoxical outcome that results from the adoption of different vantage points.

As stated above (§4.1), Braulik went further than others in taking into account the point of view of the farmers and understanding the abnormality of the consumption of a tenth of the yearly yield at the *maqom* as an incentive to meet there.[2] The abnormality of the *maqom* banquets as they are presented in Deuteronomy 14 is precisely what would convince households to make the journey *en masse* and consume their tithes at the *maqom* rather than at home. Expecting them to hurry back home in order not to deplete the revenues of the priests (§4.3) would be counterproductive. Even if the Levite joins the family pilgrimage, the foodstuffs brought to the *maqom* are for self-consumption. The Levite's share is negligible and largely compensated for by the social capital gained by public shows of munificence.[3]

The danger of the *maqom* festivities degenerating into Canaanite orgies has probably been exaggerated. Without the joy induced by the consumption of meat and wine with family and friends to your heart's desire (Deut 14:26), the pedagogical motivation of the celebration—that you may learn to fear your God always (Deut 14:23)—would hardly overcome the counter-argument that transport costs can be saved by eating and drinking 10% of one's hard-won products in one big feast at home. "Squandering" 10% of hard-won produce at one big feast is well attested (see §1.1.1). A 20–25% meat tax collected by priests may equally reflect actual practices. Nevertheless, if the aim is to convince households to

---

2   Braulik, "Joy," 59.
3   Bourdieu, "Forms of Capital."

converge on a single location to learn to fear YHWH, the encounter with tax collectors when reaching the *maqom* would have the opposite effect.

The possibility of bringing the value of yearly tithes in silver rather than in kind ensures that even the most distant households join the feast. Though the transactions entail a loss in the purchasing power of the silver (§1.1.4), the fact that these tithes are entirely for self-consumption is a weighty argument to convince any miser that he ought to join his friends and neighbors. Or he would experience intense social pressure as his absence would be obvious and would be a case of self-ostracism.

The delivery of triennial tithes at your gates corresponds to the traditional nature of tithes in the ancient Near East—and probably in Israel and Judah as well—a tax in kind for the benefit of the palace and the temples.[4] In Deuteronomy, nothing goes to the king who as an Israelite brother would be expected to bring his own tithes to the *maqom* and revel with the other tithe payers. Nothing goes to a temple either. The main challenge is to convince the audience to give up hard-won produce for the benefit of others. To this aim, the *ger*, widow and orphan are listed besides the Levite as beneficiaries of the triennial tithes. Social pressure is again at work to win the assent of the tithe payer. These tithes are delivered at your gates under the public gaze as much as those consumed at the *maqom*. To overcome any residual resistance, verse 29 concludes the presentation of the dual tithing system with a promise that delivery of triennial tithes at the gate secures divine blessing in everything you do (בכל מעשה ידך אשר תעשה Deut 14:29). The delivery of triennial tithes secures YHWH's blessing proactively on the upcoming agricultural cycle while yearly tithes consumed at the *maqom* are the result of YHWH's blessing on the previous cycle. The presence or absence of the Levite, with or without the *ger*, widow and orphan, as special guests to the *maqom* banquets is of little economic relevance to the audience, compared to the prestige derived by those who kindly invite them to join the feast. The extraction of a fifth or a fourth of the meat as priestly dues and of all first fleeces is another matter. The festive spirit implies generosity. Taxation does not. Taxation generates tax evasion.

At this point, the reader must chose between two options. Either the tithing system of chapter 14 was conceived from the start as a minor component of a sacrificial economy that includes the revenues of Levites and Levitical priests, or chapters 12, 16, 18, and 26 were penned as a corrective to the tithing system of Deuteronomy 14. The economic status of the Levite and of the Levitical priests in chapters 12, 16, 18, and 26 is far closer to the status of Aaron and his sons in Leviticus than to

---

4 Altmann, *Festive Meals*, 231.

the position of the Levite in chapter 14. The dual tithing system of Deuteronomy 14 has no biblical counterpart, except in Deuteronomy 15, 17, and 19-25 where the production and preservation of wealth is the main concern, but is it less conceivable a utopia than the economy imagined in Leviticus and Numbers?

Taking economic considerations into account answers the question. Unless Levites, priests and Levitical priests are as numerous as the non-priestly population, they have to find outlets for the fine wool they collect throughout the realm. In the absence of refrigeration, the meat cuts have to be consumed immediately and their most obvious use is the thriving sacrificial economy described in great detail by the tariffs in Leviticus and Numbers, alas an economy that focuses entirely on a single group of consumers and ignores the productive sector.

6.2 Unsacred economy?

The double tithing system in Deuteronomy 14:22-29 sets the tone of the world regulated by the laws in chapters 15-25. To present itself as YHWH worshipper and to demonstrate that it belongs to Israel, each household is invited to take stock and decide how much grain, oil, and wine to set aside for the *maqom* feast. Using Weinfeld's categories, chapter 14 reflects a "religious anthropocentric orientation", opposed to the "religious-theocentric orientation" of Deuteronomy 12, 16, and 26.[5] The lion's share of the available surplus is set apart for the pilgrimage, the climax of the year everyone looks forward to, the time that makes the daily struggles worth fighting for. It motivates the efforts to produce enough supplies for the big party and to parade one's best calf, lamb, baby, and marriageable youths in front of distant relatives, acquaintances, and God.

Having estimated the quantities to be set apart, the addressee then decides whether to bear the cost of bringing his tithes in kind or if it is preferable to travel light with silver. The know-how, practical wisdom, and flair required to put into practice the demands of these five verses (Deut 14:22-26) are easily missed, but they are only one aspect of the many other economic activities described in the next chapters.

Besides the victuals for the *maqom* festivities, an amount equal to a third of these is to be set aside for social relief (Deut 14:27-29), this time in front of shrewd neighbors who are not to be fooled by anyone trying to deliver less than his due. So much for the yearly cycle.

---

5   Weinfeld, *Deuteronomic School*, 183-185.

The whole of chapter 15 considers a seven-year cycle of credit transactions, activities as invisible and indispensable as God himself. This longer cycle involves another category besides the ordinary farmers and the four landless categories. Chapter 15 addresses a brother who is in a position to grant the short-term loans that enable ordinary farming families to survive crises. This brother can tide his neighbors over until the next harvest because he generated additional profit from the sale of a fraction of the surplus from previous years where demand is high and their worth high enough to ensure that transport costs are more than covered. The brother also diversifies his portfolio by granting long-term loans to foreigners against interest, while he borrows interest-free from fellow brothers. Nevertheless, the brother is also a farmer and a fellow Israelite who brings his best firstlings to the *maqom*, eating the less than perfect ones at home as he would game, on condition they are properly drained of their blood (Deut 15:19–23).

The distinction between ordinary farmers and the financial elite is suspended while each household eats and drinks before YHWH, declaring its allegiance to the god of Israel and thus becoming Israel together (§3.2.8). The construction of an Israelite identity requires stoning ordinary evildoers (Deut 17:2) as much as devotees of non-Yahwistic cults (Deut 17:3) who would split Israel into different sects. Nevertheless, accusations of idolatry can easily turn executions into lynchings. Hence the second call for impartiality with the imposition of a thorough enquiry and the presence of several matching witnesses who are to throw the first stones to underline their responsibility and discourage false witness (Deut 17:4–7).

Difficult cases are arbitrated during the pilgrimage in the eyes of the whole of Israel to ensure the widest publicity of the verdict (Deut 17:8–13). Levitical priests are mentioned in verse 9 besides the judge designated to arbitrate these high profile cases. These Levitical priests are unattested to in some Greek texts (§3.2.7). Given the prominent position of the Levites and of the Levitical priests in the present form of Deuteronomy, it is unlikely that the translators removed them. It is far more likely that the Levitical priests in verse 9 and the priest in verse 12 were added besides the judge. The secondary nature of the priests that arbitrate besides judges in 19:17 is less obvious, but the singular forms of the verb יהי in some manuscripts could be the last remnant of an earlier version that involved a single judge. Only the priest who harangues the troops in 20:2 displays no clue of redactional intervention. As the troop is not necessarily mustered at the *maqom*, this priest could be a clue as to the priestly functions of the Levite in your gates.

Refuge cities are set up to prevent extrajudicial homicides by blood avengers (Deut 19:1–13), except in cases of suspected premeditated murder, a matter decided by the elders of the perpetrator's home settlement who are best qualified to know of any hostile antecedents. If so, the guilty person is executed by a relative of his victim. As with the distance between one's settlement and the *maqom* (Deut 14:24) and between a city and where an unresolved murder occurred (Deut 21:1–9), the number of refuge cities is to be proportional to the size of the realm to give equal chances to all Israelites wherever they reside. Tellingly, the refuge cities bear no relation to the *maqom*, another clue that the *maqom* is no permanent sanctuary (§§3.2.2; 3.4.2). The matter of distance justifies the mention of field boundaries (Deut 19:14) before a third call to impartiality requiring the execution of false witnesses (Deut 19:15–21).

War is considered from a purely economic point of view, as a way of securing labor or spoils (Deut 20:1–14). The cities that accept the terms of peace contribute as much as those that resist the enlargement of Israelite territory. The labor required of them puts their inhabitants in regular contact with Israelites, which fosters gradual absorption of Israelite mores. Instead of viewing interaction with foreigners as a threat to purity as is the case in the second part of the war laws (Deut 20:15–18), war in Deut 20:1–14 is another means to increase available capital, as is also the case with the right to marry a desirable captive (Deut 21:10–14). As capital is liable to decrease quicker than it can increase, the orchards around a besieged city must be preserved (Deut 20:19–20).

The section on strays, lost property, clothing, secured rooftops, and the protection of the mother bird (Deut 22:5–12) interrupts matrimonial affairs that resume with cases of sexual misconduct (Deut 22:1–23:1), ending with eunuchs and bastards (Deut 23:2–3). These two categories of men are denied membership to the *qehal-YHWH*, contrary to the Edomite and the Egyptian whose sons are to be granted membership in the third generation (Deut 23:8–9). These are the only mentions of this mysterious assembly (see §3.3). However surprising the presence of the Edomites and Egyptian in it, it is coherent with the no less surprising refusal to extradite runaway slaves in the ensuing verses (Deut 23:16–17). The economic outlook of these passages continues with the interest-free loans between brothers, the advice to avoid vows and the limits on eating grapes and grain from a brother's standing crops (Deut 23:20–26). The splicing of economic and matrimonial matters continues with the ban on remarrying the wife one has previously divorced, though the motivation for such a prohibition is difficult to grasp. On the contrary, the other laws all make sense from an economic point of view: a one-year exemption from military service after marriage, followed by matters that are mostly relevant to a wealthy audience: the prohibitions on taking a grinding-stone as pledge or on kidnapping a brother's dependents and a call to pay the wages of dayworkers daily (Deut 24:1–7.10–15).

Individual liability is underlined especially between parents and their children: neither are to be put to death for sins committed by the other generation (Deut 24:16). The explicit mention of death excludes the extension of the principle to the realm of credit where heirs are responsible for the debts of their parents. Individual liability underlines the difference with the collective liability incurred by an unsolved murder (Deut 21:1–9). The elders of the closest city clear their guilt at the cost of a young heifer—the most expensive kind of livestock because the value of a cow decreases after its first calving. It is up to them to finance its cost. Individual liability also counterbalances the case of the prodigal son whose execution is motivated by the threat his behavior represents to the family's capital (Deut 21:18–21).

Unsecured loans for widows and special gleaning rights for widows, orphans, and *gerim* are presented as meritorious in the eyes of YHWH (Deut 24:17.19–21). Then, a short verse on the treading ox (Deut 25:4) interrupts issues pertaining specifically to the brotherhood: the limit of forty lashes for a brother found guilty, the marriage of the wife of the dead associate (§2.1.11), and the maiming of a "grabbing" wife (Deut 25:1–3.5–10). The collection closes with the ban on using two different weights (Deut 25:13–16), an issue particularly pertinent to the trade of victuals for and at the *maqom* (see §1.1.4; 3.2.5).

Instead of an organization in thematic sections, the progression is cyclical, with returns to similar themes. Despite their haphazard sequence, the laws provide a far more comprehensive portrayal of an Israelite society than is the case in Exodus–Numbers that focus on the function and revenues of the priesthood. Deuteronomy's laws seek the construction of a shared Israelite identity that is particularly favorable to intermarriage and to the integration of neighbors compared with most other parts of the Hebrew Bible.

All this attention to economic concerns is hardly congenial to readers who turn to the Bible for ethics that they conceive as opposed to economics. Yet, Deuteronomy's laws are no manifesto for the unrestrained accumulation of capital. The struggles to increase available capital was "a response to ever-present uncertainty rather than a strategy for profit."[6] Deuteronomic brothers who lend to one another interest-free but at unlimited interest rates to foreigners and who require pledges when they lend to neighbors belong to an elite involved in trade like Assyrian merchants (*tamkāru*). Does that make them loan-sharks?[7] Are these merchants greedier than the Levitical priests who collect priestly dues? Does

---

6   Boer, *Sacred Economy*, 67.
7   As Boer, 156 calls them.

the fact that they are collected by Levitical priests save them from being ascribed to an evil extractive regime?

The priestly dues of chapter 18 and the calendar of Deuteronomy 16 belong to "attempts to include more and more within the orbit of priestcraft."[8] Yet, professional exegetes balk at the notion that the yearly tithes of Deuteronomy 14 are for the tithes payers and not for the Levites or priests. In this sense, biblical scholarship has "internalized the ideological justifications for extraction."[9] This internalization is a tribute to the Torah's scribal artistry that managed to append Deuteronomy's laws to Leviticus–Numbers while rendering readers oblivious to the tension between priestly dues and the Levite's slender prebends in Deuteronomy 14.

Challenging the justification for extraction leads to a recognition of the systematic reinterpretation of the dual tithing system in Deut 12, 16, 18 and 26. As a result, the tithes of chapter 14 are far less extractive than is the case elsewhere in the Hebrew Bible because they imply a mere 3.33% yearly tax burden for the producers. The dual tithing system is also more allocative than is the case elsewhere in the Hebrew Bible because it allocates a theoretical fourth of 3.33% to the *ger*, the widow and the orphan rather than unspecific amounts of alms. Would that make the dual tithing system less sacred than the exploitation of the farmers by priests, which Deuteronomy 12 and 18 present as compulsory and inevitable?

The Edomite brothers and Egyptian members of the *qehal-YHWH* represent a foreigner-friendly economic regime, though it sets no limits to the interest rates charged on loans non-Israelite borrowers. This does not make the *qehal-YHWH* a brotherhood of loan sharks because interest rates are simply a reflection of the risk taken by the lender, a risk that increases proportionally to the physical and social distance between lender and borrower.[10]

6.3 Humanitarian inequality?

Contrary to Boer, who warns that the biblical vision of survival is "no festival of equality,"[11] other scholars tend to equate justice with equality of means. For instance, Ronald Simkins argues that "economic inequality has been built on capitalist's appropriation of labor and natural resources without any, or sufficient, exchange. Workers must be compensated

---

8 Boer, 142.
9 Boer, 142.
10 Jursa, *Aspects*, 490–92.
11 Boer, *Sacred Economy*, 81.

adequately for their labor with a just and equitable share in the business that their labor has built."[12]

Deuteronomy's guidelines for the regulation of human activities and the arbitration of conflicts provides no indication for what might represent just and equitable remunerations for labor, or for any form of capital for that matter. It simply relies on what Adam Smith later designated as the invisible hand of the market. There is no need to conceive ancient Levantine economies in modern terms to accept the existence of price fluctuations as adjustments to offer and demand, especially in the realm of market exchange in long-distance trade.[13] Edomite and Egyptian brothers, loans to foreigners, weight and measures are clues that the Deuteronomic writers presupposed the existence of extra-regional trade and exchange that offered opportunities for welfare maximization besides the existence of an internal credit and labor market.

There is no market for land and the single verse on the prohibition to move landmarks (Deut 19:14) deals with the flimsy delimitation of strips of communal arable land allocated to each household, landmarks that are easily moved because the location, size, and number of strips are subject to regular redistribution.[14] Arable land is not a commodity, contrary to labor for which a market exists. Workers may be hired for ploughing, weeding and harvesting.

The credit market includes loans between brothers (Deut 15:1–11; 23:20; 24:6.10–13.17), loans to foreigners, loans to neighbors and to widows, each granted on specific conditions. The labor of Hebrews is a commodity, a medium of exchange in the form of workdays that serve to reimburse loans contracted into by their initial hirer (§2.3.3).

Besides the work done by Hebrews, the labor market includes runaway slaves (23:16–17), day laborers (24:14) and corvées provided by subdued cities (Deut 20:11). All household members—including slaves and children—contribute to the production of basic necessities and surpluses. The thriving matrimonial market is a subcategory of the labor market. Divorce and remarriage are conceived as frequent. Only remarrying a wife one has previously divorced is prohibited (Deut 24:1–4). As additional or second rank wives, war captives (§1.3.4 Deut 21:10–14), and wives who did not produce a heir before the death of their husband (Deut 25:5–10) contribute labor and offspring for the household they are attached to. The wealth at the disposal of each household is the measure of the honor and rank it enjoys in Israel, which in turn defines the amount of capital to be exchanged when sons and daughters are married.

12 Simkins, *Creation & Ecology*, 290.
13 Hudson, "Review of *Macroeconomics*," 120.
14 Guillaume, *Land*, 28–52.

Triennial tithes ensure minimal redistribution as there is no attempt to attain economic equality. Credit is the answer for the needs of those who are credit-worthy, charity for those in dire straights, with no illusion about the eradication of all forms of want (Deut 15:11). Inequality of means is a prerequisite for the survival of the entire society thanks to a limited redistribution that reduces the most blatant needs without striving to attain equality of means. On the contrary, the economy relies on a general desire and hope of betterment of one's circumstances, a hope that is never entirely fulfilled and is often disappointed. Impecunious laborers may find self-indenture preferable to freedom. The inhabitants of vanquished cities are sold in slavery. The wealthy are not immune to reversals of fortune. Unfortunate brothers need to be bailed out by their creditors (Deut 15:2). The unequal distribution of wealth ensures minimal redistribution in the form of tithes, debt release and alms and prevents general collapse.

6.4 Human capital

6.4.1 Households

The harshness of economic realities is best illustrated by the execution of a prodigal son at the request of his own parents (Deut 21:22–23). It underlines the value attributed to the household, the basic unit upon which all of Israel is built. A drunken son squanders goods instead of working hard to produce them. He depletes stores and threatens his family's creditworthiness. His behavior is a taint on the family's name, a capital as crucial as stores of grain, wine, oil, animals, and silver. One must strive to accumulate economic capital and strive again to preserve the social capital of the family.

A family's social capital is epitomized in the reputation of its daughters because the value of their suitors is a reliable measure of the family's social standing. For this reason, the damage done by the accusing husband is described in Deuteronomy 22:19 as "entering a bad name on a daughter of Israel" (הוציא שם רע על בתולה ישראל). The accusations taint the family's name as much as the behavior of the drunken son and sexual misbehavior (22:13–29).[15]

---

15 "Name" is preferred here to "honor", once a popular concept that postulated the existence of a honor code applicable to the Mediterranean worlds. See Pina-Cabral, "Mediterranean as Category," 399–406; Busatta, "Honour and Shame," 75–78.

Besides these measures to preserve or restore the family's name and repute, nine verses delineate ways to gain social capital. The *maqom* reunions are public displays of the size and composition of the household. The number of servants, slaves, sons, and daughters is as significant as the amount of tithes (Deut 14:22–29) and the conformation of firstlings (Deut 15:19–22). The one-year exemption from public duties granted every time a man takes a new wife gives both partners a chance to gain honor from the birth of children (Deut 24:5).

As direct indicators of credit-worthiness and indirect indicators of power, the size of the household depends much on the number of wives, the more the better it seems. Non-Israelite war captives make perfectly acceptable Israelite wives as long as they are desirable (21:10–14). Raping unattached Israelite girls is another possible source of wives, as long as the fine is paid to their fathers (22:28–29). Having witnesses at hand to confirm the rape discovered *in flagrante delicto* placates the *pro forma* objections the girl's father would raise to save face in front of the village. Proof of non-consent preserves the girl's honor as much as her family's and provides the raped girl a life-long insurance against divorce. In these conditions, rape was an insurance premium nubile girls of families of limited means may be willing to pay in order to enter the household of men able to pay the fifty-shekel silver fine to their father. Without denying the violence involved in the transaction, the violence done to the young woman could, in some cases, function as a convenient cover-up for the pre-arranged connivence between raper and raped. Compared with the parallel in Exodus 22:15–16 that allows the father of the raped girl the option to take the fine but retain the daughter, Deuteronomy condones the well attested practice of bride abduction.[16]

Widows and divorcees are freely available for remarriage. The wife of the dead partner should be married despite the likely loss it entails for the other heirs (Deut 25:5–11; §2.1.11). The reluctant partner is to be publicly shamed, something families would avoid at any cost to preserve their honor and good name (Deut 25:9–10).

In addition to secondary wives, slaves could also be acquired on the cheap, either by welcoming runaways (Deut 23:16–17) or through simple kidnapping except at the expense of another brother (Deut 24:7). Contrary to Exodus 21:4 and Leviticus 25:44–46, Deuteronomy does not consider the matter of children born from female slaves, though that does not mean that the writers were unaware of such outcomes. They may have simply considered that the children of slaves belonged to the owner of their mother—whoever the father might have been.

---

16 See bibliography in Guillaume, *Waiting for Josiah*, 219–29.

As domestic strife increases with the number of wives and servants, divorce and remarriage are expected, the only limitation being remarriage of the same previous wife (Deut 24:3-4). As the matter of children is not evoked, one possible motivation for this limitation is the evidence of her sterility after successive marriages. As mothers compete with one another for the position of their sons, the eldest heir is to receive a double share, whatever the status of his mother (21:15-17). The likely implication of the double share is that all the other sons are to receive one share regardless of the status of their mothers. Tensions within large households are expected to the point that brawls between adult men are considered inevitable, if not normal or even honorable ways to cleanse a personal offense, as duels were in later times. The intervention of wives in such brawls is expected, but a limit is placed on the grabbing of testicles. Though an expedient means for any loving wife to rescue (להציל) her husband from the grip of her husband's opponent, a victory obtained in such a way is shameful, presumably because of the risk of castrating the opponent who would consequently be unable to sire children. The honor of the winner's family could only be restored by the maiming of the grabbing wife (25:11-12), another dent in Deuteronomy's humanitarian thrust. The avoidance of vows and the ban on astral worship complete the array of measures seeking to avoid spendings on non-essentials away from the *maqom* festivities.

6.4.2 Neighborhood

Disputes with neighbors are as detrimental to a healthy local economy as is domestic strife. Local communities use their autonomy to suppress strife. The death penalty is also required for the kidnapping, exploitation or sale of the dependents of a brother (24:7) and for premeditated murder (19:11-13). Other crimes are punished with flogging. The limitation of the number of lashes for a brother is motivated as much—if not more—by the damage done in the eyes of others (נקלה אחיך לעיניך) and thus to the family's name, as to the health of the wrongdoer himself (25:1-3).

Special loans (not gifts!) to widows and generous gleanings (24:19-22) produce social capital and contribute to a good name. The treading ox (Deut 25:4) illustrates the principle of generosity towards laborers, as does letting harvesters feed on the harvest (23:25-26). Social capital is also gained by displays of generosity towards the variety of social conditions covered by the title of *ger*—residing foreign delegates (*ubāru*, see §2.3.5), special guests granted *proxenia* (§3.1.5), the sons of non-Israelite men born from Israelite women, resident Hebrews (male and female), and other individuals living on the margins of any society.

6.4.3 Upstarts: *gerim* and slaves

Gerim are conspicuous in your gates but not in the *qehal-YHWH*. Despite the reminder that Israel was a *ger* in Egypt (Deut 23:8b), it is as brothers, i.e., equal partners that Edomites and third generation Egyptians operate within the *qehal-YHWH*. At the *maqom*, the *ger* is sometimes there as a guest.[17] In your gates, he cohabits with Israelite brothers and neighbors. As argued above (§2.3.5), the status of *ger* covers a number of economic conditions. It is non-Israelite status rather than poverty that characterizes the *ger*.

The notion that Deuteronomy builds a distinctive Israelite identity in avoidance of non-Israelites may be correct for the book as a whole,[18] but not for its core. Nevertheless, the parallel notion that Deuteronomy promotes the integration of those who are socially and economically marginalized within Israel is correct,[19] as long as the emphasis is placed on the *socially* marginalized. The integration of the *economically* marginalized is more problematic. It is too reminiscent of the old theological credo of Israel's exceptionalism—and of its modern avatar of Israel as extraordinarily progressive in its treatment of the lower classes—to be taken as granted.[20] A thrust towards the integration of the *economically* marginal is likely if those who have the power to foster the integration can expect to gain from it. What gains would the integration of the economically marginalized represent for anyone producing a set of laws in favor of the poor?

The matter of poverty and need is discussed at length above (§2.4). The admission that need—if not poverty—will remain in the land (Deut 15:11) shows that the integration of the economically marginalized was not the writers' primary concern. The integration of the socially marginalized is another matter.

A significant will to promote demographic growth has been identified in the war laws (§§1.4–6). Opening the matrimonial market to desirable war captives who are preserved from subsequent repudiation displays much concern for offspring and little concern for the preservation of a distinctive Israelite identity.[21] Certain *gerim* and slaves can play a similar role for Israelite women. As upfront as Deuteronomy is about marrying war captives, nothing indicates that the writers would consider affluent *gerim* (see §2.4.2) and successful slaves unsuitable suitors for Israelite

17 Deut 12:18 LXX instead of the Levite; 16:11.14; 26:11; but not in 14:22–26.
18 Crouch, *Making*, 218.
19 Crouch, *Making*.
20 Against Faust, *Israelite Society*, 116–22, 247–48. Noth, *History*, 2–3.
21 The law of the first born (21:15–17) is all the more significant if young men married a captive before having the means to marry a cousin.

women, in particular divorcees and bereaved wives. This is what happens in reality as a result of cohabitation with foreigners, i.e., slaves and *gerim* in your gates.[22] Trade ventures within the *qehal-YHWH* would also foster the exchange of daughters between Israelite and Edomite partners. Granted entry in the *qehal-YHWH*, the third generation Egyptian represents a *socially* marginalized person on his way to full integration. The status of his sons might hardly differ from that of Israelites, in particular when born from Israelite mothers.

As nothing indicates that the sons borne by foreign war captives were deprived of the status of son of Israel, there is little reason to consider that the writers would have agreed with the repudiation of foreign wives (Ezra 10; Neh 13). On the contrary, the list of booty taken from a besieged city that refused the terms of peace includes all women as booty along with the children, livestock and any other valuables found in the conquered city (Deut 20:14). Whatever their marital status when they were taken, female prisoners of war and their children are too precious to be wasted. The women deemed the best might be married (Deut 21:10–14, §1.3.4), the others enslaved by their captor or sold (Deut 24:7 see §1.3.5).[23]

The premium placed on reproduction does not imply the rejection of the common cultural preference for endogamous marriages. It simply implies that the preference was relaxed for second rank wives. Repudiated and bereaved women would seek remarriage (see Deut 25:7) and take the initiative as the wife of the dead brother does in Deuteronomy 25:9 where she shames the reluctant suitor in public. The text does not tell of the fate of the wife of the dead brother once she bore a son to raise the name of her deceased husband, but it is quite possible that the birth of a heir for the dead brother frees the woman to contract another marriage.[24]

---

22   A freed slave and a convert is equal to all Muslims after three generations. See Wilkinson, "Bayasirah and Bayadir," 74.

23   After the slaughter of the Heshbonites including women and children (Deut 2:34), the Deuteronomic frame including chapter 12 does not specify the slaughter of Canaanite women. Of course, it is presupposed in the *ḥerem* in Deut 7:2, but the prohibition of intermarriage in verse 3 (לא תתחתן בם) is superfluous if no Canaanite women are left alive. Chapter 12 remains equally silent over the fate of these women, focusing instead on the destruction of Canaanite altars, as though the force of chapters 20–25 was persuasive enough to prevent the writers from contradicting them frontally.

24   Verse 6 focuses on the firstborn son (הבכור), which suggests that the union between the wife of the dead with the surviving brother is intended to be temporary. The LXX suggests that much with the use of the verb συνοικέω in verse 5 instead of γαμβρεύω in Gen 38:8 that evokes a more permanent union than mere cohabitation.

Men of marginal status such as *gerim* and slaves would seek strategic unions with widowed and divorced Israelite women of higher social status as such marriages would improve their *social* standing. In this sense, privileged *gerim* and slaves represent practical kin.[25] In exchange, such a marriage improves the *economic* standing of the woman in proportion to the means of her new husband.[26] Social and economic status do not always go together. It is a collateral damage of the *personae miserae* cliché to consider that having the status of a *ger* implies poverty. Servitude and dependance accommodate varying levels of autonomy. The slaves of a powerful master had more opportunities to improve their economic condition than some freeborn men.

Instead of preserving ethnic boundaries, Deuteronomy's laws foster the integration of non-Israelites through matrimony. Within a few generation, Israel would count a number of *gerim* and sons of *gerim* in its ranks.

6.5 The Deuteronomic *Mensch* as model Israelite

The singular "you", the addressee of the core of the core, portrays an elite wealthy enough to be involved in long-term credit transactions with equals and short-term ones with neighbors. These men (capitalists?) have the means to feed extra mouths such as runaway slaves joining their workforce and self-indentured servants entering their households permanently. They have the ability to put these extra mouths to good use, something beyond the capacity of ordinary farmers as Polony's decline of Boaz's offer illustrates (Ruth 4:6).

The core of Deuteronomy's core thus portrays a virtuous man. Virtue is what makes the man, and what differentiates the ordinary man from the *Mensch*, a Yiddish term implying integrity and honor, used today to embody the qualities expected from leaders.[27] The *Mensch* has a large household, numerous herds, flocks, beasts of burden (Deut 22:1–4) and clients. All are well managed. In the Bible, his name would be Job (Job 1–2; 42). His friends come from afar. They enter his home for business involving large sums invested in joint ventures. The *Mensch* inspires confidence. He enjoys a good reputation. Wealth and reputation do not always go together, but a *Mensch* commands both. Wealth inspires confidence. Wealth both opens doors and keeps the door of the wealthy open. The *Mensch*

---

25 Bourdieu, *Outline*, 33–34.
26 For much later examples of remarriage as a strategy for social integration and economic betterment, see Glassman, *Social Rebellion and Swahili Culture*, chapter 4. Glassman, "Sorting out the Tribes"; Goitein, *Mediterranean Society*.
27 Martinuzzi, *Leader as a Mensch*.

readily opens a charitable hand to the needy (15:7–11), gives carrion to the *ger* (14:21) and makes sure to leave generous gleanings. Clients and beggars contribute to the good standing of the *Mensch*.

The neighborhood is unaware of any internecine quarrels or rumors of indecent behavior within his household, despite the number of wives, children, servants, and slaves living in his compound (Prov 31:10–31). As he does not cheat over field boundaries and weights, his neighbors readily buy from him and lend a helping hand as they know from experience that he will reciprocate by sending some of his dependents when they need help with their own harvests. When conflicts arise in the village, they turn to him for advice and arbitration.

As he pays fair wages at sunset (24:14–15), day laborers come from afar to work in his fields and to fetch wood (19:5). Or they come to work for him to repay an old debt he had helped them settle by advancing seeds, silver or livestock. When they eventually manage to repay what they owe him, he celebrates the end of the contract with gifts (15:14). If misfortune persists, they consider it a privilege to enter his reputable household permanently (15:16–17).

The *Mensch* is a role model embodied up to a point by the powerful men who form the backbone of many functional human societies. The man addressed as brother in Deuteronomy's core is akin to the wise man in biblical wisdom texts.

The Deuteronomic *Mensch* is a little too perfect to be true, but he is the kind of man whom any Israelite would want as a father-in-law. In theory, the sons of Aaron would represent even better figures, except that the Torah's priests guard their privileges by choosing their spouses from their own circle (Lev 21:14). To ordinary Israelites, the son of a *Mensch* is a desirable option; the sons of Aaron a wild dream. In other words, Exodus–Numbers offer no one with whom an ordinary Israelite might identify. The priests request their tithes by impressing upon the ordinary Israelite the fear-inducing gap that separates him from his god, a gap the priests insist on being the only ones capable of bridging. On the contrary, the Deuteronomic core is an invitation to eat one's tithes in the company of YHWH and all Israelites in mutual emulation of the *Mensch* role model.

Had the Deuteronomic core imagined an Israel where all men were brothers and equal, the *Mensch* would hardly function as a model to emulate. On the contrary, the core underlines the difference between ordinary farmers and those involved in trade besides common agricultural activities. Credit conditions differ if the borrower or lender is a brother, a neighbor (Israelite or *ger*), a widow, or a foreigner. Regular practice of the *šemiṭṭah* ensures that poverty does not prevail within the brotherhood. Poverty, however, persists in the land, a powerful motivation to behave as a *Mensch* in the hope of joining the brotherhood.

6.6 Practical effects of the model

Public shows of extravagant consumption, the execution of one's own prodigal son, the welcome of runaway slaves, and the abduction of virgins underline the importance of social capital. Being rich is not enough. The accumulation of grain and silver is dangerous when some of it is not converted into social capital.

Hence, it is ignominious to stay at home and not throw a big party at the *maqom*. It is utterly shameful to tolerate the presence of a drunken son in one's household. "Honor killing" is the solution because the protection of the family name prevails over the interests of the individual.

Within the household, extra-conjugal sexual intercourse is not an issue. Outside it is a crime. The blood of culprits must flow to remove taints on the reputation of offended households, depending where the crime occurred and on the marital status of the victim—married (Deut 22:22) or merely promised (Deut 22:23–27).

No blood is required for the rape of a girl for whom no matrimonial arrangements have yet been settled because it is impossible to ascertain the absence of connivance. Intercourse could have been consensual and both benefit from the doubt. The name of the girl is unblemished because her cries could not be heard, while the rapist clears his name by marrying the girl, never to repudiate her (22:28–29). Nevertheless, the rape is a taint on the family that has failed to protect its unmarried daughter, the most valuable embodiment of the family's social capital. Therefore, the rapist pays fifty shekels to the girl's father to compensate him for the injury he inflicted on the family. The abducted girl enters the household of a man rich enough to pay the fine and she obtains a life insurance against repudiation. The case of an impecunious rapist is ignored because the Deuteronomic *Mensch* is either rich enough to pay the penalty or wise enough to abstain from any such act.

The case of a jealous husband presents a counter-example with a hundred-shekel penalty and the same loss of the right to repudiate, enough to silence most aggrieved husbands because a bloodied sheet is always at hand as counter-proof. Whatever happens after marriage, the *Mensch* does not go back on his word. He grants a double portion to his first-born son, whatever his feelings towards the wife who bore his first son (21:15–17).

Slaves are another domain in which the *Mensch* proves his mettle. Deuteronomy ignores the case of the slave owner who injures or kills his own slave (Exod 21:20–21) but condones the welcome of runaway slaves who are granted the extraordinary luxury of deciding which household they want to enter. This case underlines a hierarchy of forms of capital. The number of slaves is one indicator of the household's net worth, but economic capital is subservient to social capital. It is better to own a single slave who stays than many slaves who require constant supervision and beatings to deter escape. Besides the simple fact that willing slaves and employees are more productive, the escape of a slave is a taint on the owner's repute as much as on his wealth. The runaway slave proves that his owner is no *Mensch.* The escape is an ignominy for the master, a loss of reputation that adds to the loss of workforce.

In an ideal world, all slaves would have escaped harsh masters and found asylum in the households of generous ones. As a mere theoretical principle, the idea that runaway slaves ought to be granted asylum rather than being forcefully returned to their master constitutes a serious warning against the harsh treatment of slaves. In real conditions, losing a slave would be a clue, if not a proof, of mismanagement as damning for the household as any drunken son in its midst. Would the slave master report his loss to the elders at the gate of his town?

This is what seems to have been the standard procedure at Babylon when a slave had escaped. It was reported immediately and Hammurabi's laws threaten with the death penalty anyone hiding or not producing a runaway slave when the alarm was raised (CH 15–16, 19).[28] What would the slighted owner of Deuteronomy 23 do? Would he raise the alarm? What should the elders do when the escapee seeks asylum in their town?

The case of the prophet in Deuteronomy 18 is key: that prophet claimed he spoke in the name of YHWH but what he foretold did not occur. Therefore, verse 22 argues that the prophet spoke presumptuously (בזדון) a word in YHWH's name that YHWH had (obviously) not spoken because it did not turn out as foretold. The point is that instead of blaming the prophet, the fault lies with the person who trusted the prophet, which is the reason not to "be frightened by it" (NRSV) or afraid of him (לא תגור ממנו). The prophet is not liable, his oracle turned out to be useless to the person who asked for it. The elders at the gate would not even consider a complaint lodged against this prophet. Only a fool would approach the elders with such a complaint. He would be publicly rebuffed and ridiculed, becoming a byword in the entire community.

Hammurabi's and Deuteronomy's slave-laws indicate that slave theft existed in Babylon as much as in Israel. Neither Hammurabi nor Deuteronomy threaten the slave, but Deuteronomy threatens the slave owner rather than the asylum giver. The question of practicality is hardly relevant. Hammurabi's threats are not necessarily more effective in curbing the escape of slaves than Deuteronomy's threat of loss of face. In practice, some slaves will get beaten, some will escape—in Israel as much as

---

28 Richardson, *Hammurabi's Laws*, 47–48.

in Babylon. It is impossible to ascertain whether runaway slaves would be a more prevalent phenomenon in Israel than in Babylon. Deuteronomy is simply more economical in its treatment of the problem than Hammurabi.

In what appears to be an effort to enhance the efficacy of his threats, Hammurabi adds a reward of two shekels of silver for the return of a lost slave (CH 17).[29] Loopholes remain, so Hammurabi then considers the case of the captor of a runaway slave who escaped again before the captor could return the slave to its owner. In this case, the careless captor is to swear a solemn oath "by the god to the slave's owner" (CH 20) to clear himself from the suspicion that he was harboring a runaway slave with the intent of passing him or her on to an accomplice.[30] Deuteronomy simply puts the blame onto the slave owner and dispenses itself from the need to consider loopholes, an endless task that keeps legislators busy adapting regulations to ever new challenges.

Whereas Hammurabi opens his code by charging those who make unsubstantiated allegations with the penalty that would have applied had the accusations been substantiated (CH 1–4), Deuteronomy insists on personal liability (Deut 24:16).[31] The example of the death penalty (איש בחטו יומתו) is applicable to all cases. Personal guilt is not soluble within the group: "Parents shall not be put to death for their children, nor shall children be put to death for their parents" (NRSV). Personal guilt is not mitigated by appealing to corporate guilt.

Personal liability increases individual responsibility, a mark of the *Mensch* ethos. Deuteronomy ignores unsubstantiated allegations because the number of admissible complaints is sharply reduced. Impartiality is required when the evidence is strong enough to require the arbitration of a lawsuit (Deut 16:18–20). The *Mensch*, however, abstains from disclosing many of the wrongs he may have suffered, seeking private arbitration and avoiding public disclosure. Quibbling, pettifogging and insisting on one's right is unworthy of the *Mensch* who makes the first move towards resolving a dispute, magnanimously going the extra mile, *noblesse oblige*.

Repute is far more valuable than rights. When victim of a heinous crime, the *Mensch* insists on the prompt return of the corpse of the executed criminal to its family (Deut 21:22–23). The pedagogical exemplarity of public punishments is lost if the execution feeds a desire for revenge within the clan of the criminal. The same principle of benevolence applies to floggings (Deut 25:1–3). The *Mensch* has more to gain from asking

---

29   Richardson, 49.
30   Richardson.
31   Richardson, 41–43.

the judge to reduce the number of lashes than by insisting on the harshest possible punishment.

6.7 Beyond common usage

The *Mensch* model may provide an alternative to the question of whether the Deuteronomic core reflects actual practice or a utopian ideology. To escape the dilemma, Milstein proposes that the Deuteronomic laws represent a deviation from common law.[32] Milstein got her cue from clay tablets found in Late Bronze Emar that record the testamentary dispositions of men who willed their estate to their wives or daughters.[33] Tablets were probably drawn up because such dispositions differed from common usage. Contestation could be expected from the other parties that would appeal to custom to establish their rights as heirs, hence the need to produce a tablet.

The implication is that the Deuteronomic laws were not meant to regulate practice by listing obligations and prohibitions known to everyone because they were customary. On the contrary, the Deuteronomic laws encourage comportments that depart from the unwritten rules of common law. Good, normal practice is not the issue. What Deuteronomy calls for is best practice, beyond the ordinary. It sets down a practical model that differs significantly from accepted mores. The *Mensch* is expected to go beyond the call of duty and beyond what is merely acceptable.

Therefore, the Deuteronomic *mišpaṭim*[34] are practical illustrations of the behavior of a model Israelite. They do not consider all possibilities or deal with all known loopholes. They list examples to inspire behavior that goes against the natural preference for options that involve less effort and promise immediate gratification. In this sense, the *Mensch* ethos recalls the old notion of Israelite exceptionalism, a notion that erred by taking biblical laws as descriptions of practice instead of models.[35] Yet, it would be equally erroneous to assume that Deuteronomy can merely be regarded as a utopian project. In fact, the *Mensch* model was and still is the backbone of most Near Eastern societies, if not beyond. Hence, it is not Israel that was exceptional, it was and still is the elite that provides the backbone of these societies, societies that survive crises because the

---

32 Milstein, "Will," 53.
33 Démare-Lafont, "Éléments," 52–53: "*volonté de déroger au droit commun.*"
34 Rendered as "decisions, judgement, dispute, case, legal claim, measure, blueprint, law" (*HALOT* 2:651–52).
35 Noth, *History*, 2–3.

non-elite know to whom to turn when needed. They know which door to knock at because the elite must display their riches.

To be rich is not enough to be awarded elite status. Riches have to be shared. The ordinary rich are sharks (§1.3.3), but Deuteronomy ignores sharks because the *Mensch* ethos sets the Deuteronomic brother on a footing above the average.

Deuteronomy's *Mensch* is rich and the tithes he brings at the *maqom* prove it. Being rich, he is respected and envied by his peers and by the rank and file that may well see him as a loan shark. Yet, bringing less than a theoretical ten percent of the yearly yield of his household at the *maqom* to avoid exciting envy would be as bad as not turning up at all. The Deuteronomic core envisages no egalitarian utopia.[36] The Deuteronomic core relies on an elite of rich patrons for *kol* Israel to prosper. In times of need, the purported loan shark is expected to intervene. He taps his stores to provide seed and food to the rank and file who must put away pride and be thankful. The purported loan shark must remit the arrears of a brother after seven years, but he is free to go beyond his legal obligations and remit the arrears of a neighbor at any time.

Therefore, the distinction between the Deuteronomic brother and the ordinary Israelite is fundamental. The Deuteronomic *Mensch* can only offer a viable model for Israel as a whole if his daily practice is significantly above what is expected from ordinary Israelites.

6.8 Results of the focus on tithes

Scholarship has downplayed the tension between the passages that delineate priestly prebends and the dual tithing system of Deuteronomy 14:22–29 that seriously curtails them. Yet, this tension points to the existence of a previous version of the Deuteronomic laws that limited the support of its Levite to a share of the social relief stored in your gates. Such a limitation is coherent with the fact that Deuteronomy grants no revenues to the king or to the House of YHWH (Deut 23:18). The coherence, however, is missed when Deuteronomy's *maqom* is conceived as Jerusalem and a cypher for its temple. In this case, it is so obvious that some—if not most—of the annual tithes brought to the *maqom* are set apart for the priesthood, that it was not necessary to note it. This kind of *argumentum ex silentio* is what makes a scholarly consensus and ensures

---

36   In fact, the double share granted as birthright (Deut 21:17) fosters inequality in order to secure the elite status of a father for one of his heir. Compare Hammurabi §170 that merely grants the eldest son first choice of equalized shares. See Richardson, *Hammurabi's Laws*, 95.

its faithful reproduction over two centuries as happened with de Wette's hypothesis.

As long as the *maqom* is conceived as the temple at Jerusalem, these tithes are obviously brought there to feed the priests. Once the obvious is not obvious anymore, the dual tithing system of Deuteronomy 14:22–29 sticks out like a sore thumb. If the sacrifices are delivered at the *maqom* to feed the priests (and YHWH), the stern warning in Deuteronomy 12:19 that these offerings are to be brought to the *maqom* makes sense. The beneficiaries of the foodstuffs seek to curtail tax evasion by the farmers who might bring less than required to the *maqom*. If, however, the tithes brought to the *maqom* are consumed entirely by the tithes payers, as Deuteronomy 14:22–26 states explicitly, the farmers are likely to bring more than required rather than less.

The warning not to abandon the Levite in Deuteronomy 14:27 is immediately answered by granting the Levite a share of triennial tithes in your gates. On the contrary, the similar warning in Deuteronomy 12:19 is a protest that a share of triennial tithes is insufficient.

Deuteronomy mentions no Jerusalem and only once a House of YHWH (23:18), to which it forbids to offer prostitution fees. It is with the help of echoes of holocausts, offerings and festivals from Leviticus 23 and elsewhere that Deuteronomy 12 and 16 shore up the Levite's presence at the *maqom* festivities. Then, the priestly dues of 18:1–8 further contradict the dual tithing system by granting the Levites equal shares with Levitical priests who arrive at the *maqom* out of the blue because neither Deuteronomy 12, 14 or 16 mention any Levitical priests there. It is only in chapter 26 that a synthesis somewhat integrates the dual tithing system into a broader presentation of the *maqom* feasts with a single priest who merely receives a basket of first fruits for hearing an oath that all triennial tithes were duly delivered in your gates. This priest does not state that the other tithes brought to the *maqom* are for the maintenance of the temple and for the upkeep of his family and those of Levitical priests.

Instead of integrating the dual tithing system into a coherent presentation of the *maqom* festivities, Deuteronomy 12; 16; 18:1–8; and 26 add details upon details that blur the clear differentiation between yearly and triennial tithes in Deuteronomy 14:22–29, without ever challenging the notion that yearly tithes are for the enjoyment of the tithe payers. Hence, the dual tithing system of chapter 14 remains an erratic bloc in the Torah's overall presentation of YHWH's cult.

Instead of arguing from silence, Part II has thus read Deuteronomy 12; 16; 18:1–8; and 26 as part of a effort to align Deuteronomy's laws with the previous books of the Pentateuch and make it Torah compatible. That Deuteronomy 12; 16; 18:1–8; and 26 rely on echoes of passages in Exodus, Leviticus and Numbers (calendars, sacrifices, priestly prebends) to increase the revenues of the priesthood supports the contention that these chapters oppose the dual tithing system that grants the lion's share of the tithes to the tithes payers as an incentive to join the feast.

Other less extensive passages were probably inserted into previous versions of the Deuteronomic Code, but no attempt to identify secondary material besides Deuteronomy 12; 16; 18:1–8; and 26 have been made here because that would inevitably end up with hypothetical delimitations due to the lack of reliable criteria once the historical anchor of Josiah's cultic reform is abandoned.

Nevertheless, the outcome of Part I and Part II ought to be tested against recent proposals on the origins of the Deuteronomic Code.

PART III

PROBING THE HISTORY OF THE DEUTERONOMIC CORE

CHAPTER 7
URDEUTERONOMIUM AFTER DE WETTE

Limiting YHWH's cult to one centralized location has long been held as something particularly innovative if not revolutionary in Deuteronomy.[1] Read in the framework of the Josianic reform, Deuteronomy's centralization is revolutionary if Josiah obeyed Deuteronomy's command to close local sanctuaries and compensate the disenfranchised Levites with positions at the Jerusalem temple. This is probably how the writers of the story of Josiah's reform interpreted Deuteronomy, but it has no bearing on the formation of the Deuteronomic legal collection itself.

Therefore, this final chapter considers the results obtained of the previous parts in light of recent proposals regarding the origins of Deuteronomy 12–26.

7.1 A matter of linchpins (Bill Arnold)

Arnold provides a convenient overview of the Deuteronomic innovations based on Kilchör's identification of the Deuteronomic *Sondergut* (§4.1), which he generally accepts as valid.[2] Arnold recognizes the exultant character of the celebrations at the *maqom* as a most innovative element in Deuteronomy though he regards Braulik's festive theory as an overstatement.[3] Other Deuteronomic innovations include:

- Humanitarian concern for the *personae miserae* and the non-Jerusalem Levite.
- Lending laws to protect destitute brother-Israelites.
- Altruism extended to the runaway slave.
- Essential fairness to the owner of standing crops, newly weds, treading oxen, mother birds, field boundaries, corpses, flogging, conquered cities, fruit trees, female captives, heirs of polygamous families and the widow's essential implements.

---

1   Wellhausen, *Prolegomena*, 33–34.
2   Arnold, "Innovations," 164.
3   Arnold, 181; See Braulik, "Joy," 27–65.

- Honesty in court proceedings, witness and unsolved murder.
- Acceptance of royal institutions qualified by abhorrence of Canaanite practices.

Innovative as they are in regard to the other biblical legal collections, these Deuteronomic innovations are less innovative compared to other ancient Near Eastern corpora that equally insist on the requirements of fairness in legal proceedings and the protection of property.

As discussed previously (§3.4.1), setting the legitimate place of the Levite in your gates, a point the framing reiterates in Deuteronomy 26:12, keeps Levites away from the *maqom*, despite the mitigation of the Levite's confinement in chapters 12, 16 and 18. The central point is the hegemony of the priesthood. Humanitarianism is more problematic.

As discussed already, no lending laws, as humanitarian as they may be, can ever protect the destitute (§2.1.13). As nothing indicates that the runaway slave is manumitted upon arrival in Israel, self-interest offsets altruism. Welcoming a runaway slave is a direct gain to his new owner and to the slave himself who is looking for a better master. The interests of the owner from whom the slave escaped are ignored (§1.3.5).

The purported humanitarian thrust of Deuteronomy's approach to nestlings, war captives, and rebellious sons is equally motivated by self-interest. These are minor issues of vocabulary compared with the main conclusion that arises from Arnold's analysis of Deuteronomic innovations.

There is no doubt that the centralization of the cult is important, but the lack of connection of the other purported innovations with the theme of centralization is striking. The "centralization of the cult is merely one subject among others in Deuteronomy."[4] Even the legal proceedings that take place at the *maqom* display no desire to suppress the autonomy of each locality in settling its own disputes.

Cultic centralization covers 40 verses of the 180 verses in Kilchör's *Sondergut*, a mere 22.22%.[5] The rest deals with matters that have nothing to do with the *maqom*. The disconnection between the central theme and the bulk of the literary material is blatant. The protection of the destitute, altruism, essential fairness, and honesty are relevant whether the cult is centralized or not.

The bulk of the innovations relevant to cultic centralization is found in chapter 12 with some echoes in chapters 16, 18 (verses 1–8). The rest

---

4   Levin, "Rereading," 50.
5   Deut 12:6–12.17–19.26.28 (22 verses) + Deut 14:22 (1 verse) + Deut 15:20–22 (3 verses) + Deut 16:2.5.12.14.17 (5 verses) + Deut 17:8–13 (6 verses) + Deut 18:6–8 (3 verses) = 40 verses.

of the core displays no influence from chapter 12. Arnold notes that Deuteronomy 12 may be understood as innovating the *maqom* festivities that were first conceived as they are presented in 14:22–29.[6] This is what Part II above has tried to demonstrate. Arnold, however, refuses to view in chapter 12 a secondary phase of the development of the Deuteronomic core. He takes Deuteronomy 12:2–28 "as the rhetorical cornerstone of the legal core".[7] Yet, nothing in Arnold's demonstration of the role of chapter 12 as the linchpin of the core discounts the presence of an older version of the core.[8]

It is remarkable that the concluding chapter of the core, the liturgy that crowns the framing process of the core of the core, echoes Deuteronomy 14:28–29 rather than chapter 12. Each Israelite swears that he has set apart the whole of his triennial tithes and given them for the Levite, the *ger*, the orphan, and the widow at the gate of his town (Deut 26:12). The oath is an innovation, but it reaffirms the presentation of the triennial tithes in Deuteronomy 14:28–29. Significantly, the oath is sworn in front of a priest, not in front of a Levite or of a Levitical priest, though the framing material strove to introduce them at the *maqom* festivities (Deut 12:12.18; 16:11.14; 17:9; 18:6).

As much as it synthesizes the innovations introduced by chapters 12, 16, and 18, chapter 26 pays homage to the dual tithing system of chapter 14. Instead of insisting on the privilege of the Levitical priest to collect dues at the *maqom* and at home (Deut 18:1–8), chapter 26 concludes with a reminder that the legitimate place of the Levite is not at the "Place", the *maqom*, but in your gates. A Levite may join the *maqom* festivities, but he remains a guest there. Hence, the main innovation of the Deuteronomic *Sondergut* as defined by Kilchör is not the centralization of the cult but the rise of a Levitical priesthood in control of all aspects of Israelite life, including the Crown.

Chapter 12 is thus the linchpin of the innovations introduced in the earlier version of the laws that confined the Levite in your gates and

---

6   Wellhausen, *Prolegomena*, 33–34: "Now, in this point also Deuteronomy has left the old custom, on the whole, unchanged. According to xiv. 22 seq. the tithe of the produce of the soil, or its equivalent in money, must be brought year by year to the sanctuary, and there consumed before Jehovah, that is, as a sacrificial meal; only every third year it is not to be offered in Jerusalem, but is to be given as alms to the people of the locality who have no land, to which category the Levites in particular belong. This last application is an innovation, connected on the one hand with the abolition of the sanctuaries, and on the other with the tendency of the Deuteronomist to utilize festal mirth for humane ends." Here, Wellhausen envisages not a previous version of Deuteronomy but an old custom.
7   Arnold, "Innovations," 165.
8   Arnold, "Israelite Worship," 161–75.

probably ignored other cultic specialists such as Levitical priests. Accepting Deuteronomy 14:22–15:23 as the linchpin of an earlier version of *Urdeuteronomium* challenges the standard Josianic scenario.

7.2 The trouble with a Manassite *Urdeuteronomium*

Arnold proposes a compositional history of Deuteronomy that begins before Josiah's reign:

1. A late eighth century BCE list of texts (ספרים) transcribed, compiled, expended, and invented from previous models and inspired by some version of the Book of the Covenant (oldest part Exod 21:1–22:16). This short list was motivated by social, political, and religious developments in Hezekiah's reign.
2. Seventh century scribes expanded the list with the *Sondergut*, introduced possibly by the *shema'* of Deuteronomy 6:4–5 [9] followed by 12:1–26:15*, i.e., *Urdeuteronomium*. What now became a proper document reacted to Manasseh's pro-Assyrian policies and was influenced by the Holiness school without directly copying Priestly texts.
3. *Urdeuteronomium* was expanded in a Josianic edition comprising Deuteronomy 4:44–28:69*, turning the previous statutes and ordinances into "this Torah".
4. A historical introduction and conclusion was added during the exilic era, thus amounting to a composition fairly similar to the current book of Deuteronomy.

According to Arnold, stage two was motivated by a conservative movement nostalgic for Hezekiah's reforms, which explains the use of Assyrian parallels in Deuteronomy 13 that make *Urdeuteronomium* an "essential call for loyalty to one YHWH in the face of Assyrian demands for loyalty and service". Altogether, the core would have contributed to shape "a community of YHWH loyalists". The innovative character of the humanitarian, altruistic, and fair measures of YHWH-serving people would shape the YHWH-serving Israel.

The presupposition is that the advocated measures were markedly different from actual practices in the days of Manasseh. That *Urdeuteronomium* fosters the acceptance of royal institutions on the basis of abhorrence of Canaanite practices implies that Canaanite practices are a cypher for Manasseh's Assyrianizing policies. This presupposition requires ascribing a high degree of historical reliability to the very negative assessment of Manasseh's reign in 2 Kings 21. In fact, the so-called humanistic thrust of Deuteronomy could have been used by any king to justify his policies. Had Hezekiah and Josiah prescribed greater levels of altruism and fairness to compensate the deleterious effects their reforms had for certain groups, Manasseh would have been as likely to prescribe them to foster the acceptance of his pro-Assyrian policies.

The most relevant part of the Deuteronomic *Sondergut* for a Manassite *Urdeuteronomium* would be the law of the king. It stands to reason that a conservative movement nostalgic for Hezekiah's reforms would have wished that royal policies were dictated by the Levitical priests. That they would do so by supplying a copy of a Torah scroll is, however, more difficult as it is most likely anachronistic for any part of the seventh century. The cultural level attained then in Jerusalem was advanced enough for a compilation such as *Urdeuteronomium*, but the notion of the Torah as a body of binding laws is problematic.

If so, the law of the king does not belong to the Deuteronomic *Sondergut* that Kilchör identified. Or *Urdeuteronomium* is several centuries later than Manasseh's days. This issue adds another layer of unsupported assumptions to the difficulties generated by de Wette's hypothesis with its focus on Jerusalem and its temple.

Among the innovations Arnold identifies in Deuteronomy 12 are

> the focus on eating in the presence of YHWH together with the whole household in joyful celebration, cf. vv. 7,12,17,18; (2) the inclusion of the male and female servants, and Levites for humanitarian reasons, cf. vv. 12, 18, 19; and (3) above all of course, the idea of centralization, vv. 8-11, 26. In addition, it might be observed that the stock Deuteronomic phraseology of "carefully hearing" the words being commanded, and the purpose clause, that "it may go well" may be another innovation of the chapter (v. 28).[9]

"Innovation" is correct inasmuch as it introduces new concepts, in particular priestly personnel designated as "Levitical priests". These innovations, however, are harmonizations because they introduce notions from the previous scrolls of the Pentateuch. In the framework of the Pentateuch, these harmonizations are not revolutionary. They are a return to biblical tradition, i.e., the notion that the reforms supposedly implemented by Hezekiah and Josiah were a return to the Mosaic heritage. If, as stated by Arnold, the critique of Manasseh's policies and the Josianic reform were the work of a movement nostalgic for Hezekiah's reforms, the attitude is conservative rather than innovative. According to the biblical scenario, Hezekiah's reform was motivated by a return to the ancestral practices prescribed by Moses and implemented by King David (2 Kgs 18:3–6).

---

9   Arnold, "Innovations," 166.

Arnold deviates from the biblical scenario when he reaches Hezekiah. Instead of claiming that Hezekiah returned to the Mosaic tradition of old, Arnold's scheme has the changes operated during Hezekiah's reign motivated by social, political, and religious developments. "Developments" can either be innovative or conservative. In an implicit shift from the literary to the historical level, what the Bible considers traditional becomes innovatory. The shift from the literary to the historical level is the consequence of de Wette's hypothesis and the fascination for the Josianic reform centered around the temple of Jerusalem read in light of the *maqom* festivities depicted in Deuteronomy 12.

As the turning point for the shift from tradition to innovation is the "event" of Hezekiah's reform according to 2 Kings 18, why not remain faithful to the biblical scenario? If the story of Hezekiah's "reform" in 2 Kings 18 is given that much historical credence, why not give as much credence to 2 Kings 17?

7.3 An Israelite cradle for the core of the Deuteronomic core (Philip Davies)

The fascination with Jerusalem produced a tunnel vision in Deuteronomic research. Arnold is oblivious to anything happening beyond the walls of Jerusalem. Hence, Arnold screens the reigns of Hezekiah, Manasseh, and Josiah for events motivating the rise of *Urdeuteronomium*, despite Deuteronomy's low valuation of the royal office, despite its systematic reference to Israel and the silence over Jerusalem and Judah.

Yet, Arnold accepts a significant influence from Israelite traditions, "from northern refugees".[10] That the notion of Israelite refugees in Hezekiah's Judah is fallacious has been convincingly demonstrated.[11] As building hypothesis upon hypothesis leads nowhere, these refugees are best avoided. The northern refugees are "an overly convenient means to explain how Judah absorbed northern traditions."[12]

7.3.1 The *maqom* in Samerina

An alternative to Israelite refugees fleeing advancing Assyrian troops about to storm Samaria in 720 BCE has been proposed by Philip Davies.[13]

---

10 See already Clements, "Jerusalem Cult Tradition," 300–312; Nicholson, *Deuteronomy and Tradition*.
11 Na'aman, "Myth of a Flood," 1–14.
12 Edenburg and Müller, "Northern Provenance," 157.
13 Davies, "Where Deuteronomy?" Already, Davies, "Josiah and the Law Book," 65–77.

Davies set the relevance of the strong Israelite identity thrust of the Deuteronomic core in Israel itself. Instead of a diffuse literary influence of northern traditions, Davies used the scenario of 2 Kings 17 as the backdrop of actual conditions pertaining in Samerina in the wake of the Assyrian take-over of Samaria in 722–720 BCE. In this way, the "penchant for hypothetical life settings" taken as reflections of particular historical realities "employed to reconstruct still more life settings for literary works" is cut short.[14]

Instead of a reaction to Manasseh's pro-Assyrian policies, the *maqom* pilgrimage and the delineation of Israelite mores answer the need to built a strong Israelite identity following the settlement of immigrants in Samerina. As biblical (2 Kgs 17) and Assyrian (Sargon)[15] sources agree over the settlement of non-Israelites in post-720 BCE Samerina, the hypothesis rests on firmer historical ground than any cultic reforms initiated by Judahite kings.

Whether or not the Assyrian king sent a deported priest back to Bethel to quench YHWH's wrath and placate the lions he plagued the immigrants with need not be taken literally (2 Kgs 17:25–28). As a story, it illustrates the need felt in Samerina to integrate the immigrants and create a shared Israelite identity that differed from the cultic practices mentioned in Deuteronomy 17:2–3 (animals inappropriate for sacrifice to YHWH) and 17:2–5 (common divinatory practices). Phrases such as "the land YHWH is giving you" (Deut 15:4; 19:10.14; 21:1; 23:20; 25:15) were as relevant to the newcomers as to the Israelites who were not deported.

According to Davies, the Exodus tradition "was already an intrinsic part of Israelite identity and so could not be effaced."[16] In fact, there was no need to efface the Exodus tradition. It was relevant to the new immigrants as much as to the old Israelites because being immigrants "is no bar to being Israelites. Rather, they can claim the land equally as theirs by divine gift."[17] Hence the references to the Exodus (Deut 15:4; 16:18; 17:2; 19:1–14; 21:1.23; 24:4; 25:15).

Davies' scenario for the rise of the earliest phase of Deuteronomy has the significant advantage of being anchored in a social-political context confirmed by biblical and Assyrian sources. The scope of Davies' scenario is limited to the rise of the core of the core. It does not explain the role

---

14   Edenburg and Müller, "Northern Provenance," 161.
15   See *CoS* II.293 and 298. Whether the people Sargon relocated were Arabs is irrelevant here. Byrne, "Assyrian Contacts," 12 considers that the Assyrians encountered the people they resettled in Samerina in southwestern Syria, Gilead or at the northern end of Wadi Sirhan.
16   Davies, "Where Deuteronomy?", 19.
17   Davies, 19.

of the Levites in the core of the core, contrary to the scenario proposed by Mark Christian.

7.3.2 Other proposals

For Christian, the Levites began as middle-tier cultic specialists subordinated to regional peers from the eighth century BCE until the Babylonian period. In Babylon, the Levites would have enjoyed a higher status. Therefore, their priestly-prophetic brand of Deuteronomism infiltrated elite priestly classes in Israel, a phenomenon that continued with Nehemiah's activities in Jerusalem in the latter part of the fifth century BCE and the increase in cultic activity there.[18] Such a scenario is more comprehensive than Davies', but far more hypothetical. What corroborating evidence is there for Levites in late monarchic Israel and in Babylon?

Sandra Richter presents another attempt to shake the Josianic yoke from the neck of Deuteronomic scholarship. She claims that "the genesis of *Urdeuteronomium* cannot be located in the post-collapse era of the Neo-Babylonian period, the recovering early Persian period, or the complex economic realities of the late Persian period."[19] Instead of the post-collapse era of the Neo-Assyrian period, Richter locates the economic profile of *Urdeuteronomium* "in the transition period between the Iron I and Iron IIA period."[20] She thus pushes back the origins of Deuteronomy to an even more obscure era than Josiah's reign and the eighth century Levites of Christian's scenario.

Davies' setting of *Urdeuteronomium* in the context of Neo-Assyrian Samerina focuses on times that are more propitious for the production of such a work. The question is whether or not this context could have given rise to the concept of a quasi autonomous Israel with an elite of brothers at its center.

7.3.3 Imperial control and local elites

Greek oligarchies were specific constitutional alternatives that arose between the late sixth century and the mid-fifth century BCE. In Athens, the catastrophic Peloponnesian War against Sparta sparked a short-lived oligarchic revolution in 411 BCE.[21] Could the Assyrian takeover of Samaria have sparked a similar reaction in Israel?

---

18   Christian, "Priestly Power," 4–8.
19   Richter, "Money," 317. See also Richter, "Question of Provenance."
20   Richter, 317.
21   Trevett, "Status and Class," 212.

Despite the lack of evidence, the rise of new elites in post-720 BCE Israel can be expected. The transfer of local royal elites in other regions of the Babylonian empires fostered the rise of dynasties of local big men upon whom the Empires relied to run their peripheries. Efficient control of distant and economically secondary areas required, however, preventing local big men from becoming more autonomous—as happened for instance when Babylonia revolted in Xerxes' fifth regnal year.[22] Local political scenes were best maintained in a constant state of instability by regular shifting of the favors of the imperial administration to different big men. As they vied with one another for the favors granted by imperial residents, local big men did not join forces to seek political support elsewhere.

The books of Ezra and Nehemiah tell with glee how Sanballat, Tobiah and Geshem failed to resist their (partial) demotion in the wake of the transfer of (some) imperial support to Jerusalem (Neh 4–6). The powers of the new Jerusalem elite is itself constrained by the concomitant rise of the Gerizim elite. The fragmentation of local autonomy between different rival groups—older elites and newcomers—is visible at the heart of Deuteronomy. Besides the elders at the gate, chapter 18 introduces Levi's brotherhood that imposes a heavy tax burden on the rest of Israel. The authority of this elite is nevertheless challenged by the Levitical priests who assert their status by claiming exclusive control over the Torah.[23] Hence, Deuteronomy displays the struggle of rival elites for the control of Israel at the local level as much as the *maqom*. The identification of a democratic stance in Deuteronomy is in large part illusory.[24]

From the vantage point of whoever produced the Deuteronomic core, the political powers of the elders at the gate of each local settlement did not encroach on the mostly economic activities of the *qehal-YHWH* brotherhood. As long as the Empire—any empire—maintained home stability and kept trade routes open, the integration of the Israelite hills into the global market—Assyrian and any others—fostered elite cooperation with Edomite and Egyptian peers.[25]

7.3.4 *Maqom* banquets and Greek patronage networks

The notion of a mobile *maqom* can also be put in parallel with Greek networks of patronage. In eighth century BCE Attika, big men served as

---

22 Hackl, "Esangila," 175–177.
23 Rossi, "Not by Bread Alone," 329–64 on Deut 10:6–9 and 18:1–8.
24 Against Crüsemann, "Theokratie," 199–214.
25 Simonton, *Oligarchy*, 33.

individual patrons by hosting lavish *symposia* in their homes to accumulate social capital from ritual sacrifice and sacrificial feasting. In the first part of the seventh century BCE, however, the

> banqueting was removed to sacred precincts where no individual could claim patronage of the feast. Transferring the ceremonial consumption of meat to neutral *temene* of the gods deprived individuals of the benefits of individual patronage and the status enhancement of hosting a meat feast. The transfer of patronage to the divine realm seems to have had the advantage of stabilizing society by diminishing the threat of prominent individuals monopolizing the system [...] it also allowed the system to be much more inclusive and capable of operating on an ever-larger scale, since feasting was no longer limited to a single individual's feasting network. The neutral venue of the sacred precinct could combine multiple patronage networks, as individuals were ranked according to their status and assigned an increasing variety of ritual roles.[26]

The participation of all Israelites in the *maqom* banquets—whatever their means—enabled the Israelite members of the *qehal-YHWH* to service and broaden their patronage networks while underlining their ordinary Israeliteness to their Israelite clients.

Patronage networks were maintained and broadened as the Israelite members of the *qehal-YHWH* were the same Israelites who commanded the largest households and thus brought the largest amount of yearly tithes at the *maqom*. The *maqom* banquets were ideal venues to make a show of their wealth; but as the other producers also brought ten percent of their annual yield, the ability of the biggest contributors to patronize the feast was limited by the overall abundance of victuals. Hence, instead of the clue of the impractical and utopian character of the Deuteronomic laws, the festive consumption of 10% of the yearly yield together in front of YHWH actually reflects the shift of private feasts towards neutral *temene* of the gods.[27]

The anonymity of the *maqom* meeting ground and the injunction to seek its location through divination (דרשׁ) also contributed to prevent the rise of a single group around a central sanctuary benefiting year after year from the windfalls of the pilgrimage. The Deuteronomic core thus extends the notion of *isonomia* beyond the *qehal-YHWH* in order to maintain the three loci of power—gates, *maqom* and *qehal*—in tension and prevent one from prevailing over the others.

---

26 Van den Eijnde, "Power Play," 84.
27 On the use of the banquets as proof of Deuteronomy's lack of concern for actual life conditions, see already Hölscher, "Komposition," 161 and Reuss, *Histoire sainte*, 2.308.

Though no Greek example can make up the lack of sources on the early history of Samerina, for the time being they argue in favor of Davies' scenario. It is a viable option because it presents a far less hypothetical historical context than the other scenarii. It is more modest than Arnold's as it does not seek to explain the entire literary history of Deuteronomy. It leaves a gap between the formation of the Deuteronomic core and its framing to produce a scroll of Deuteronomy, but it is not difficult to imagine why the Deuteronomic core of the core was turned into Moses' final words.

7.4 Why integrate a northern core into a shared Torah?

Apart from 2 Kings 17, the Bible is silent over what happened in Samerina between the Assyrian take-over and Alexander the Great. Archaeological data is equally meagre. The interpretation of the excavations of Samaria is a major challenge in itself.[28] In any case, coinage and the Wadi Daliyeh papyrii indicate that life went on, as could be expected.[29] As the Benjamin plateau suffered less than Jerusalem at the hands of the Neo-Babylonians, it also remained an important contributor to the survival of Israel. Despite claims to the contrary, the role of Bethel as a bridge between the Israelite heritage and Jerusalem's is far more likely than the hypothetical northern refugees fleeing the advance of Assyrian troops (§7.2).[30] Given the number of issues surrounding the history of Samaria and Samerina between 720 and, say, 350 BCE, any attempt to set the literary history of Deuteronomy in precise historical contexts is too hypothetical to be of use. Instead, it is more useful to ask what would have motivated the inclusion of the Deuteronomic legal core into what became the Torah.

A Torah comprising a Tetrateuch without Deuteronomy would have been less appropriate as a means to a shared proto-Jewish/Samaritan identity in Palestine and across the Diaspora. Deuteronomy's model *Mensch* had a greater appeal for the non-priestly segments of communities in various imperial realms than Leviticus–Numbers, the burden of which is to justify the hegemonic position of the priesthood and the revenues it claims from the non-priests. As a code of honor rather than a collection of legally binding regulations or a compendium of common laws,[31]

---

28 See Franklin, "Samaria," 189–202; Franklin, "Review," 148–151.
29 See Dušek, "Importance," 1–12.
30 On the issues around the role of Bethel in the formation of biblical literature, see Anderson and Guillaume, "Benjamin."
31 Berman, "History of Legal Theory," 19–39.

the splicing of the *Mensch* and priestly figures in Deuteronomy 12–26 was best suited to open the brotherhood to all Israelites in imperial contexts.

As the replication of the Edomite in Deuteronomy 2:4.8 shows, the presence of an Edomite brother was no hindrance to the project of identity formation even in its latter stages. The Edomite became the symbol of the benevolence towards a selection of neighbors. The Deuteronomic *qehal-YHWH* became identified with Israel as a whole. Hence, the meekest member of the target community entered the elite by simply identifying with the model Israelite.

In Palestine, however, the *maqom* was gradually anchored at the temples of Jerusalem and Gerizim. The duplication of the *maqom* did not weaken the identity-building potential of the Pentateuch, except that it contributed to the formation of two identities—Jewish and Samaritan—constructed in opposition to one another.

In other words, Deuteronomy 14–25 (minus 14:1–21; 16; and 18:1–8 at least) represents the overthrow of the monarchy and of the church by the bourgeoisie. Deuteronomy 1–13 and 26–34 align chapters 14–25 with Exodus–Numbers and represent the revenge of the church. Leading the counter-revolution, the clergy goes further than claiming back its previous position. It claims an undisputed hegemony by eliminating the royalty in partnership with which it had ruled before the Deuteronomic revolution.

7.5 Exodus 21–23 as parent text?

Kilchör tried to demonstrate that Exodus 21:2–23:19 was the template of the Deuteronomic Code.[32] Table 7.1 places the similar laws side by side and sets the closest parallels together in the centre to underline their similarity. The italics in the right-hand side column signal Deuteronomic passages Kilchör presents as similar, though the similarity is rather stretched.

The closest parallels between the Covenant Code and Deuteronomy concern passages that are likely to belong to the alignment of a previous version of Deuteronomy with the Torah: the kid boiled in its mother's milk (Deut 14:21), the festal calendar (Deut 16), zoophilia (Deut 27:21) and first fruits (Deut 26:2). To these close parallels, the influence of Exodus 20:24; 23:24, and 34:13 on Deuteronomy 12 can be added.[33] Therefore, Kilchör's view that "the laws in Exodus, Leviticus and Numbers were available more or less in their present form when the Deuteronomic law was composed, and they had a quasi-canonical status"[34] is valid for Deu-

32 Kilchör, *Mosetora*, 310–11.
33 Kilchör, 76–79.
34 Kilchör, 340.

Table 7.1 Reception of Exod 21:2-23:19 in Deuteronomy according to Kilchör

Exodus	Deuteronomy
21:2-11 purchase and manumission of Hebrew	15:12-18 Hebrews' labour in brothers' antichretic loans
21:12-14 homicides	19:1-13 cities of refuge
21:15 patricide and matricide	*21:18-21 rebellious son*
21:16 kidnapping	24:7 sale of person abducted from an Israelite brother
21:17 slander of father or mother	21:18-21 rebellious son
21:18-19 bodily harm in brawl	*25:1-3 punishment by flogging*
21:20-21.26-27 injured slave	23:16-17 welcome of runaway slaves
21:22-25 abortion, talion	19:21; *25:11-12 brother's grabbing wife*
21:28-36 goring ox, open pit	—
21:37-22:7 theft, grazing, fire	—
22:8 loss of pledges	22:3 *brother's stray donkey*
22:9-14 ownership, animals	—
22:15-16 abducted virgin	22:28-29 abducted virgin cannot be divorced
22:17 execution of sorceress	18:10-11 list of forbidden diviners
22:18 zoophilist executed or cursed (Deut 27:21)	
22:19 idolatry	(13:7-19) 17:2-7 execution of idolater at the gate
22:20-23 protect *ger*, widow, orphan	24:17-18 protect orphaned *ger*, unsecured loan to widow
22:24 interest-free loans to needy ἀδελφός	23:20-21 interest-free loans to a brother
22:25-26 pawned cloak	24:[10-]13 pawned cloak, 10-12 pledge for loan to neighbour
22:27 reviling god and cursing a leader	—
22:28-29 firstborn sons and animals for YHWH	15:19-23 firstlings males eaten before YHWH at the *maqom*
22:30 torn carcass for the dogs	14.2.21 carrion for *ger* or foreigner
23:1-2 impartiality in court	19:16-17 punishment of false witnesses
23:3.6-8 not favouring the poor	16:18-20; 24:17 impartiality in court, protect *ger's* orphan
23:4-5 helping enemy's donkey	22:1-4 return of brother's strays
23:9 protection of *ger*	24:22 gleanings for *ger*, orphan and widow
23:10-13 fallow on seventh year	15:1-11 release of brother's debt at the end of seventh year
Deut 16:1-17 // Exod 23:14-18 festival calendar	
23:19a first fruits to YHWH's house	26.2 basket of first fruits to priest at the *maqom*
23:19b // 14:21 boiling kid in mother's milk	

teronomy 12, 14, 16 and 26 but invalid for the core chapters. The influence of Exodus on the Deuteronomic core is limited to Exodus 21, in particular the five laws with similar Deuteronomic counterparts. The questionable parallels between brawl and flogging (Exod 21:18–19; Deut 25:1–3) and between abortion resulting from a brawl and the woman who grabs the testicles of her husband's opponent (Exod 21:22–25; Deut 19:21; 25:11–12) are too stretched to convince. The same pertains to Kilchör's placement of the rebellious son (Deut 21:18–21) on the same line as the patricide/matricide of Exodus 21:15. Placing it is where it belongs, i.e., in parallel with the slanderer of father and mother (Exod 21:17) breaks the sequence Kilchör tried to demonstrate (Table 7.1).

Moreover, Table 7.2 shows that the sequence of five close enough thematic parallels is broken in Deuteronomy as kidnapping appears in chapter 24 before the rebellious son (Deut 21) and the runaway slave (Deut 23).

A closer look at the thematic similarities shows that one may have inspired the other, but with much reinterpretation (Table 7.3).

Compared to Exodus, the scope of the laws of the Hebrews, of the kidnapped, and of runaway slaves in Deuteronomy is narrowed to the circle of the brotherhood, which neatly illustrates the essence of the Deuteronomic thrust. The identification of a thrust in Exodus 21 is more difficult, however.

Though the Hebrew is bought (קנה) and is designated as a slave (עבד) in Exodus 21:2, the fact that his service is limited to six years shows that he is no slave *per se*. The supply of a wife reads as an incentive to self-indenture motivated by the love of the "slave" for his master and for his own sons borne from the wife the master provided (Exod 21:5). The indenture ceremony at the gate is common to both texts, but apart from that, the differences are many. The Hebrew and Hebrewess in Deuteronomy 15:12–18 are not designated as slaves. Their labor is traded (מכר) between two brothers (§2.3.3). Logically, Deuteronomy 15 ignores the matter of the ownership of children born during the service of the Hebrews precisely because they are not slaves. Exodus 21:7 does use the notion of trade (מכר), but applies it to a daughter who, contrary to most translations, is not sold but supplied as a kind of housemaid by her father in repayment of antichretic loans as is the case for the Hebrews in Deuteronomy 15. The main difference is that the daughter's duties can include sexual services that automatically change her status at the end of the unspecified period of her service. She becomes a secondary spouse who acquires marital rights if the master decides to keep her for himself or for his son (Exod 21:10). Hence neither dowry nor bride price are mentioned as counterparts for the end-of-contract gifts (Deut 15:14). Instead, the contract includes the prohibition of trading (מכר) her to foreigners, something that makes much sense as an echo of the two brothers (Deut 15:12) and as an echo of the promise that brothers will lend to foreigners

Table 7.2 Similarities between Exodus 21 and Deuteronomy 15-24

Exodus	Deuteronomy
21:2–11 purchase and manumission of Hebrew	15:12–18 Hebrews' labour in brothers' antichretic loans
21:12–14 homicides	19:1–13 cities of refuge
21:16 kidnapping	24:7 sale of person abducted from an Israelite brother
21:17 slander of father or mother	21:18–21 rebellious son
21:20–21.26–27 injured slave	23:16–17 welcome of runaway slaves

Table 7.3 Differences in the treatment of cases in Exodus 21 and Deuteronomy 15-25

Exodus	Deuteronomy
21:2–11 purchase and manumission of Hebrew	15:12–18 Hebrews' labour in brothers' antichretic loans
21:12–14 refuge at the altar	19:1–13 cities of refuge
21:15 patricide and matricide	*21:18–21 rebellious son*
21:16 kidnapping	24:7 sale of person abducted from an Israelite brother
21:17 slander of father or mother	21:18–21 rebellious son
21:18–19 bodily harm in brawl	*25:1–3 punishment by flogging*
21:20–21.26–27 injured slave	23:16–17 welcome of runaway slaves
21:22–25 abortion, talion	19:21; 25:11–12 *grabbing wife*
21:28–32.34–36 goring ox, open pit	22:8 parapet
21:37 livestock theft	22:1 brother's stray livestock

but never borrow from them (Deut 15:6). Therefore, the notion of "reception" is correct, but not necessarily as the reception of Exodus 21 in Deuteronomy. The order of influence may be bi-directional. What is clear is that Exodus 21 considers the case of the daughter from the point of view of her father whose economic situation makes him consider arrangements that the wealthy brothers in Deuteronomy would never envisage for their daughters.

Nor would the Deuteronomic *Mensch* injure expensive commodities such as his own slave. The owner of a single slave ought to treat him as a brother (Sirach 33:31). A good beating might be necessary to keep one's household in order, including sons and oxen. If the rod proves insufficient, Deuteronomy advises parents to condemn their own prodigal son to death (Deut 21:18–21). Daughters present no risk of turning into drunkards and gluttons. The contrast with Exodus 21 is eloquent. Exodus 21 lists a number of cases that would be utterly shameful in the household of the Deuteronomic *Mensch*: the murder and slander of parents presumably by daughters as much as by sons (Exod 21:17.19); a goring ox that may have long been known to be dangerous (Exod 21:28–32.34–36) and slave beating by the master (Exod 21:20–21) that leads to immediate death or death in the following days. Why should the slave owner be punished in the first case and not in the second case is not any clearer than who should punish such a senseless slave owner. The distinction reads like an exercise in casuistic finery from a scribe showing off his compositional skills.

In fact, the presentation of cases in Exodus 21:12–37 displays a careful imbrication of cases somewhat similar to Deuteronomic sandwiched between cases that are not found in Deuteronomy. Patricide/matricide (verse 15) and father/mother slander (verse 17) are interrupted by kidnapping (verse 16, see Deut 24:7). Slave beating (Exod 21:20–21.26–27) is interrupted by the case of abortion resulting from injuries received during a brawl between men (Exod 21:22–24). The corresponding case in Deuteronomy 25:11–12 concerns the maiming of the wife who grabbed testicles to save her husband, not necessarily a more common occurrence in real life, but something that makes sense to model a *Mensch* (§6.5). The goring ox (Exod 21:28–32.34–36) is also interrupted by the case of the dangerous pit left open, to which corresponds the parapet to secure the roof on one's house (Exod 21:33; Deut 22:8). One could only tentatively conclude that these three Deuteronomic cases were purposefully spliced with cases listed in a previous version of Exodus 21. Therefore, reception goes both ways; a reception of Deuteronomy 22–24 in Exodus 21 besides a reception of Exodus 21 in Deuteronomy 15–24. Dependence, influence and reinterpretation between the legal collections makes the unravelling of the order of dependence too hypothetical to be useful. The consensus about the dependence of the Deuteronomic Code on the the oldest part of the Covenant Code (Exod 21:1–22:16) is certainly correct,[35] but only as a general principle.

---

35 See Otto, *Politische Theologie*, 236–364; Otto, *Deuteronomium 1–11*, 231–38; Arnold, "Innovations."

Conclusion

Approaching Deuteronomy 12–26 without the presupposition that the *maqom* represents Jerusalem and its temple in the days of Josiah reshuffles the actors' roles and position. The priests are sent back into the background and give way to brothers to whom Deuteronomic laws pay far more attention than to the priests. This process triggers a chain reaction that challenges a number of other common presuppositions: that tithes are obviously revenues for the temple personnel, that allowing tithe payers to eat and drink their tithes before YHWH would turn into Canaanite orgies, that the *qehal-YHWH* is Israel, that Israel is a people of brothers and sisters, that Israelite identity is constructed in isolation from other peoples, that the poor need loans and, lastly, that debt releases are impracticable. None of these presuppositions turns out to be as obvious as has been the case so far in Deuteronomic scholarship.

Instead of a brotherhood where men and women, slave and master are equals, Israel's portrayal is closer to attested ancient Near Eastern practices, albeit markedly different from the sacred economy of Exodus-Leviticus. Nevertheless, eating and drinking joyfully in the presence of YHWH is the high point of the Deuteronomic view of the cult at the chosen Place. Cultic centralization remains a key Deuteronomic concept, except that it serves the interest of two different groups. Deuteronomy 12, the introduction of the legal collection, favors Levitical priests who extract revenues at the chosen Place, revenues specified in chapter 18, while chapter 16 delineates the festivals to be celebrated there. Apart from these passages, priests, Levites and Levitical priests are secondary figures in the bulk of Deuteronomy 12–26, which is dedicated to the activities of brothers.

Sometimes a sibling, other times a partner, usually an Israelite—though Edomites are not excluded—the Deuteronomic brother is the backbone of the Deuteronomic Israel. At home, he is a husband, a father, a farmer, a slave owner and an employer. In the village, he contributes to communal affairs, giving a helping hand or a loan to neighbors, arbitrating a conflict, providing tithes for the Levite, the widow and the orphan, alms for the destitute, and waging war in foreign lands. At the central place, he parades the best produce of the year in the eyes of *kol* Israel. When he can afford it, he is involved in trade with Edomite and Egyptian partners.

Contrary to his ancestors in the wilderness, the Deuteronomic brother works hard to keep his household afloat. Life in Deuteronomy is unforgiving. Debtors default, witnesses lie, arbitrators are partial. Accidents happen, people fall off roofs, cases are complex, evidence is not forthcoming, insults turn to assault and murder, mobs crave to lynch culprits on the spot. Husbands are jealous or inconsiderate or rapists, or refuse to marry a needy relative. Others die before fathering a son. When sons are born, they might drink, daughters might flirt. Donkeys and slaves escape or are raided, crops are pilfered, warriors go amiss, salaries are overdue, weights and measures are not always fair. But reveling before YHWH at the central place makes the challenges of the rest of the year worth struggling for. Supporting local Levites, aliens, widows and orphans at home is normal. These have no other revenues other than gleaning rights.

Scholarship also view the 25 percent tax levied by the priest on meat and the 100 percent tax on the best wool as normal. Ever since de Wette identified the *maqom* as the temple of Jerusalem, it stands to reason that 10 percent of the harvest of any given year is brought to the chosen place to feed the priests. Having the tithe payers gorge themselves there in front of YHWH is inconceivable. It would squander precious resources and be a case of abandoning the Levite (Deut 12:9.18; 14:27), though Deuteronomy 14:22–29 and 26:12 only grant the Levite a share of the triennial tithes with the alien, the widow and the orphan.

Hence, the economic reading in Part I of this study brought to the fore the tension between the allocation of tithes in Deuteronomy 14:22–29 and what chapters 12; 16; and 18:1–8 add to the revenues of the Levites and Levitical priests. Part II then focused on the tension and its implications. Deuteronomy 12; 16; and 18:1–8 imply that a mere quarter of triennial tithes is sufficient for the *ger*, the widow and the orphan but insufficient for the Levite—but not for the other so-called *personae miserae*!

Tithe payers should not squander their yearly tithes in front of YHWH, but the tribe of Levi may gorge itself with a quarter of all sacrificial meats. Tithe payers are expected to hand out alms for the destitute but the priests are not called to do so. Scholars even expect tithe payers to relinquish joyfully the tithes they deliver at the *maqom* to the priesthood because they have fully internalized the Torah's ideological justification for the levying of revenues by the priesthood.

The Torah expects its readers to consider exactions of meat, wool, grain, oil and wine by the priesthood as essential to pacify YHWH. The Torah equally expects its readers to ignore the effect of such exactions on the producers. Hence, instead of identifying the purpose of

Deuteronomy's laws according to conventional expectations, the economic approach to Deuteronomy 12–26 reveals two antagonistic agendas, each one with a specific cultic theory: on the one hand, the common biblical wisdom that rests on paying cultic specialists to secure YHWH's blessings; on the other hand, a theory unique to Deuteronomy 14 that calls for the tithe payers to eat and drink their tithes before YHWH in gratitude for his blessings.

The traditional identification of the Deuteronomic Code as Deuteronomy 12–26 is misleading because it suggests that the legal collection is a coherent whole, which blinds readers to the tension between the interests of the priesthood and those of the producers. A similar tension exists in Exodus–Numbers as a constant tension between Moses and the Israelite mob, but Exodus–Numbers ignore the point of view of the mob.

Deuteronomy 1–11 and 27–34 ensure that Moses' voice resonates throughout Deuteronomy, but the priest is a minor figure in Deuteronomy, a figure that only makes sense in the broader context of the Torah. At the heart of the book, the constitutive figure is a *Mensch*, a figure that functions as a model for every Israelite because he belongs to a worthy but non-priestly elite.

Despite the unforgiving nature of the economy it displays, Deuteronomy's world is prosperous because it is not geared to provide for a temple but relies instead on the skills of brothers who are more than ordinary farmers. Laws such as the *šemiṭṭah* do not concern ordinary farmers. The template for the new Israelite is the brother of the *qehal-YHWH*, a circle that one may potentially enter, provided one has accumulated enough capital to risk some of it in trade ventures. Instead of a people of brothers, Israel is a mosaic of individuals from differing social and economic conditions, including foreign wives, Edomite partners, Hebrews, slaves and immigrants of various origins.

Having considered the interplay between the different economic players and institutions in Part II, Part III compared Davies' proposal for the rise of the Deuteronomic collection in Samerina in the wake of the Assyrian take-over with alternative views on the compilation of *Urdeuteronomium* in Jerusalem. Davies' scenario best accounts for the inherent difficulties pertaining to the low valuation of the royal office and the silence over Jerusalem and Judah in Deuteronomy and the Torah. The earliest version of Deuteronomy responded to the need to create a new Israelite identity, a need reflected in the story of the Bethel priest sent back to teach the new immigrants how to worship YHWH (2 Kgs 17). The *maqom* celebrations, as described in Deuteronomy 14–15, make a better fit with a post-monarchic Israel, i.e., after 720 BCE, than does the Jerusalem temple at any time of its existence.

Instead of a priest in the guise of Aaron's successors, Deuteronomy presents a *Mensch* who embodies comportments that are essential to success in trade and at home. Hence, the Deuteronomic laws do not greatly differ from the traditional mores of the elite the Assyrians deported from Samaria and those of the immigrants Sargon brought in. A common Israelite identity had to be built upon similarities. The laws did not have to be taught and disseminated by a public reading, as is the case in Deut 31:10-13, because the ethos they inspire did not radically differ from custom but asked its primary audience to go beyond the call of duty. The spirit of the Deuteronomic laws is modeled on the daily behavior of the members of the most successful households, the brother addressed throughout as "you", i.e., those Israelites that display the largest and finest tithes at the *maqom* and embody Israeliteness at its best. These households would provide the largest contributions for the upkeep of the local Levite, *ger*, widow and orphan. It is at their door that anyone in need would knock.

The indefectible point is the place of YHWH as the god of the land. The only cultic practices deemed incompatible with YHWH's primacy are related to astral bodies (Deut 17:2-5). Expecting everyone to become exclusively YHWH worshipers overnight would have been counterproductive. The mission of the Bethel priest (2 Kgs 17:28) is to teach (מורה) so that the new immigrants fear YHWH (ייראו את יהוה). The aim of the *maqom* festivities is no different: to learn (למד) to fear YHWH (ליראה את יהוה Deut 14:23). Apart from that, the primacy of the brotherhood as an economic elite is an appeal to immigrants, most of whom were members of the elite in their place of origin and selected for this reason for resettlement in other parts of the Empire (2 Kgs 24:14; 25:12).

The strategy envisaged for the formation of a new Israelite identity is integration from above. The *qehal-YHWH* is the inner circle that brings together merchants in risky trade and credit operations. The financial means of these merchants allow them to grant agricultural loans to neighbors—old Israelites and new immigrants—and to open their hands in charitable gestures, as is expected from any local patron. The common meals at the *maqom* foster the integration of the immigrants, without threatening the autonomy of each local settlement ruled by its elders. The immigrants were settled either in ethnically pure settlements spread across the province or as single families within Israelite settlements. In either case, the immigrants—*gerim*—participated in the imperial control of the province, while a local Levite plays a role in the inculturation of the immigrants as 2 Kings 17 suggests. Up to this point, the Deuteronomic *mišpatim* did not need a written text any more than arbitrators needed a law code to render just verdicts. Davies' point that Deuteronomy is "the literary by-product of an enterprise that was actually undertaken"[1] gains credibility if the enterprise reflected daily practices that elite merchant traders set as a model for all Israelites to emulate.

The big men addressed in the Deuteronomic core provide a model for a broader audience than their own circle because they too are involved in the production of basic food staples on their estates (with the help of slaves and day laborers), but they are also involved in the trade of agricultural surpluses, an activity that leads them to buy from their Israelite, non-Israelite and quasi Israelite neighbors, and to lend to them too.

The need for a written form arose when a slot in the foundation myth of the Exodus had to be found for the Deuteronomic ethos. The Torah could hardly become the charter of a Judaic *ethnos* without Deuteronomy's central notion of brotherhood. Integrating Deuteronomy as the fifth scroll of the Pentateuch broadened the outlook of the Torah with an appeal to non-priests. Therefore, the double tithing system of Deuteronomy 14 represents the quintessence of the oldest biblical festival theory Braulik was looking for elsewhere in Deuteronomy.

---

1 Davies, "Where Deuteronomy?".

Bibliography

Achenbach, Reinhard. "Zur Systematik der Speisegebote in Leviticus 11 und in Deuteronomium 14," *Zeitschrift für Altorientalische und Biblische Rechtsgeschichte* 17 (2011): 161–209.

Adamczewski, Bartosz. *Retelling the Law. Genesis, Exodus–Numbers, and Samuel–Kings as Sequential Hyper Textual Reworking of Deuteronomy*. Frankfurt: P. Lang, 2012.

Akiyama, Kengo. *The Love of Neighbour in Ancient Judaism: The Reception of Leviticus 19:18 in the Hebrew Bible, the Septuagint, the Book of Jubilees, the Dead Sea Scrolls, and the New Testament*. Leiden: Brill, 2018.

Albertz, Rainer. "A Possible *terminus ad quem* for the Deuteronomic Legislation – A Fresh Look at Deut 17:16." In *Homeland and Exile*, ed. Gershon Galil, Markham Geller, and Alan R. Millard, 271–96. Leiden: Brill, 2009.

Altmann, Peter. *Economics in Persian-Period Biblical Texts*. Tübingen: Mohr Siebeck, 2016.

—. *Festive Meals in Ancient Israel: Deuteronomy's Identity Politics in Their Ancient Near Eastern Context*. Berlin: de Gruyter, 2011.

—. "What do the 'Levites in your Gates' have to do with the 'Levitical Priests'? An Attempt at European-North American Dialogue on the Levites in the Deuteronomic Law Corpus." In *Levites and Priests in Biblical History and Tradition*, ed. Mark Leuchter and Jeremy M. Hutton, 135–54. Atlanta, GA: SBL, 2011.

Anderson, Bradford A. *Brotherhood and Inheritance*. London: T. & T. Clark, 2011.

Anderson, Gary A. *Sin: A History*. New Haven, CT: Yale University Press, 2009.

Anderson, James and Guillaume, Philippe. "If I Ever Forget You, Benjamin…" In *The Hunt for Ancient Israel - Essays in Honour of Diana V. Edelman*, ed. Cynthia Shaffer-Elliott, Kristin Joachimsen, Ehud Ben Zvi, and Pauline A. Viviano, 336–59. Sheffield: Equinox, UK, 2022.

Aristophanes. *Aristophanes with an English Translation by Benjamin Bickley Rogers*. Loeb Classical Library 180. Cambridge, MA: Harvard University Press, 1991.

—. *Wealth*. Translated by G. Theodoridis. Accessed December 15, 2015 at http://www.poetryintranslation.com/PITBR/Greek/Wealth.htm.

Arnold, Bill T. "Deuteronomy and the Law of the Central Sanctuary noch einmal," *Vetus Testamentum* 64 (2014): 236–48.

—. "Innovations of the Deuteronomic Law and the History of its Composition." In *Deuteronomy in the Making: Studies in the Production of Debarim*, ed. D. Edelman, Benedetta Rossi, K. Berge, and P. Guillaume, 163–94. Berlin: de Gruyter, 2021.

—. "Israelite Worship as Envisioned and Prescribed in Deuteronomy 12." *Zeitschrift für Altorientalische und Biblische Rechtsgeschichte* 22 (2016): 161–75.

Awabdy, Mark A. *Immigrants and Innovative Law: Deuteronomy's Theological and Social Vision for the* גר. Tübingen: Mohr Siebeck, 2014.

Baker, David L. *Tight Fists or Open Hands? Wealth and Poverty in Old Testament Law*. Grand Rapids, MN: Eerdmans, 2009.

Bartos, Michael and Bernard M. Levinson. "'This is the Manner of the Remission': Implicit Legal Exegesis in 11QMelchizedek as a Response to the Formation of the Torah," *Journal of Biblical Literature* 132 (2013): 351–71.

Beattie, Daren R. G. "What does 'Hebrew' Mean?" Paper presented in Belfast, May 23 2007.

Becker, Gary S. *The Economic Approach to Human Behavior*. Chicago: University of Chicago, 1976.

—. "The Economic Way of Looking at Life. Nobel Lecture, December 9, 1992. Accessed November 12, 2016 at http://www.nobelprize.org/nobelprizes/economic-sciences/laureates/1992/becker-lecture.pdf.

Bedford, Peter R. "Temple Funding and Priestly Authority in Achaemenid Judah." In *Exile and Return*, ed. Jonathan Stökl and Caroline Waerzeggers, 336–51. Berlin: de Gruyter, 2015.

Bekins, Peter and Alexander T. Kirk. "A Thorny Text: The Use of את and the Subversion of Form in Ezek 2:6." *Vetus Testamentum* 67 (2017): 357–371.

Ben Zvi, Ehud. "Utopias, Multiple Utopias, and Why Utopias at All? The Social Roles of Utopian Visions in Prophetic Books within Their Historical Context." In *Utopia and Dystopia in Prophetic Literature*, ed. Ehud Ben Zvi, 5–85. Helsinki/Göttingen: Finnish Exegetical Society/Vandenhoeck & Ruprecht, 2006.

Bennett, Harold V. "Triennial Tithes and the Underdog : A Revisionist Reading of Deuteronomy 14:22–29 and 26:12–15." In *Yet with a Steady Beat Contemporary U.S. Afrocentric Biblical Interpretation*, ed. Randall C. Bailey, 7–18. Atlanta, GA: SBL, 2003.

Berge, Kåre. "Literacy, Utopia and Memory: Is there a Public Teaching in Deuteronomy?" *Journal of Hebrew Scripture* 12 (2012): 1–19.

Bergsma, John S. *The Jubilee from Leviticus to Qumran. A History of Interpretation*. Leiden: Brill, 2007.

Berlejung, Angelika. "Social Climbing in the Babylonian Exile." In *Wandering Arameans: Arameans Outside Syria. Textual and Archaeological Perspectives*, ed. Angelika Berlejung, Aren M. Maeir and Andreas Schüle, 101–24. Wiesbaden: Harrassowitz, 2017.

Berlin, Adele. "Sex and the Single Girl in Deuteronomy 22." In *Mishneh Todah: Studies in Deuteronomy and Its Cultural Environment in Honor of Jeffrey H. Tigay*, ed. Nili Sacher Fox, David A. Glatt-Gilad and Michael J. Williams, 95–112. Winona Lake, IN: Eisenbrauns, 2009.

Berman, Joshua. "The History of Legal Theory and the Study of Biblical Law," *Catholic Biblical Quarterly* 76 (2014): 19–39.

Biga, Maria G. "Feste e fiere a Ebla." In *Mercanti e politica nel mondo antico*, ed. Carlo Zaccagnini, 55–68. Rome: L'Erma di Bretschneider, 2003.

Bird, Phyllis A. "Of Whores and Hounds: A New Interpretation of the Subject of Deuteronomy 23:19," *Vetus Testamentum* 65 (2015): 352–64.

Block, Daniel I. *The Gospel according to Moses*. Eugene, OR: Cascade, 2012.

Blok, Josine. *Citizenship in Classical Athens*. Cambridge; New York: Cambridge University Press, 2017.

Boer, Roland. *The Sacred Economy of Ancient Israel*. Louisville, KY: Westminster John Knox, 2015.

Bodi, Daniel. "Outraging the Resident-Alien: King David, Uriah the Hittite, and an El-Amarna Parallel." *Ugarit-Forschungen* 35 (2003): 29–56.

Bourdieu, Pierre. *"The Forms of Capital."* In *Handbook of Theory and Research for the Sociology of Education*, ed. John G. Richardson, 241–49. New York: Greenwood, 1986.

—. Outline of a Theory of Practice. New York: Cambridge University, 1977.

Boyer, Robert and Yves Saillard. "Summary of *Régulation* Theory." In *Régulation Theory: the State of the Art*, ed. Roger Boyer and Yves Saillard, translated by Carolyn Shread, 36–44. London: Routledge, 2002.

Braulik, Georg. "The Joy of the Feast: The Conception of the Cult in Deuteronomy, the Oldest Biblical Festival Theory." In *The Theology of Deuteronomy: Collected Essays of Georg Braulik*, 27–65. North Richland Hills, TX: BIBAL, 1994. Translation of Braulik, Georg, "Die Freude des Festes: Das Kultverständnis Des Deuteronomium - Die älteste Biblische Festtheorie," in *Leiturgia - Koinonia - Diakonia. Festschrift für Kardinal Franz König zum 75. Geburtstag*, ed. Raphael Schulte, 127–79. Vienna: Herder, 1980. Previous versions in *Theologisches Jahrbuch* (1983): 13–54 and in Studien zur Theologie des Deuteronomiums (Stuttgarter biblische Aufsatzbände 2. Stuttgart: Katholisches Bibelwerk, 1988), 161–218.

Brueggemann, Walter. *Deuteronomy*. Nashville, TN: Abingdon, 2001.

Bultmann, Christoph. *Der Fremde im antiken Juda, eine Untersuchung zum sozialen Typenbegriff "ger" und seinem Bedeutungswandel in der alttestamentlichen Gesetzgebung*. Göttingen: Vandenhoeck & Ruprecht, 1992.

Busatta, Sandra. "Honour and Shame in the Mediterranean,"*Antrocom* 2 (2006): 75–78.

Byrne, Ryan. "Early Assyrian Contacts with Arabs and the Impact of Levantine Vassal Tribute," *Bulletin of the American Schools of Oriental Research* 331 (2003): 11–25.

Carmichael, Calum M. *The Laws of Deuteronomy*. Ithaca, NY: Cornell University Press, 1974.

Chavel, Simeon. "The Literary Development of Deuteronomy 12." In *The Pentateuch: International Perspectives on Current Research*, ed. Thomas B. Dozeman, Konrad Schmid and Baruch J. Schwartz, 85–108. Tübingen: Mohr Siebeck, 2011.
Chirichigno, Gregory C. *Debt-Slavery and the Ancient Near East*. Sheffield: JSOT Press, 1993.
Christian, Mark A."Priestly Power that Empowers: Michel Foucault, Middle-Tier Levites, and the Sociology of 'Popular Religious Groups' in Israel," *Journal of Hebrew Scriptures* 9 (2009), article 1, doi: 10.5508/jhs.2009.v9.a1.
Claburn, W. Eugene. "The Fiscal Basis of Josiah's Reforms," *Journal of Biblical Literature* 92 (1973): 11–22.
Clements, Ronald E. "Deuteronomy and the Jerusalem Cult Tradition," *Vetus Testamentum* 15 (1965): 300–312.
Coin-Longeray, Sandrine. "Πενία et πένης: Travailler pour vivre?," *Revue de philologie, de littérature et d'histoire anciennes* 75 (2001): 249–56.
Cook, Stephen L. "Those Stubborn Levites: Overcoming Levitical Disenfranchisement." In *Priests and Levites in History and Tradition*, ed. Mark A. Leuchter and Jeremy. M. Hutton, 155–70. Atlanta, GA: SBL, 2012.
Craigie, Peter C. *The Book of Deuteronomy*. Grand Rapids, MN: Eerdmans, 1976.
Crawford, Sidnie W. "4QDeut^c." In *Qumran Cave 4 IX Deuteronomy, Joshua, Judges, Kings*, DJD XIV, ed. Eugene Ulrich, Frank M. Cross, Sidnie W. Crawford and Julie A. Duncan. Oxford: Clarendon, 1995.
Crouch, Carly L. *Israel and the Assyrians. Deuteronomy, the Succession Treaty of Esarhaddon, and the Nature of Subversion*. Atlanta, GA: SBL, 2014.
—. *The Making of Israel: Cultural Diversity in the Southern Levant and the Formation of Ethnic Identity in Deuteronomy*. Leiden: Brill, 2014.
—. "The Threat to Israel's Identity in Deuteronomy: Mesopotamian or Levantine?" *Zeitschrift für die alttestamentliche Wissenschaft* 124 (2012): 541–54.
Crüsemann, Frank. "Theokratie als Demokratie. Zur politischen Konzeption des Deuteronomiums." In *Anfänge politischen Denkens in der Antike: die nahöstliche Kulturen und die Griechen*, ed. Kurt Raaflaub and Elisabeth Müller-Luckner, 199–214. München: Oldenbourg, 1993.
Cullen, John. *The Book of the Covenant in Moab: A Critical Inquiry into the Original Form of Deuteronomy*. Glasgow: James Maclehose and Sons, 1903.
D'Eichthal, Gustave. *Mélanges de critique biblique: le texte primitif du premier récit de la création. Le Deutéronome, le nom et le caractère du Dieu d'Israël Yahveh*. Paris: Hachette, 1886.
Dalman, Gustaf. *Arbeit und Sitte*. Gütersloh: Bertelsmann, 1939.
Davies, Philip R. "The Authority of Deuteronomy." In *Deuteronomy-Kings as Emerging Authoritative Books: A Conversation*, ed. Diana V. Edelman, 27–47. Atlanta, GA: SBL, 2014.

—. "From Where Did Deuteronomy Originate?" In *Deuteronomy in the Making: Studies in the Production of Debarim*, ed. D. Edelman, Benedetta Rossi, K. Berge, and P. Guillaume, 13–24. Berlin: de Gruyter, 2021.

—. "Josiah and the Law Book." In *Good Kings and Bad Kings: The Kingdom of Judah in the Seventh Century*, ed. Lester L. Grabbe, 65–77. London: T&T Clark, 2005.

—. *The Origins of Biblical Israel*. New York: T.&T. Clark International, 2007.

De Wette, Wilhelm. M. L. *Dissertatio critico-exegetica qua Deuteronomium a prioribus libris Pentateuchi diversum, alius cuiusdam recentioris auctoris opus esse monstratur*. PhD diss., University of Jena: Etzdorf, 1805.

Démare-Lafont, Sophie. "Eléments pour une diplomatique juridique des textes d'Émar." In *Trois millénaires de formulaires juridiques*, ed. Sophie Démare-Lafont and André Lemaire 43–84. Genève: Droz, 2010.

—. "Les « frères » en Syrie à l'époque du Bronze récent: réflexions et hypothèse." In Organization, Representation, and Symbols of Power in the Ancient Near East: Proceedings of the 54th Rencontre Assyriologique Internationale, ed. Gernot Wilhelm, 129–41. Winona Lake, IN: Eisenbrauns, 2012.

Duncan-Jones, Richard. Economy of the Roman Empire. Cambridge: Cambridge University, 1974.

Dušek, Jan. "The Importance of the Wadi Daliyeh Manuscripts for the History of Samaria and the Samaritans," *Religions* 11 (2020): 1–12, doi.org/10.3390/rel11020063

Ebach, Ruth. *Das Fremde und das Eigene*. Berlin: de Gruyter, 2014.

—. "'You shall Walk Exactly on the Way which YHWH Your God has Commanded You': Characteristics of Deuteronomy's Concepts of Leadership." In *Debating Authority*, ed. Katharina Pyschny and Sarah Schulz, 159–77. Berlin: de Gruyter, 2018.

Edelman, Diana V. "Deuteronomy as Instructions of Moses and Yahweh Literature versus a Framed Legal Code." In *Deuteronomy in the Making: Studies in the Production of Debarim*, ed. D. Edelman, Benedetta Rossi, K. Berge, and P. Guillaume, 25–76. Berlin: de Gruyter, 2021.

—. "Different Sources, Different Views: Snapshots of Persian-Era Yehud Based on Texts and on Archaeological Data," *Estudios Biblicos* 76 (2018): 411–51.

Edenburg, Cynthia and Reinhard Müller. "A Northern Provenance for Deuteronomy?," *Hebrew Bible and Ancient Israel* 4 (2015): 148–61.

Eissfeldt, Otto. *Erstlinge und Zehnten im Alten Testament*. Leipzig: Hinrich, 1917.

Elat, Moshe. "The Economic Relations of the Neo-Assyrian Empire with Egypt." *Journal of the American Oriental Society* 98 (1978): 20–34.

—. "Der tamkāru im neuassyrischen Reich." *Journal of the Economic and Social History of the Orient* 30 (1987): 233–54.

Eldevik, John. *Episcopal Power and Ecclesiastical Reform in the German Empire. Tithes, Lordship, and Community, 950–1150*. Cambridge: Cambridge University Press, 2012.

Epstein, Steven. A. "Economics in Dante's Hell." In *In laudem hierosolymitani*, ed. Iris Shagrir, Ronnie Ellenblum and Jonathan C. Riley-Smith, 437–46. Aldershot: Ashgate, 2007.

Fabry, Heinz-Josef. "Deuteronomium 15. Gedanken zur Geschwister-Ethik im Alten Testament," *Zeitschrift für Altorientalische und Biblische Rechtsgeschichte* 3 (1997): 92–111.

Faust, Avraham. *Israelite Society in the Period of the Monarchy. An Archaeological Perspective.* Jerusalem: Yad Ben Zvi, 2005.

Fitzpatrick-McKinley, Anne. *The Transformation of Torah from Scribal Advice to Law.* Sheffield: Sheffield Academic Press, 1999.

Fleishman, Joseph. "Spreading the Cloth in Deuteronomy 22:17b. Conclusive Evidence of the Beginning of the Evidential Procedure?" *Zeitschrift für Altorientalische und Biblische Rechtsgeschichte* 18 (2012): 295–308.

Foldvari Peter and Bas van Leeuwen. "Market Performance in Early Economies: Concepts and Empirics with an application to Babylon." In *A History of Market Performance from Ancient Babylonia to the Modern World*, ed. Bert van der Spek, Jan L. van Zanden and Bas van Leeuwen, 19–44. London: Routledge, 2015.

Franklin, Norma. "Review of *The Archaeology of the Ostraca House at Israelite Samaria: Epigraphic Discoveries in Complicated Contexts* by Ron E. Tappy," *Journal of Eastern Mediterranean Archaeology and Heritage Studies* 6 (2018): 148–151.

—. "Samaria: From the Bedrock to the Omride Palace," *Levant* 36 (2004): 189–202.

Friedland Roger and Richard Hecht. "The Nebi Musa Pilgrimage and the Origins of Palestinian Nationalism." In *Pilgrims and Travelers to the Holy Land*, ed. Bryan F. Le Beau and Menahem Mor, 89–118. Omaha, NB: Creighton University, 1996.

Fries, Samuel, *Die Gesetzesschrift des Königs Josia. Eine kritische Untersuchung.* Leipzig: Georg Böhme, 1903.

Frymer-Kensky, Tikva. "Israel." In *Security for Debt in Ancient Near Eastern Law*, ed. Raymond Westbrook and Richard Jasnow, 251–63. Leiden: Brill, 2001.

Gallagher, Edmon L. "Cult Centralization in the Samaritan Pentateuch and the Origins of Deuteronomy," *Vetus Testamentum* 64 (2014): 561–72.

Garlan, Yvon. "War and Peace." In *The Greeks*, ed. Jean-Pierre Vernant. Chicago, IL: University of Chicago, 1995.

Glanville, Mark R. *Adopting the Stranger as Kindred in Deuteronomy.* Atlanta, GA: SBL, 2018.

Glassman, Jonathon P. *Social Rebellion and Swahili Culture: The Response to German Conquest of the Northern Mrima, 1888–1890.* PhD thesis, University of Wisconsin-Madison, 1988.

—. "Sorting out the Tribes: The Creation of Racial Identities in Colonial Zanzibar's Newspaper Wars," *Journal of African History* 41 (2000): 395–428.

—. *War of Words, War of Stones: Racial Thoughts and Violence in Colonial Zanzibar.* Bloomington: Indiana University, 2011.
Goitein, Shlomo Dov, *A Mediterranean Society: The Jewish Communities of the Arab World as Portrayed in the Documents of the Cairo Geniza.* Berkeley, CA: University of California, 1967–1993.
Gottheil, Richard J. H. "On קושיהו and קישי," *Journal of Biblical Literature* 17 (1898): 199–202.
Graber, D. "The גר (gēr) in Deuteronomy." In Deuteronomy in the Making: Studies in the Production of Debarim, ed. D. Edelman, Benedetta Rossi, K. Berge, and P. Guillaume, 365–82. Berlin: de Gruyter, 2021.
Greenspahn, Frederick E. "Deuteronomy and Centralization." *Vetus Testamentum* 64 (2014): 227–35.
Greifenhagen Franz V. *Egypt on the Pentateuch's Ideological Map.* Sheffield: Sheffield Academic Press, 2002.
Guillaume, Philippe. "Binding 'Sucks': A Response to Stefan Schorch," *Vetus Testamentum* 61 (2011): 335–37.
—. *Land, Credit and Crisis.* Sheffield: Equinox, 2012.
—. "Thou shalt not Curdle Milk with Rennet," *Ugarit Forschungen* 34 (2002): 213–15.
—. *Waiting for Josiah: The Judges.* London: T. & T. Clark International, 2004.
—. "פְּרוּ וּרְבוּ and the Seventh Year: Complementary Strategies for the Economic Recovery of Depopulated Yehud." In *The Economy of Judah in its Historical Context*, ed. Marvin. L. Miller, Ehud Ben Zvi and Gary N. Knoppers, 123–50. Winona Lake, IN: Eisenbrauns, 2015.
Hackl, Johannes. "The Esangila Temple during the Late Achaemenid Period and the Impact of Xerxes' Reprisals on the Northern Babylonian Temple Households." In *Xerxes and Babylonia*, ed. Caroline Waerzeggers and Maarja. Seire, 165–88. Leuven: Peeters, 2018.
Hagedorn, Anselm C. *Between Moses and Plato: Individual and Society in Deuteronomy and Ancient Greek Law.* Göttingen: Vandenhoeck & Ruprecht, 2004.
. "Placing (a) God. Central Theory in Deuteronomy 12 and at Delphi." In Temple and Worship in Israel and the Ancient Near East. Proceedings of the Oxford Old Testament Seminar, 188–211. London: T. & T. Clark International, 2005.
Halabi, Awad Eddie "The Nabi Musa Festival Under British-Ruled Palestine," *ISIM Newsletter* 10, 27 (2002): https://corescholar.libraries.wright.edu/history/30.
Hall, Gary. H. *Deuteronomy.* Joplin, MO: College Press, 2000.
Halpern, Baruch. "The Centralization Formula in Deuteronomy," *Vetus Testamentum* 31 (1981): 20–38.
—. "What does Deuteronomy Centralizes?" In *Deuteronomy in the Making: Studies in the Production of Debarim*, ed. D. Edelman, Benedetta Rossi, K. Berge, and P. Guillaume, 97–162. Berlin: de Gruyter, 2021.

Hamilton, Jeffries M. *Social Justice in Deuteronomy: The Case of Deuteronomy 15.* Atlanta, GA: Scholars, 1992.
Havely, Nicholas R. "Poverty in Purgatory: from *Commercium* to *Commedia*," *Dante Studies* 114 (1996): 229–43.
Haworth, Marina. "The Wolfish Lover: The Dog as a Comic Metaphor in Homoerotic Symposium Pottery," *Archimède* 5 (2018): 7–23: https://archimede.unistra.fr/revue-archimede/.
Henkelman, Wouter F. M. "Parnakka's Feast: šip in Pārsa and Elam." In *Elam and Persia*, ed. Javier Álvarez-Mon and Mark B. Garrison, 89–166. Winona Lake, IN: Eisenbrauns, 2011.
—. "Practice of Worship in the Achaemenid Heartland." In *A Companion to the Achaemenid Persian Empire*, ed. B. Jacobs and R. Rollinger, chapter 86. Malden, MA: Wiley-Blackwell, 2021.
—. *The Other Gods Who Are: Studies in Elamite-Iranian Acculturation Based on the Persepolis Fortification Tablets.* Leiden: Brill, 2008.
Hensel, Benedikt. *Juda und Samaria.* Tübingen: Mohr Siebeck, 2016.
Herman, Menahem. "Tithes as Gift: The Biblical Institution in Light of Mauss's Prestation Theory," *Association for Jewish Studies Review* 18 (1993): 51–73.
Hertz, J. H. *The Pentateuch and the Haftorahs.* Oxford: Oxford University Press, 1960, original version 1936.
Himbaza, Innocent. "«Le lieu que YHWH aura choisi». Une perspective narrative, historique et philologique," *Semitica* 58 (2016): 115–34.
Hölscher, Gustav. "Komposition und Ursprung des Deuteronomiums," *Zeitschrift für die alttestamentliche Wissenschaft* 40 (1922): 161–255.
Horst, Louis. "Etudes sur le Deutéronome: II – Les sources et la date du Deutéronome (suite et fin)," *Revue de l'histoire des religions* 27 (1893): 119–76.
Houston, Walter. J. *Contending for Justice.* London: T. & T. Clark, 2006.
—. *Purity and Monotheism: Clean and Unclean Animals in Biblical Law.* Sheffield: Sheffield Academic Press, 1993.
Hudson, Michael. "Reviewed Work: *Macroeconomics from the Beginning: The General Theory, Ancient Markets, and the Rate of Interest* by David A. Warburton," *Journal of the Economic and Social History of the Orient* 48 (2005): 118–22.
Humbert, Paul. "Le mot biblique *èbyôn*," *Revue d'histoire et de philosophie religieuse* 32 (1952): 1–5 = *Opuscules d'un hébraïsant*, 187–92. Neuchâtel: Secrétariat de l'Université, 1958.
—. "*Laetari et Exultare* dans le vocabulaire religieux de l'Ancien Testament," *Revue d'histoire et de philosophie religieuse* 22 (1942): 185–214 = *Opuscules d'un hébraïsant*, 119–45. Neuchâtel: Secrétariat de l'Université, 1958.
Hurowitz, Victor. "Temporary temples." In *kinattūtu ša dārâti. Raphael Kutscher Memorial Volume*, ed. Anson F. Rainey, 37–50. Tel Aviv: Tel Aviv University, 1993.

Jagersma, H. "The Tithes in the Old Testament," *Old Testament Studies* 21 (1981): 116–28.
Japhet, Sara. "The Relationship between the Legal Corpora in the Pentateuch in Light of Manumission Laws." In *Studies in Bible*, ed. Sara Japhet, 63–89. Jerusalem: Magnes, 1986.
Joannès, Francis and André Lemaire. "Contrats babyloniens d'époque achéménide du Bît-abi Râm avec une épitaphe araméenne," *Revue d'assyriologie et d'archéologie orientale* 90 (1996): 41–60.
—. "Trois tablettes cunéiformes à l'onomastique ouest-sémitique," *Transeuphratène* 17 (1999): 17–34.
Jones, Donald W. *Economic Theory and the Ancient Mediterranean*. Malden, MA: Chichester, 2014.
Joüon, Paul and Takamitsu Muraoka. *A Grammar of Biblical Hebrew*. Rome: Pontificio Istituto Biblico, 2008.
Jursa, Michael (ed.) *Aspects of the Economic History of Babylonia in the First Millennium*. Münster: Ugarit-Verlag, 2010.
—. "Silver and Other Forms of Elite Wealth in Seventh Century BC Babylonia." In *Silver, Money and Credit. A Tribute to Robartus J. van der Spek on the Occasion of his 65th Birthday on 18th September 2014*, ed. Kristin Kleber and Reinhard Pirngruber, 61–71. Leiden: Nederlands Instituut voor het Nabije Oosten, 2016.
—. "Talking of Eating and Food in Iron-Age Babylonia." In *Libiamo ne' lieti calici. Ancient Near Eastern Studies Presented to Lucio Milano on the Occasion of his 65th Birthday by Pupils, Colleagues and Friends*, ed. PaolavCorò, Elena Devecchi, Nicla De Zorzi, and Massimo Maiocchi, 181–98. Münster: Ugarit Verlag, 2016.
Jursa, Michael and Sven Tost, "Greek and Roman Slaving in Comparative Ancient Perspective: The State and Dependent Labour in the Ancient Near East and in the Graeco-Roman World." In *Imperium & Officium: Comparative Studies in Ancient Bureaucracy and Officialdom IOWP*: http://iowp.univie.ac.at/node/2.
Kaufman, Stephen A. "The Structure of the Deuteronomic Law," *Maarav* 1 (1978): 105–58
—. "Deuteronomy 15 and Recent Research on the Dating of P." In *Deuteronomium: Entstehung, Gestalt und Botschaft*, ed. Norbert Lohfink, 273–76. Leuven: Leuven University Press, 1985.
Kessler, Rainer. "Debt and the Decalogue: The Tenth Commandment," *Vetus Testamentum* 65 (2015): 1–9.
Kilchör, Benjamin. *Mose Tora und Jahwetora*. Wiesbaden: Harrassowitz, 2015.
Kletter, Raz. *Economic Keystones: The Weight System of the Kingdom of Judah*. Sheffield: Sheffield Academic Press, 1998.
—. "Vessels and Measures: The Biblical Liquid Capacity System," *Israel Exploration Journal* 64 (2014): 22–37.
Kline, Meredith. G. *Treaty of the Great King*. Grand Rapids, MN: Eerdmans, 1963.

Kloppenborg, John S. "New Institutional Economics, Euergetism, and Associations." In *The Extramercantile Economies of Greek and Roman Cities: New Perspectives on the Economic History of Classical Antiquity*, ed. David B. Hollander, Thomas R. Blanton IV and John T. Fitzgerald, 117–29. London and New York: Routledge, 2019.

Knauf, Ernst Axel. "Observations on Judah's Social and Economic History and the Dating of the Laws in Deuteronomy," *Journal of Hebrew Scriptures* 9 (2009): article 18.

Knight, Donald A. "Whose Agony? Whose Ecstasy? The Politics of Deuteronomic Law." In *Shall not the Judge of All the Earth Do Right? Studies on the Nature of God in the Tribute to James L. Crenshaw*, ed. D. Penchansky and Paul L. Redditt. 97–112. Winona Lake, IN: Eisenbrauns, 2000.

Knoppers, Gary N. "Establishing the Rule of Law? The Composition Num 33,50 –56 and the Relationships Among the Pentateuch, the Hexateuch, and the Deuteronomistic History." In *Das Deuteronomium zwischen Pentateuch und Deuteronomistischem Geschichtswerk*, ed. Eckart Otto and Reinhard Achenbach, 135-152. Göttingen: Vandenhoeck & Ruprecht, 2004.

—. *Jews and Samaritans.* Oxford: Oxford University Press, 2013.

—. "The Northern Context of the Law Code of Deuteronomy," *Hebrew Bible and Ancient Israel* 4 (2014): 162–83.

—. "Rethinking the Relationship between Deuteronomy and the Deuteronomistic History: The Case of Kings," *Catholic Biblical Quarterly* 63 (2001) 393–415.

Kratz, Reinhard G. *The Composition of the Narrative Books of the Old Testament.* London: T. & T. Clark International, 2005.

Lambert, Wilfred. G. "The Qualifications of Babylonian Diviners." In *Festschrift für Rykle Borger zu seinem 65. Geburtstag am 24. Mai 1994*, ed. S. M. Maul, 141-158. Groningen: Styx, 1998.

Lauinger, Jacob. "Esarhaddon's Succession Treaty at Tell Tayinat: Text and Commentary," *Journal of Cuneiform Studies* 64 (2012): 87–123.

Lawson Younger, K. Jr., "Ninurta-Kudurrī-uṣur." In *The Context of Scripture* 2, ed. William W. Hallo, 2.115B. Leiden: Brill, 2003.

Lemaire, André. "New Aramaic Ostraca from Idumea and their Historical Interpretation." In *Judah and the Judeans in the Persian Period*, ed. Oded Lipschits and Manfred Oeming, 413–56. Winona Lake, IN: Eisenbrauns, 2006.

Lemche, Nils P. "'Hebrew' as a National Name for Israel," *Studia Theologica* 33 (1979): 1–23.

Levin, Christoph. "Rereading Deuteronomy in the Persian and Hellenistic Periods: The Ethics of Brotherhood and the Care of the Poor." In *Deuteronomy-Kings as Emerging Authoritative Books: A Conversation*, ed. Diana V. Edelman, 49–71. Society of Biblical Literature Ancient Near East Monographs 6, Atlanta, GA: Society of Biblical Literature, 2014.

Levin, Y. "From Lists to History: Chronological Aspects of the Chronicler's Genealogies," *Journal of Biblical Literature* 123 (2004): 601–636.

—. "The Role of the Levites in Chronicles: Past, Present, Utopia?" in Ben Porat Yosef, ed. M. Avioz, O. Minka and Y. Shemesh. Münster: Ugarit-Verlag, 2019) 133–46.

Levinson, Bernard M. "The Manumission of Hermeneutics: The Slave Laws of the Pentateuch as a Challenge to Contemporary Pentateuchal Theory." In *Congress Volume Leiden 2004*, ed. A. Lemaire. 281-324. Leiden: Brill, 2006.

Lipínski, Edouard. "L'esclave hébreu," *Vetus Testamentum* 26 (1976): 120–24.

Lipton, Diana. "Legal Analogy in Deuteronomy and Fratricide in the Field." In *Studies on the Text and Versions of the Hebrew Bible in Honour of Robert Gordon*, ed. Geoffrey Khan and Diana Lipton, 21–38. Leiden: Brill, 2011.

Liverani, Mario. "La ceramica e i testi: commercio miceneo e politica orientale." In *Traffici micenei nel mediterraneo*, ed. Massimiliano Marazzi, Sebastiano Tusa, Lucia Vagnetti, 405–12. Taranto: Istituto per la storia e l'archeologia della Magna Grecia, 1986.

—. "Early Caravan Trade between South-Arabia and Mesopotamia," *Yemen* 1 (1992): 111–15.

—. "The Influence of Political Institutions on Trade in the Ancient Near East (Late Bronze to Early Iron Age)." In *Mercanti e politica nel mondo antico*, ed. Carlo Zaccagnini, 126–27. Rome: L'Erma di Bretschneider, 2003.

Livingstone, Alasdair. *Court Poetry and Literary Miscellanea.* Helsinki: Helsinki University Press, 1989.

Lohfink, Norbert. "Das deuteronomische Gesetz in der Endgestalt - Entwurf eine Gesellschaft ohne marginale Gruppen," *Biblische Notizen* 51 (1990): 25–40.

—. "Poverty in the Laws of the Ancient Near East and of the Bible," *Theological Studies* 52 (1991): 34–50.

—. "The Destruction of the Seven Nations in Deuteronomy and the Mimetic Theory," Contagion: Journal of Violence, Mimesis, and Culture 2 (1995): 103–17.

—. "Distribution and Functions of Power: the Laws concerning Public Offices in Deuteronomy 16:18–18:22." In *A Song of Power and the Power of Song*, ed. Duane L. Christensen, 345–49. Winona Lake, IN: Eisenbrauns, 1993.

Lundbom, Jack R. *Deuteronomy: A Commentary.* Grand Rapids, MN: Eerdmans, 2014.

Lynch, Kathleen. "The Hellenistic Symposium as Feast." In *Feasting and Polis Institutions*, ed. Floris van den Eijnde, Josine H. Blok and Rolf Strootman, 233–56. Leiden: Brill, 2018.

Martinuzzi, Bruna. *The Leader as a Mensch: Become the Kind of Person Others Want to Follow.* Six Seconds Emotional Intelligence Press, 2009.

Mattison, Kevin. *Rewriting and Revision as Amendment in the Laws of Deuteronomy.* Tübingen: Mohr Siebeck, 2018.

Mayes, Andrew D. H. *Deuteronomy*. Grand Rapids, MN: Eerdmans, 1981.
McCarthy, Carmel. *Biblia hebraica quinta 5*. Stuttgart: Deutsche Bibelgesellschaft, 2007.
McConville, J. Gordon. *Deuteronomy*. Leicester: Apollos, 2002.
Milgrom, Jacob. *Leviticus 23-27*. New York: Doubleday, 2000.
—. "Profane Slaughter and a Formulaic Key to the Composition of Deuteronomy," *Hebrew Union College Annual* 47 (1976): 1-17.
Miller, Marvin L. "Methods and Models for Understanding Ancient Economies." In *The Economy of Ancient Judah in its Historical Context*, ed. Marvin L. Miller, Ehud Ben Zvi and Gary N. Knoppers, 3-26. Winona Lake, IN: Eisenbrauns, 2015.
Milstein, Sara J. "Will and (Old) Testament: Reconsidering the Roots of Deuteronomy 25,5-10." In *Writing, Rewriting, and Overwriting in the Books of Deuteronomy and the Former Prophets. Essays in Honour of Cynthia Edenburg*, ed. Ido Koch, Thomas Römer and Omer Sergi, 49-64. Leuven: Peeters, 2019.
Miralles Maciá, Lorena. *Marzeaḥ y thíassos. Una institución convival en el Oriente Próximo Antiguo y el Mediterráneo*. Madrid: Publicationes Univesidad Complutense de Madrid, 2007.
Monson, Andrew. "The Ethics and Economics of Ptolemaic Religious Associations," *Ancient Society* 36 (2006): 221-38.
Moran, William L. "A Note on the Treaty Terminology of the Sefîre Stela," *Journal of Near Eastern Studies* 22 (1963): 173-76.
Morrow, William S. *An Introduction to Biblical Law*. Grand Rapids, MN: Eerdmans, 2017.
—. *Scribing the Center. Organization and Redaction in Deuteronomy 14:1-17:13*. Atlanta, GA: Scholars, 1995.
Mukenge, André K. "«Toutefois, il n'y aura pas de nécessiteux chez toi». La stratégie argumentative de Deut. 15:1-11," *Vetus Testamentum* 60 (2010): 69-86.
Muraoka, Takamitsu. *Emphatic Words and Structures in Biblical Hebrew*. Jerusalem: Magnes, 1985.
—. *A Greek-English Lexicon of the Septuagint*. Leuven: Peeters, 2009.
Mutius, Hans-Georg von. "Die Zinsgesetzgebung in der Septuaginta zu Deuteronomium 23,21. Übersetzungs- und Sachprobleme aus nicht drittmittelgestützter Forschungsperspektive," *Biblische Notizen* 163 (2014): 19-24.
Na'aman, Nadav. "Dismissing the Myth of a Flood of Israelite Refugees in the Late Eighth Century BCE," *Zeitschrift für die alttestamentliche Wissenschaft* 126 (2014): 1-14.
—. "The Discovered Book and the Legitimation of Josiah's Reform," *Journal of Biblical Literature* 130 (2011): 47-62.

—. "Four Notes on the Ancient Near Eastern Marzeaḥ." In *Open-Mindedness in the Bible and Beyond. A Volume of Studies in Honour of Bob Becking*, ed. Marjo C. A. Korpel and Lester L. Grabbe, 215–22. London: T.&T. Clark, 2015.

—. "Resident-Alien or Residing Foreign Delegate," *Ugarit Forschungen* 37 (2005): 475–78.

—. "Sojourners and Levites in the Kingdom of Judah in the Seventh Century BCE," *Zeitschrift für Altorientalische und Biblische Rechtsgeschichte* 14 (2008): 237–79.

Nakanose, Shigeyuki. *Josiah's Passover: Sociology and the Liberating Bible*. Maryknoll: Orbis, 1993.

Nestor, Dermot. "We Are Family: Deuteronomy 14 and the Boundaries of an Israelite Identity," *Bible and Critical Theory* 9 (2013): 38–53.

Nicholson, Ernest. W. *Deuteronomy and the Judaean Diaspora*. Oxford: Oxford University, 2014.

—. *Deuteronomy and Tradition*. Oxford: Blackwell, 1967.

Nihan, Christophe. "Laws about Clean and Unclean Animals in Leviticus and Deuteronomy." In *The Pentateuch: International Perspectives on Current Research*, ed. Thomas B. Dozeman, Konrad Schmid and Baruch J. Schwartz, 401–34. Tübingen: Mohr Siebeck, 2011.

—. *From Priestly Torah to Pentateuch*. Tübingen: Mohr Siebeck, 2007.

—. "Resident Aliens and Natives in the Holiness Legislation." In *The Foreigner and the Law*, ed. Reinhard Achenbach, Rainer Albertz and Jacob Wöhrle, 111–34. Wiesbaden: Harrassowitz, 2011.

Noth, Martin. *History of Israel*. London: Black, 1960.

Oestreicher, Theodor. *Das deuteronomische Grundgesetz*. Gütersloh: Gütersloher Verlag, 1923.

Olivier, Johannes P. J. "Restitution as Economic Redress: The Fine Print of the Old Babylonian mēšarum-Edict of Ammiṣṣduqa," *Zeitschrift für Altorientalische und Biblische Rechtsgeschichte* 3 (1997): 12–25.

Olmo Lete, Gregorio del and Joaquín Sanmartín. *A Dictionary of the Ugaritic Language in the Alphabetic Tradition*. Leiden: Brill, 2004.

Oosthuizen, Martin J. "Deuteronomy 15:1–18 in Socio-Rhetorical Perspective," *Zeitschrift für Altorientalische und Biblische Rechtsgeschichte* 3 (1997): 64–91.

Otto, Eckhart, *Deuteronomium 1–11*. Freiburg in Brisgau: Herder, 2012.

—. *Deuteronomium 12–34*. Freiburg: Herder, 2016.

—. *Deuteronomium 12,1–23,15*. Freiburg in Brisgau: Herder, 2016.

—. *Das Deuteronomium im Pentateuch und Hexateuch*. Tübingen: Mohr Siebeck, 2000.

—. *Das Deuteronomium: Politische Theologie und Rechtsreform in Juda und Assyrien*. Berlin: de Gruyter, 1999.

—. "Deuteronomy as the Legal Completion and Prophetic Finale of the Pentateuch." In *Paradigm Change in Pentateuchal Research*, ed. Matthias Armgardt, Benjamin Kilchör and Markus Zehnder, 179-88. Wiesbaden: Harrassowitz, 2019.

—. "False Weights in the Scale of Biblical Justice? Different Views of Women from Patriarchal Hierarchy to Religious Equality in the Book of Deuteronomy." In *Gender and Law in the Hebrew Bible and the Ancient Near East*, ed. Victor H. Matthews, Bernard M. Levinson and Tikva Frymer-Kensky, 128-46. Sheffield: Sheffield Academic Press, 1998.

—. *Das Gesetz des Moses.* Darmstadt: Wissenschaftliche Buchgesellschaft, 2007.

—."Programme der sozialen Gerechtigkeit," *Zeitschrift für Altorientalische und Biblische Rechtsgeschichte* 3 (1997): 26-63.

Paganini, Simone. "Ein Gesetz zum Schutz der korrekten Kulthandlungen. Zauberei, Magie und andere verbotene Praktiken in Dtn 18,8-14." In *Zauber und Magie im antiken Palästina und seiner Umwelt,* ed. Jens Kamlah, Rolf Schäfer and Markus Witte, 309-42. Wiesbaden: Harrassowitz, 2017.

Pagolu, Augustine. *The Religion of the Patriarchs.* Sheffield: Sheffield Academic Press, 1998.

Pardee, Dennis. "The Meṣad Ḥashavyahu (Yavneh Yam) Ostracon." In *The Context of Scripture*, ed. William W. Hallo, 3.41. Leiden: Brill, 2002.

Pearce, Laurie E. and Cornelia Wunsch, *Documents of Judean Exiles and West Semites in Babylonia in the Collection of David Sofer.* Cornell University Studies in Assyriology and Sumerology 28. Bethesda, MD: CDL Press, 2014.

Perlitt, Lothar. "'Ein einzig Volk von Brüdern': Zur deuteronomischen Herkunft der biblischen Bezeichnung 'Brüder'." In *Kirche: Festschrift für Günther Bornkamm zum 75. Geburtstag*, ed. Dieter Lührmann and Georg Strecker, 27-52. Tübingen: J.C.B. Mohr, 1980; reprint in Lothar Perlitt, *Deuteronomium Studien*. Tübingen: J.C.B. Mohr, 1994, 50-73.

Pina-Cabral, João de. "The Mediterranean as a Category of Regional Comparison: A Critical Review," *Current Anthropology* 30 (1989) 399-406.

Pitkänen, Pekka. *Central Sanctuary and Centralization of Worship in Ancient Israel.* Piscataway, NJ: Gorgias, 2004.

Porten, Bezalel and Ada Yardeni, *Textbook of Aramaic Documents from Ancient Egypt.* Jerusalem: Hebrew University Press, 1986-1999.

Pury, Albert de. "Steinigt den störrischen Sohn!" - "Geißelt die Ehebrecher!" Überlegungen zum Sinn von "problematischen" Geboten in der biblischen und der koranischen Überlieferung." In *Propheten der Epochen. Prophets during the Epochs. Festschrift für István Karasszon for his 60th birthday / Studies in Honor of István Karasszon for his 60th Birthday.* ed. Viktor K. Nagy and Lásló. S. Egeresi, 151-60. Münster: Ugarit-Verlag, 2015.

Pyschny, Katharina. "From Core to Centre: Issues of Centralization in Numbers and Deuteronomy," *Hebrew Bible and Ancient Israel* 8 (2019): 287-312.

Rad, Gerhard von. *Das 5. Buch Mose – Deuteronomium.* Göttingen: Vandenhoeck & Ruprecht, 1983.

—. *Deuteronomy.* Philadelphia, PA: Westminster, 1966.

Radner, Karen. "Assyrische uppi adê als Vorbild für Deuteronomium 28:20–44?" In *Die deuteronomistischen Geschichtswerke: Redaktions- und religionsgeschichtliche Perspektiven zur 'Deuteronomismus'-Diskussion in Tora und Vorderen Propheten,* ed. Markus Witte, Konrad Schmid, Doris Prechel and Jan C. Gertz, 251–78. Berlin: de Gruyter, 2006.

—. "Traders in the Neo-Assyrian Period." In *Trade and Finance in Ancient Mesopotamia,* ed. Jan G. Dercksen, 101–26. Leiden: Nederlands Historisch-Archaeologisch Instituut te Istanbul, 1999.

Renger, Johannes M. "Comments on Economic Structures in Ancient Mesopotamia," *Orientalia* 63 (1994): 157–208.

Reuss, Eduard. *L'histoire sainte et la Loi: Pentateuque et Josué.* Paris: Librairie Sandoz et Fischbacher, 1879.

Reuter, Eleonore. *Kultzentralisation. Entstehung und Theologie von Dtn 12.* Frankfurt am Main: Hain, 1993.

Ribichini, Sergio. "A servizio di Astarte. Hierodulia e prostituzione sacra nei culti fenici e punici." In *El mundo púnico,* ed. Antonino González Blanco, Gonzalo Matilla Séiquer and Alejandro Egea Vivancos, 33–68. Murcia: Universidad de Murcia, 2004.

Richardson, Mervyn E. J. *Hammurabi's Laws.* Sheffield: Sheffield Academic Press, 2000.

Richter, Sandra L. "The Place of the Name in Deuteronomy," *Vetus Testamentum* 57 (2007): 342–66.

—. "Placing the Name, Pushing the Paradigm." In *Deuteronomy in the Pentateuch, Hexateuch, and the Deuteronomistic History,* ed. Konrad Schmid and R. F. Person, 64–78. Tübingen: Mohr Siebeck, 2012.

—. "What's Money got to do with It?" In Paradigm Change in Pentateuchal Research, ed. Matthias Armgardt, Benjamin Kilchör and Markus Zehnder, 301–22. Wiesbaden: Harrassowitz, 2019.

Ro, Johannes U. *Poverty, Law, and Divine Justice in Persian and Hellenistic Judah.* Atlanta, GA: SBL, 2018.

—. "The Question of Provenance and the Economics of Deuteronomy: The Neo-Babylonian and Persian Periods," *Catholic Biblical Quarterly* 82 (2020): 547–566.

Rogerson, John W. *W.M.L. de Wette. Founder of Modern Biblical Criticism.* Sheffield: JSOT Press, 1992.

Romano, Immanuel. *L'inferno e il paradiso,* ed. and transl. Giorgio Battistoni and Emanuele Weiss Levi. Florence: La Giuntina, 2000. English version Immanuel Ben Solomon Romi, Tophet and Eden (Hell and Paradise): in imitation of Dante's Inferno and Paradiso, from the Hebrew of Dante's contemporary (translated and edited by Hermann Gollancz). London: University of London Press, 1921.

Römer, Thomas C. "Cult Centralization in Deuteronomy 12." In *Das Deuteronomium zwischen Pentateuch und Deuteronomistischen Geschichtswerk*, ed. Eckart Otto and Reinhard Achenbach, 168–80. Göttingen: Vandenhoeck & Ruprecht, 2004.

—. "How to Date Pentateuchal Texts – Some Case Studies." In *Dating the Pentateuch*, ed. Jan C. Gertz, Bernard M. Levinson, Dalit Rom-Shiloni and Konrad Schmid, 357–70. Tübingen: Mohr Siebeck, 2016.

—. *The So-Called Deuteronomistic History*. London: T. & T. Clark, 2005.

Rossi, Benedetta. "Not by Bread Alone (Deut 8:3): Elite Struggles over Cultic Prebends and Moses's Torah in Deuteronomy," In *Deuteronomy in the Making: Studies in the Production of Debarim*, ed. D. Edelman, Benedetta Rossi, K. Berge, and P. Guillaume, 329–64. Berlin: de Gruyter, 2021.

Rossi, Benedetta and Philippe Guillaume. "An Alternative Reading the Law of the Hebrew 'Slave' (Deuteronomy 15:12-18)," *Res Antiquae* 15 (2018): 1–28.

Rütersworden, Udo. "Concerning Deut 14." In *What Is Bible?*, ed. Karin Finsterbusch and Armin Lange, 95–103. Leuven: Peeters, 2012.

—. "Purity Conceptions in Deuteronomy." In *Purity and the Forming of Religious Traditions in the Ancient Mediterranean World and Ancient Judaism*, ed. Christian Frevel and Christophe Nihan, 413–28. Leiden: Brill, 2013.

—. *Von der politischen Gemeinschaft zur Gemeinde. Studien zu Dt 16,18-18,22*. Frankfurt: Athenäum, 1987.

Sacher Fox, Nili. "Prohibition of Cross-Dressing in Deuteronomy 22:5." In *Mishneh Todah*, ed. Nili Sacher Fox, David A. Glatt-Gilad and Michael J. Williams, 49–71. Winona Lake, IN: Eisenbrauns, 2009.

Salonen, Erkki. "Über den Zehnten in Alten Mesopotamien: ein Beitrage zur Geschichte der Besteuerung,' *Studia Orientalia* 43 (1972): 1–62.

Samuel, Harald. *Von Priestern zum Patriarchen: Levi und die Leviten im Alten Testament*. Berlin: de Gruyter, 2014.

Schaper, Joachim. "Geld und Kult im Deuteronomium," *Jahrbuch für Biblische Theologie* 21 (2006): 45–54.

Scheffler, Eben. "Criticism of Government: Deuteronomy 17:14-20 between and beyond Synchrony and Diachrony." In *South African Perspectives on the Pentateuch between Synchrony and Diachrony*, ed. Jurie H. Le Roux and Eckart Otto, 124–37. New York: T. & T. Clark, 2007.

Schenker, Adrian. "Warum gibt es literalistische Übersetzungen in der Septuaginta?" In *Brennpunkt: die Septuaginta. Studien zur Entstehung und Bedeutung der Griechischen Bibel*, ed. Siegfried Kreuzer and Hans Joseph Lesch, 151–62. Stuttgart: Kohlhammer, 2004.

—. "Le Seigneur choisira-t-il le lieu de son nom ou l'a-t-il choisi? L'apport de la Bible grecque ancienne à l'histoire du texte samaritain et massorétique." In *Scripture in Transition*, ed. Anssi Voitila and Jutta Jokiranta, 339–51. Leiden: Brill, 2008.

—. "Textgeschichtliches zum Samaritanischen Pentateuch und Samareitikon." In *Samaritans: Past and Present: Current Studies*, ed. Menachem Mor and Friedrich V. Reiterer, 105–21. Berlin: de Gruyter, 2010.

Schiffman, Lawrence H. "The Septuagint and the Temple Scroll: Shared 'Halakhic Variants," *Septuagint and Cognate Studies* 33 (1992): 277–97.

Schmid, Konrad. *Literaturgeschichte des Alten Testaments*. Darmstadt: Wissenschaftliche Buchgesellschaft, 2008.

Schorch, Stephan. "The Construction of Samari(t)an Identity from the Inside and from the Outside." In *Between Cooperation and Hostility. Multiple Identities in Ancient Judaism and the Interaction with Foreign Powers*, ed. Rainer Albertz and Jacob Wöhrle, 135–50. Göttingen: Vandenhoeck & Ruprecht, 2013.

—. "The Samaritan Version of Deuteronomy and the Origin of Deuteronomy." In *Samaria, Samarians, Samaritans*, ed. J. Zsengellér, 23–37. Berlin: de Gruyter, 2011.

Sider, Ronald. J. "Evaluating the Triumph of the Market." In *The Jubilee Challenge. Utopia or Possibility?*, ed. Hans Ucko, 112–33. Geneva: WCC Publications, 1997.

Silverman, Jason M. "Judaeans under Persian Forced Labor and Migration Policies," *Anabasis Studia Classica et Orientalia* 6 (2015): 14–34.

Simkins, Ronald A. *Creation & Ecology. The Political Economy of Ancient Israel and the Environmental Crisis*. Eugene, OR: Cascade, 2020.

Simonton, Matthew. *Classical Greek Oligarchy. A Political History*. Princeton and Oxford: Princeton University Press, 2017.

Smelik, Klaas A. D. "The Inner Cohesion of Jeremiah 34:8–22, on the Liberation of Slaves during the Siege of Jerusalem, and its Relation to Deuteronomy 15." In *Torah and Tradition. Papers read at the Sixteenth Joint Meeting of the Society for Old Testament Study and the Oudtestamentisch Werkgezelschap, Edinburgh, 2015*, ed. Klaas Spronk, 239–50. Leiden: Brill, 2017.

Smith, William Roberston. *Lectures on the Religion of the Semites. Fundamental Institutions. First Series* (London: Adam & Charles Black 1889); second edition edited by J. S. Black (1894), reprint 1956 by Meridian Library, New York; third edition, introduced and additional notes by S. A. Cook (1927), reprint 1969 by Ktav, New York, with prolegomenon by James Muilenberg. Republished with an Introduction by Robert A. Segal. New Brunswick, NJ: Transaction Publications, 2002.

Snijders, Lambertus. A. *The Meaning of* זר *in the Old Testament*. Leiden: Brill, 1954.

Soss, Neal M. "Old Testament Law and Economic Society," *Journal of the History of Ideas* 34 (1973): 323–44.

Stackert, Jeffrey. "The Cultic Status in the Temple Scroll: Between History and Hermeneutics." In *Levites and Priests in Biblical History*, ed. Mark Leuchter and Jeremy M. Hutton. 199–214. Atlanta, GA: SBL, 2011.

—. *Rewriting the Torah*. Tübingen: Mohr Siebeck, 2007.
Steinberg, Naomi. "Romancing the Widow: The Economic Distinctions between the ʾalmānâ, the ʾiššâ-ʾalmānâ and the ʾēšet-hammēt." In *God's Word for Our World*, ed. Deborah L. Ellens, J. Harod Ellens, Isaac Kalimi and Rolf Knierim, 327–46. London: T. & T. Clark, 2004.
Steinkeller, Piotr. "Money-Lending Practices in Ur III Babylonia: the Issue of Economic Motivation." In *Debt and Economic Renewal in the Ancient Near East*, ed. Michael Hudson and Mark van de Mieroop, 109–37. Bethesda, MD: CDL, 2002.
Steymans, Hans Ulrich. "Deuteronomy and Tell Tayinat," *Verbum et Ecclesia* 12 (2012): 1–13 DOI: 10.4102/ve.v34i2.870.
Stolz, Fritz. *Strukturen und Figuren im Kult von Jerusalem. Studien zur altenorientalischen, vor- und frühisraelitischen Religion*. Berlin: de Gruyter, 1970.
Stulman, Louis. "Encroachment in Deuteronomy: An Analysis of the Social World of the D Code," *Journal of Biblical Literature* 109 (1990): 613–32.
Sulzbach, Carla. "Building Castles on the Shifting Sands of Memory: From Dystopian to Utopian Views of Jerusalem in the Persian Period." In *Memory and the City in Ancient Jerusalem*, ed. Diana V. Edelman and Ehud Ben Zvi, 309–20. Winona Lake, IN: Eisenbrauns, 2014.
Talmon, Shemaryahu. "Double Readings in the Massoretic Text," *Textus* 1 (1960): 144–84.
Thelle, Rannfrid I. *Approaches to the "Chosen Place": Accessing a Biblical Concept*. New York: T. & T. Clark International, 2012.
Tigay, Jeffrey H. *Deuteronomy*. Philadelphia, PA: JPS, 1996.
—. "The Role of the Elders in the Laws of Deuteronomy." In *A Common Cultural Heritage: Studies on Mesopotamia and the Biblical World in Honor of Barry L. Eichler*, ed. Grant Frame, Erle Leichty, Karen Sonik, Jeffrey Tigay, and Steve Tinney, 89–96. Bethesda, MD: CDL Press, 2011.
—. "'To Place His Name There': Deuteronomy's Concept of God Placing His Name in the Temple." In *'Now It Happened in Those Days' Studies in Biblical, Assyrian and Other Ancient Near Eastern Historiography Presented to Mordechai Cogan on his 75th Birthday*, ed. Amittai Baruchi-Unna, Tova L. Forti, Shmuel Ahituv, Israel Eph'al, and Jeffrey H. Tigay, 1.17–26. Winona Lake, IN: Eisenbrauns, 2017.
Tilly, Charles. *Trust and Rule*. Cambridge: Cambridge University, 2005.
Trevett, Jeremy. "Status and Class." In *Themes in Greek Society and Culture: An Introduction to Ancient Greece*, ed. Allison Glazebrook and Christina Verster. Don Mills, Ontario: Oxford University Press, 2017.
Trundle, Matthew. "Coinage and the Economics of the Athenian Empire." In *Circum Mare: Themes in Ancient Warfare*, ed. Jeremy Armstrong, 65–79. Leiden: Brill, 2016.
Tsai, Daisy. Y. *Human Rights in Deuteronomy*. Berlin: de Gruyter, 2014.

Tsevat, Matitiahu. "The Hebrew Slave According to Deuteronomy 15:12–18: His Lot and the Value of His Work with Special Attention to the Meaning of מִשְׁנֶה," *Journal of Biblical Literature* 113 (1994): 587–95.
Tugendhaft, Aaron. "How to Become a Brother in the Bronze Age: An Inquiry into the Representation of Politics in Ugaritic Myth," *Fragments* 2 (2012): 89–104.
Ulrich, Eugene. "4QJoshua^a and Joshua's First Altar in the Promised Land." In *New Qumran Texts and Studies*, ed. Georges J. Brooke and F. García Martínez, 89–104. Leiden: Brill, 1994.
—. *Biblical Qumran Scrolls: Transcriptions and Textual Variants*. Leiden: Brill, 2010.
Van den Eijnde, Floris. "Power Play at the Dinner Table: Feasting and Patronage between Palace and Polis in Attika." In *Feasting and Polis Institutions*, ed. Floris Eijnde, Josine H. Blok and Rolf Strootman, 60–92. Leiden: Brill, 2018.
Van der Brugge, Caroline. "Production, Profit and Destruction: Of Production, Trade, Profit and Destruction: An Economic Interpretation of Sennacherib's Third Campaign," *Journal of the Economic and Social History of the Orient* 60 (2017): 292–335.
Van Leeuwen, Marco. H. D. *The Logic of Charity*. New York: St Martin's Press, 2000.
Van Seters, John. *A Lawbook for the Diaspora: Revision in the Study of the Covenant Code*. Oxford: Oxford University Press, 2003.
—. "The Law of the Hebrew Slave: A Continuing Debate," *Zeitschrift für die alttestamentliche Wissenschaft* 119 (2007): 169–83.
—. *The Pentateuch*. Sheffield: Sheffield Academic Press, 1999.
Vargyas, Peter. "Babylonian Interest Rates: Weren't they Annual?" In *Studi sul Vicino Oriente Antico*, ed. Simonetta Graziani and Luigi Cagni, 1095-1105. Naples: Istituto Universitario Orientale, 2000.
Veijola Timo. *Das 5. Buch Moses*. Göttingen: Vandenhoeck & Ruprecht, 2004.
Venter, Pieter. M. "The Dietary Regulations in Deuteronomy 14 within its Literary Context," *HTS Teologiese Studies / Theological Studies* 58 (2002): 1240–62.
Vernes, Maurice. *Une nouvelle hypothèse sur la composition du Deutéronome. Examen des vues de M. G. d'Eichthal*. Paris: Ernest Leroux, 1887.
—. *Précis d'histoire juive*. Paris: Hachette, 1889.
Villard, Pierre. "L'(an)darāru à l'époque néo-assyrienne," *Revue d'assyriologie et d'archéologie orientale* 101 (2007): 107–23.
Von Gall, August (ed.), *Der hebräische Pentateuch der Samaritaner*. Berlin: de Gruyter, 1966.
Waerzeggers, Caroline. *The Ezida Temple of Borsippa: Priesthood, Cult, Archives*. Leiden: Nederlands Instituut voor het Nabije Oosten, 2010.
—. "Review Article Laurie E. Pearce and Cornelia Wunsch, Documents of Judean Exiles and West Semites in Babylonia in the Collection of

David Sofer Cornell University Studies in Assyriology and Sumerology (CUSAS) 28," *Strata: Bulletin of the Anglo-Israel Archaeolocial Society* 33 (2015) 179–94.

—. and Michael Jursa. "On the Initiation of Babylonian Priests," *Zeitschrift für Altorientalische und Biblische Rechtsgeschichte* 14 (2008): 1–38.

Wagner-Tsukamoto, Sigmund A. "An Economic Reading of the Exodus: On the Institutional Economic Reconstruction of Biblical Cooperation Failures," *Scandinavian Journal of the Old Testament* 22 (2008): 114–34.

Wallace, Robert W. "Greek Oligarchy and the pre-Solonian Aeropagos Council in [Aristotle] *Ath. Pol.*2.2–8.4," *Polis* 31 (2014): 191–205.

Waltke, Bruce K. and Michael P. O'Connor, *An Introduction to Biblical Hebrew Syntax*. Winona Lake, IN: Eisenbrauns, 1990.

Weigert, Sebastian. *Hebraica veritas*. Stuttgart: Kohlhammer, 2016.

Weinfeld, Moshe. *Deuteronomy 1–11*. New York: Doubleday, 1991.

—. *Deuteronomy and the Deuteronomic School*. Oxford: Clarendon, 1972.

—. "Deuteronomy: The Present State of the Field." In *A Song of Power and the Power of Song*, ed. Duane L. Christensen, 21–35. Winona Lake, IN: Eisenbrauns, 1993.

Welch, Adam. *The Code of Deuteronomy. A New Theory of its Origin*. London: James Clarke and Co., 1924.

—. *Deuteronomy: the Framework to the Code*. London: Oxford University, 1932.

Wellhausen, Julius. *Prolegomena to the History of Israel*. Translated by J. Sutherland Black and Allan Enzies, with preface by William Robertson Smith. Edinburgh: Black, 1885. Reprinted as *Prolegomena to the History of Israel*. Atlanta, GA: Scholars, 1994.

Wells, Bruce. *The Law of Testimony in the Pentateuchal Codes*. Wiesbaden: Harrassowitz, 2004.

—. "The Interpretation of Legal traditions in Ancient Israel," *Hebrew Bible and Ancient Israel* 4 (2015): 234–66.

—. "Sex Crimes in the Laws of the Hebrew Bible," *Near Eastern Archaeology* 78 (2015): 294–303.

Welton, Rebekah. *'He is a Glutton and a Drunkard'. Deviant Consumption in the Hebrew Bible*. Leiden: Brill, 2020.

Welwei, Karl-Wilhelm. "Proxenia, proxenos", in *Brill's New Pauly*, 2006, Antiquity volumes, ed. Hubert Cancik and Helmuth Schneider, English Edition by Christine F. Salazar, Classical Tradition volumes http://dx.doi.org/10.1163/1574-9347_bnp_e1011640.

Wenham, Gordon J. "Deuteronomy and the Central Sanctuary," *Tyndale Bulletin* 22 (1971): 103–18.

Westbrook, Raymond. *Property and Family in Biblical Law*. Sheffield: JSOT Press, 1991.

Wevers, John. W. *Notes on the Greek Text of Deuteronomy*. Atlanta, GA: Scholars, 1995.

Weyde, Karl. W. "The Narrative of King Solomon and the Law of the King: On the Relationship between 1 Kings 3-11 and Deut 17:14-20." In *Enigmas and Images. Studies in Honor of Tryggve N. D. Mettinger*, ed. Göran Eidevall and Blaženka Scheuer, 75-91. Winona Lake, IN: Eisenbrauns, 2011.

Wijngaards, John. N. M. *The Dramatization of Salvific History in the Deuteronomic Schools*. Leiden: Brill, 1969.

Wilcke, Claus. "Markt und Arbeit im Alten Orient am Ende des 3. Jahrtausends v. Chr." In *Menschen und Märkte: Studien zur historischen Wirtschaftsanthropologie*, ed. Wolfgang Reinhard and Justin Stagl, 71-132. Vienna: Böhlau, 2006.

Wilkinson, John C. "Bayasirah and Bayadir," *Arabian Studies* 1 (1974): 75-85.

Willis, Timothy M. *The Elders of the City: A Study of the Elders-Laws in Deuteronomy*. Atlanta, GA: SBL, 2001.

Wilson, James. D. *Redefining the Roles of the Rural Levites in Deuteronomy*. PhD diss., Asbury Theological Seminary, 2018.

Wright, Jacob L. "Warfare and Wanton Destruction," *Journal of Biblical Literature* 127 (2008): 423-58.

Wunsch, Cornelia. "Judeans by the Waters of Babylon: New Historical Evidence in Cuneiform Sources from Rural Babylonia in the Schøyen Collection," *Babylonische Archive* 6. Dresden: ISLET, forthcoming.

Yamauchi, Edwin M. and Marvin R. Wilson. *Dictionary of Daily Life in Biblical & Post-biblical Antiquity*. Peabody: Hendrickson, 2014.

Younger, Lawson K. Jr., "Ninurta-Kudurrī-uṣur – Suḫu Annal." In *The Context of Scripture*, ed. William W. Hallo, 2.282-83. Leiden: Brill, 1997.

Yu, Suee Yan. *Tithes and Firstlings in Deuteronomy*, PhD thesis Union Theological Seminary in Virginia, 1997.

Zaccagnini, Carlo. "Nuzi." In *Security for Debt in Ancient Neareastern Law*, ed. Raymond Westbrook and Richard Jasnow, 223-36. Leiden: Brill, 2001.

Zehnder, Markus. *Umgang mit dem Fremden in Israel und Assyria*. Stuttgart: Kohlhammer, 2005.

Index of Authors

Achenbach, R. 38
Adamczewski, B. 115
Akiyama, K. 144
Albertz, R. 121
Altmann, P. 10, 19, 43, 76, 122, 127, 164, 176
Anderson, B. A. 131, 140, 142
Anderson, G. A. 6
Anderson, J. S. 209
Aristophanes 102
Arnold, B. T. 118, 169, 199–205, 214
Awabdy, M. A. 17, 32, 63, 105, 106
Baker, D. L. 47, 10
Bartos, M. 10
Beattie, D. R. G. 93
Becker, G. S. 7
Bedford, P. R. 117
Bekins, P. 85
Ben Zvi, E. 115
Bennett, H. V. 63, 111, 125
Berge, K. 4
Bergsma, J. S. 83
Berlejung, A. 89
Berlin, A. 113
Berman, J. 209
Biga, M. G. 128
Bird, P.-A. 35
Block, D. I. 122
Blok, J. 132
Boer, R. 40, 42, 44, 50–53, 79, 110, 114, 180, 181
Bodi, D. 99
Bourdieu, P. 175, 188
Boyer, R. 110
Braulik, G. 5, 157, 158, 164–166, 175, 199
Brueggemann, W. 33
Bultmann, C. 95, 98, 140
Busatta, S. 183
Byrne, R. 205
Carmichael, C. M. 46,

Chavel, S. 38
Chirichigno, G. C. 26
Christian, M. A. 206
Claburn, W. E. 33
Clements, R. E. 204
Coin–Longeray, S. 102
Cook, S. L. 23, 174
Craigie, P. C. 47
Crawford, S. W. 68
Crouch, C. L. 47, 61, 100, 127, 138–140, 146, 148, 186
Crüsemann, F. 131, 207
Cullen, J. 2
D'Eichthal, G. 2
Dalman, G. 21
Davies, P. R. 2, 9, 10, 93, 117, 127, 204–206, 219
de Wette, W. M. L. 1
Démare-Lafont, S. 71, 135, 193
Ducan-Jones, R. 44
Dušek, J. 209
Ebach, R. 17, 59
Edelman, D. V. 20, 59, 95, 129
Edenburg, C. 204, 205
Eissfeldt, O. 160
Elat, M. 134
Eldevik, J. 32
Epstein, S. A. 6, 7
Fabry, H.-J. 143
Faust, A. 96, 186
Fitzpatrick-McKinley, A. 9
Fleishman, J. 113
Foldvari P. 107
Franklin, N. 209
Friedland R. 128
Fries, S. 2
Frymer-Kensky, T. 151
Gallagher, E. L. 120
Garlan, Y. 46
Glanville, M. R. 95
Glassman, J. P. 188

Goitein, S. D. 188
Gottheil, R. J. H. 141
Graber, D. 172
Greenspahn, F. E. 118
Greifenhagen F. V. 138
Guillaume, P. 26, 30, 39, 48, 50, 64, 80, 83, 113, 145, 182, 184, 209
Hackl, J. 140, 207
Hagedorn, A. C. 46, 115–118
Halabi, A. 128
Hall, G. H. 33
Halpern, B. 118, 172
Hamilton, J. M. 144
Havely, N. R. 6
Haworth, M. 35
Hecht, R. 128
Henkelman, W. F. M. 118, 150
Hensel, B. 130
Herman, M. 16, 33
Hertz, J. H. 123
Himbaza, I. 120
Hölscher, G. 2, 3, 68, 208
Horst, L. 2
Houston, W. J. 38, 119
Hudson, M. 182
Humbert, P. 103, 104, 158
Hurowitz, V. 117
Jagersma, H. 18
Joannès, F. 39
Joüon, P. 85, 86
Jursa, M. 7, 8, 25, 48, 51, 65, 79, 94, 107, 129, 181
Kaufman, S. A. 83
Kessler, R. 108
Kilchör, B. 159–162, 170, 171, 201, 203, 210–212
Kirk, A. T. 85
Kletter, R. 25
Kline, M. G. 123
Kloppenborg, J. S. 141, 151
Knauf, E. A. 96–98
Knight, D. A. 112
Knoppers, G. N. 2, 23, 120, 121
Kratz, R. G. 10
Lambert, W. G. 65
Lauinger, J. 9
Lemaire, A. 39
Lemche, N. P. 93
Liverani, M. 134, 135, 141
Levin, C. 41, 42, 47, 58, 96, 136, 145, 200
Levin, Y. 149
Levinson, B. M. 10, 60, 83, 84, 89, 90

Lipínski, E. 146
Lipton, D. 113
Liverani, M. 134, 135, 141
Livingstone, A. 151
Lohfink, N. 5, 32, 34, 63, 100, 105, 151, 165
Lundbom, J. R. 17, 18, 22, 38, 118, 124, 144
Lynch, K. 141, 216
Martinuzzi, B. 187
Mattison, K. 163
Mayes, A. D. H. 18
McCarthy, C. 69, 92
McConville, J. G. 33, 47, 169
Milgrom, J. 33, 171
Miller, M. L. 54
Milstein, S. J. 65, 66, 193
Miralles Maciá, L. 141
Monson, A. 151
Moran, W. L. 59
Morrow, W. S. 16, 56, 118
Mukenge, A. K. 150
Müller, R. 204, 205
Muraoka, T. 85, 86, 102
Mutius, H.-G. von 40
Na'aman, N. 95, 96, 98
Nakanose, S. 33
Nestor, D. 15
Nicholson E. W. 144, 204
Nihan, C. 38, 170
Noth, M. 186, 193
Oestreicher, T. 116
Olmo Lete, G. del 122
Olivier, J. P. J. 27
Oosthuizen, M. J. 108
Otto, E. 9, 10, 17, 38, 58, 67, 72, 73, 80, 108, 115, 130, 137, 146, 148, 170, 214
Paganini, S. 35
Pagolu, A. 16
Pardee, D. 59
Pearce, L. E. 39, 89
Perlitt, L. 61, 83, 131, 136, 137
Pina-Cabral, J. de 183
Pitkänen, P. 118
Pury, A. dE 112
Pyschny, K. 119
Rad, G. von 118, 165
Radner, K. 9, 51, 52
Renger, J. M. 44
Reuss, E. 3, 208
Ribichini, S. 35
Richardson, M. E. J. 191, 192, 194

Richter, S. L. 117, 118, 206
Ro, J. U. 8, 41
Rogerson, J. W. 1
Romano, I. 6
Römer, T. C. 9, 119, 130, 137
Rossi, B. 65, 83, 126, 207
Rütersworden, U. 10, 36, 38, 46, 117, 132
Sacher Fox, N. 35
Saillard, Y. 110
Salonen, E. 16
Samuel, H. 174
Sanmartín, J. 122
Schaper, J. 16
Scheffler, E. 34
Schenker, A. 67, 118, 120
Schiffman, L. H. 37
Schmid, K. 7
Schorch, S. 118-121
Sider, R. J. 44
Silverman, J. M. 48
Simkins, R. A. 182
Simonton, M. 133, 207
Smelik, K. A. D. 88
Snijders, L. A. 95, 99
Soss, N. M. 17, 146
Stackert, J. 15-18, 83, 160-162, 174
Steinberg, N. 79, 80
Steinkeller, P. 26, 29
Steymans, H. U. 9
Stolz, F. 158
Stulman, L. 139
Sulzbach, C. 117
Talmon, S. 143
Thelle, R. I. 115
Theophratus 135
Tigay, J. H. 2, 32-34, 47, 71, 115, 123
Tilly, C. 115
Tost, S. 94, 107
Trevett, J. 206
Trundle, M. 46
Tsai, D. Y. 100

Tsevat, M. 82
Tugendhaft, A. 59
Ulrich, E. 68, 120
Van den Eijnde, F. 208
Van der Brugge, C. 134
Van Leeuwen, B. 107
Van Leeuwen, M. H. D. 104
Van Seters, J. 58, 61, 83-85, 90-94
Vargyas, P. 44
Veijola T. 158, 165
Venter, P. M. 38
Vernes, M. 2
Villard, P. 146
Von Gall, A. 68
Waerzeggers, C. 22, 65, 79, 135
Wagner-Tsukamoto, S. A. 7, 8
Wallace, R. W. 132
Waltke, B. K. 85
Weigert, S. 37
Weinfeld, M. 3, 93, 177
Welch, A. C. 95, 116
Wellhausen, J. 199, 201
Wells, B. 9, 10, 94
Welton, R. 112
Welwei, K.-W. 114
Wenham, G. J. 116
Westbrook, R. 71
Wevers, J. W. 37, 92
Weyde, K. W. 34
Wijngaards, J. N. M. 116
Wilkinson, J. C. 187
Willis, T. M. 34
Wilson, J. D. 162-163
Wilson, M. R. 4
Wright, J. L. 46
Wunsch, C. 39, 89
Yamauchi, E. M. 4
Yardeni, A. 59
Younger, L. K. Jr. 134
Yu, S.-Y. 127
Zaccagnini, C. 26
Zehnder, M. 95

Index of Biblical References

Genesis
1:28	113
9:1–7	113
13:10	85
14:21	85
19:16	85
19:30–38	138
20:7	85
31	88
38:8	74

Exodus
20:24	118, 121, 169, 210
21–23	9, 10, 88, 94, 97, 210
21:1–22:16	214
21:2	84, 212
21:4–10	184, 212
21:16	47
21:18–25	212, 214
22:15–16	184
22:31	99
23:3–4	148
23:20–24	169, 210
32:9	167
32:28	76
33:3 5	167
34	159, 169, 210

Leviticus
7	21, 39
11	15, 169–170
17–27	9, 10, 94, 97
17:13–14	169
19	159
19:18	145
21:14	189
21:20–21	190
23	128
25	17, 42, 61, 88, 91, 184
27	16, 25, 33; 160

Numbers
3:4	23
16:3	129
18:21–26	16, 20, 21, 33, 160, 162, 171, 172
20:4	129

Deuteronomy
1:16–28	56, 62, 136
2:4–8	58, 60, 61, 135, 140, 210
3:18–20	56, 136
4:44–28:69	202
5:21–22	54, 130
6:4–9	9, 202
7:2–3	47
7:6	117
7:15	39
9:15–21	167
9:10	130
10:4	130
10:6	23
10:8–9	56, 77
10:12	34
12–26	9, 10, 24, 95, 110, 136, 152, 159, 210
12	116, 118, 152, 170
12:2–28	201
12:2–5	121
12:12	21, 54–55, 77, 81, 110, 132, 168
12:14	119
12:15–22	36–38, 112
12:18	21, 54–55, 81, 110, 168, 171
12:19	163
12:27	23, 117
13	2, 9, 56, 127, 136, 169, 202
14–25	210
14:1–21	15, 85, 112
14:2	117
14:21	55, 98, 189, 210

14:22–15:23	202	20:2–15	34, 45–46, 54, 62, 76, 169, 172, 179, 182, 187
14:22–28	3, 16, 18, 32, 33, 77, 81, 85, 110, 115, 128, 158, 166–167, 170, 174, 195	20:16–20	39, 45–46
		21:1–9	34, 50, 76, 85, 179
14:22	19	21:10	54, 184, 187
14:23	161, 175	21:11	46, 185
14:24	46, 122, 179	21:14	81
14:27	21, 77, 152, 163	21:15–17	185
14:28–29	19, 23, 55, 64, 73, 78, 95, 125, 165, 176, 177	21:18–21	34, 112, 213
		21:22–23	183
15–25	76	22:1–23:1	179
15:1–18	87	22:1–5	35, 58, 62, 144, 148, 188
15:1–12	3, 17, 26, 41, 45, 51, 54–55, 58, 147	22:5–12	179, 214
		22:10–29	34, 54, 85, 94, 110, 113, 125, 184, 190
15:2–4	60, 62, 64, 66–70, 95, 136, 140–144	22:19	183
15:5–25:1	86–87	22:22	190
15:4–11	93, 101, 105, 108, 110–112, 142–143, 182	23:2–9	80, 129, 132–141, 179, 186
		23:8–14	40, 46, 58–60, 65, 130
15:6	133, 145	23:15–16	46–47, 54, 81, 182, 184
15:7–11	189	23:17	94, 114, 129
15:11–16	28, 55, 63, 64, 80, 82–88, 90–91, 101, 173, 183, 189, 212	23:18–21	35, 39–40, 51, 55, 60, 62, 92, 100, 112, 145, 148, 179, 182, 194
15:16	48, 93, 189	23:19	115
15:17	54, 81	23:22–26	50, 54, 94, 185
15:18	93	24:1–15	179
15:19	85, 178, 184	24:3–4	185
15:22	36–38, 85, 112	24:5–9	46, 54–55, 58, 65, 85, 113, 180, 182, 184, 185, 187
15:23	116		
16:1–16	116, 123, 170–171, 181, 210	24:10–15	26, 40, 43–44, 54–55, 63, 95, 98, 101–104, 114, 182
16:1–8	36, 110		
16:11–14	21, 36, 54–55, 78, 81, 163–164, 168	24:14–22	29–30, 55, 80, 93, 96, 99, 105–108, 110, 112, 180, 182, 189
16:16	167, 168		
16:18	34, 192	24:16	192
16:21	23, 117, 173	24:19	102, 185
17:2–3	178	25:1–2	34, 185, 192
17:8–12	23, 34, 35, 55, 76, 78, 85, 110, 126, 169, 172, 173	25:3–11	55, 65, 71–76, 79, 100, 110, 144, 180, 182, 184, 187
17:13	127	25:11–14	25, 65, 71, 75, 214
17:14–20	1, 34, 55, 58, 85, 93, 98, 100, 121, 136, 173	25:17–19	173
		26:2–8	22, 23, 116, 117, 173, 210
17:17	97	26:11–13	18, 20, 55, 64, 78, 168, 172, 201
18:1–8	19, 21–23, 36, 38, 55, 56, 76, 78, 112, 116, 171		
		26:15–19	117
18:6	116	27:1–4	117, 118, 121
18:10–11	35	27:5–9	23, 55, 112, 117
18:15–18	56, 130, 152	27:12	119
18:22	191	27:17–24	54, 99, 210
19:3–11	46, 54, 62, 85, 94, 131, 189	28	9, 54, 55, 56
19:12–15	34, 50, 54, 94, 179, 182, 185	29:7	55
19:16–21	23, 34, 62, 75, 85, 173, 212	29:21	55

Index of Biblical References **247**

31	4, 23, 55, 115, 116, 126, 130
32:50	56
33	56, 76, 112

Joshua
22:10–11	122

Judges
21:11–12	45

2 Kings
17	205, 209, 218
18:3–6	203–204
21	202
22–23	1–2, 115, 117, 150
23:27	120
24–25	218

Isaiah
22:13	165
44:28	58
45:1	58

Jeremiah
7:14–16	120
25:9	58
27:6	58
34	94
43:10	58
49	59, 138

Hosea
9:1	165

Micah
2:5	129, 130

Zephaniah
1	2

Zechariah
8:19	165

Malachi
3:8–10	33

Psalms
37:11	145
78:60–68	120
140:12	42

Proverbs
28:27	102
31:10–31	189

Job
1–2	188

Ruth 30, 80
1:4	74
4:6	188

Qohelet
1:13	102
2:4–15	103
3:10	102

Ezra
10	187

Nehemiah
1:8–9	120
8	126
9:36–37	117, 145
10:39	20, 21
13:1–2	130, 138, 187

1 Chronicles
15:17	141
28:4	130
28:9	129
31:11–12	124

Tobit
1:7	18

Sirach
33:31	213
38:24–34	102

Matthew
5:5	145
19:24	42

Josephus
Antiquities IV.8.22 18

Index of Subjects

alms/charity 15, 18, 31, 41–45, 53, 55, 57, 70, 80, 101–104, 108, 109, 123, 125, 144, 181, 183, 201, 215
antichresis/tic 26, 28, 48, 64, 81, 88–94, 106, 114, 146, 211–213
Asarhaddon 9
barley 8, 25, 30, 31, 39
capital (social) 27, 29, 43–45, 111, 125, 140, 175, 185, 190, 208
capital (means) 8, 41, 45, 48, 73, 88, 94, 104, 151, 179, 180, 182–184, 217
carrion 38–40, 49, 53, 55, 98–100, 112, 189, 211
cooperation 8, 207
credit 3–6, 17, 27, 40, 44, 46, 51–55, 64, 70, 88, 90, 107, 127, 142–151, 178, 180, 182, 188, 218
creditworthiness 41, 43, 81, 91, 109, 183
debt (see release)
default 40–44, 108, 109, 216
destitution 5, 41–45, 73, 100–104, 108–109, 199, 215
fear 20, 33, 34, 46, 50, 74, 114, 116, 141, 161, 164, 175, 189, 218
first fruits 15, 21–23, 31, 78, 116, 150, 158, 167, 172, 195, 210
firstlings 15, 16, 19, 22–28, 31, 124, 126, 163, 165, 171, 178, 184, 211
fleece (*see* wool)
foreigner 38–41, 55, 58, 72, 100, 136, 142, 147, 181
gift 38–43, 51–53, 87, 92, 98, 99, 104, 108, 109, 167, 189, 205, 213
gleaning(s) 15, 29–31, 55, 80, 98–100, 174, 180, 185, 189, 211, 216

guild 60, 61, 131, 134, 135, 140–145, 149, 151
harvest 18, 26–31, 39, 80, 111, 123, 169, 178, 185, 216
holiness 117, 148
humanitarian/ism 3, 27, 30, 43, 48, 58, 65, 66, 68, 75, 80, 92–96, 114, 181, 185, 200–203
indenture 48, 49, 54, 81–84, 89, 93, 127, 183, 212
interest 15, 26–29, 39–44, 49–57, 60–63, 70, 89, 92, 95, 100, 103, 108, 140, 142, 145, 178–181, 211
isonomia 133, 208
Josiah 1–3, 9, 21, 23, 96, 115, 121, 199, 203, 204
loan/s 26, 28, 40–45, 51–55, 66, 72, 81, 88–93, 102–108, 144–146, 211, 215
loan-shark 79, 180, 194
Manasseh (king) 97, 202–204
manumission 26, 82–84, 87, 88, 94, 213
marriage 46, 72, 74, 137, 166, 180, 187, 189, 190
meat 17, 19, 21, 22, 31, 36–39, 50, 55, 78–81, 98, 112, 116, 118, 125, 150, 165, 175, 176, 208, 216
merchant/trade 24, 25, 46, 51–53, 66, 71, 79, 127, 134, 135, 141, 149, 151, 180–182, 187, 189, 207, 212, 216–219
mišarum 53
Moses 2–3, 7, 23, 35, 55, 56, 61, 117, 119, 122, 151, 152, 167, 203, 209, 217
neighbor 54–69, 94, 95, 100, 101, 105, 109, 142–149, 171, 189, 194, 211

Index of Subjects

Northern origin of Deuteronomy 2, 95, 96, 204, 205, 209

oil 16-18, 21, 27, 31, 51, 55, 78, 151, 162, 168, 172, 177, 183, 216

orphan (*see* widow)

personae miserae 5, 63, 64, 77, 79, 81, 95, 99, 100, 104, 106, 128, 131, 188, 199, 216.

pledge 11, 26, 40-43, 48, 54, 62, 80, 89, 95, 103, 108, 145, 146, 189, 211

poverty, poor 3, 8, 16, 18, 32, 41-45, 51, 53, 57, 63, 68, 78, 93-98, 100-112, 123, 125, 140, 143-147, 150, 186, 188, 189, 211

prebend 19, 21, 23, 49, 57, 167, 181, 194, 195

priest/s 16, 18, 19-23, 31, 35-38, 55, 76-79, 81, 86, 110, 112, 116, 121, 122, 126-128, 135, 149, 150-153, 163-169, 171-181, 189, 195, 201-211, 216-219

debt release/*šemiṭṭah* 3, 4, 27, 28, 41, 48, 54, 60, 62-72, 82, 87, 91, 95, 100, 107-109, 111, 136, 142-147, 151, 183, 189, 217

risk 27, 28, 40-44, 72, 103, 108, 146, 181, 213, 217

Sargon 51, 52, 134, 205, 218

shekel/silver 6, 15, 24, 25, 30, 31, 39, 49-53, 62, 67, 88-92, 97, 104, 122-125, 127, 160, 168, 175-177, 183, 189-192

slave/ry 5, 8, 15, 26, 36, 45-54, 61-64, 77, 81-84, 87-93, 105, 106, 187, 190-192, 199, 200, 211-219

tax/ation 16-19, 21-25, 33, 36, 38, 50-53, 79, 151, 164, 175-177, 181, 195, 207, 216

Torah 1-11, 21, 24, 32-34, 55, 71, 86, 93, 115, 119, 126-129, 137, 151-152, 160, 166, 167, 170-175, 195, 202-209, 216-219

transport 5, 15, 24, 31, 49, 107, 122-124, 175, 178

im/practicality 2-4, 45, 67-69, 106, 126, 127, 142, 146, 168, 190-193, 208

Urdeuteronomium 1-2, 9, 96, 115, 137, 199-213, 217

usufruct 26, 50, 71, 79, 80

Utopian/idealistic 3-5, 9, 25, 39, 126, 174-177, 193, 194, 208

wage/s 15, 29, 55, 57, 63, 64, 82, 88, 89-94, 100, 103-106, 110, 114, 179, 189

war 5, 8, 34, 45, 46, 54, 57, 75, 81, 94, 113, 114, 166, 169, 179, 182, 184, 186, 187, 200, 206, 215

weight 15, 25, 31, 180, 182, 189, 216

welfare 7, 44, 55, 104, 112, 131, 182

wheat 16, 17, 30, 31, 168, 172

widow 5, 17-23, 30, 31, 50, 55, 63, 71, 73, 74, 77-81, 98-100, 105, 111-114, 125-128, 131, 145 164, 172, 176, 180-185, 188, 189, 201, 211, 215, 216, 218

wisdom 35, 43, 102, 103, 177, 189, 217

wine 17, 18, 21, 28, 31, 50, 55, 78, 125, 151, 158, 162, 165, 167, 168, 172, 175, 177, 183, 216

wool 8, 17, 19, 21, 22, 29, 31, 39, 50, 55, 78, 79, 116, 150, 168, 172, 176, 177, 216

Xerxes 207

www.ingramcontent.com/pod-product-compliance
Lightning Source LLC
Chambersburg PA
CBHW050849230426
43667CB00012B/2213